Henry Satterlee

New Testament Churchmanship and the Principles

upon which it was founded

Henry Satterlee

New Testament Churchmanship and the Principles
upon which it was founded

ISBN/EAN: 9783337368555

Printed in Europe, USA, Canada, Australia, Japan

Cover: Foto ©Lupo / pixelio.de

More available books at **www.hansebooks.com**

New Testament
Churchmanship

And the

Principles Upon Which It Was Founded

BY THE RIGHT REV.

Henry Y. Satterlee, D.D., LL.D.

Bishop of Washington

AUTHOR OF "A CREEDLESS GOSPEL AND
THE GOSPEL CREED," ETC.

NEW YORK
LONGMANS, GREEN AND CO.
LONDON AND BOMBAY
1899

TO THE

Communicants and Church Workers
OF CALVARY PARISH, NEW YORK

WHOSE INTELLIGENT SYMPATHY AND COÖPERATION
WERE AN UNFAILING HELP AND INSPIRATION TO
THE AUTHOR DURING HIS RECTORSHIP,
THIS VOLUME IS

AFFECTIONATELY AND GRATEFULLY DEDICATED

PREFACE

WESTERN Christendom, through the dominating influences of the Church of Rome, during the past thousand years has witnessed the gradual substitution of another type of Christianity for that of apostolic days. In the Apostolic Church itself, a true balance was preserved between the inward or subjective, and the outward or objective, religious life of the Church, and we read that, under the influences of the Holy Ghost, the Spirit of Truth, those baptized on the Day of Pentecost continued steadfastly in the Apostles' doctrine and fellowship and in the breaking of bread and in prayers. This is a fundamental principle of the religion of Christ. The inward and outward are so bound together in His Incarnation that they are mutually dependent upon one another; nor can the highest spiritual life, which is life in Christ, be fully attained save through their union. Each, without the other, gives rise to an abnormal, one-sided development of religion; and this has been the error into which the Roman Church has fallen. By unduly exaggerating the outward at the expense of the inward, she not only lost that which St. Paul calls *the proportion or analogy of the Faith*,[1] but also acquired an untrue, unspiritualized

[1] εἴτε προφητείαν, κατὰ τὴν ἀναλογίαν τῆς πίστεως (Rom. xii. 6).

conception of the outward. It is true that she preserves outwardly the form of the Faith once for all delivered to the saints, but while she boasts of her orthodoxy and challenges the world to find a flaw of heresy in her apostolic doctrine, she has lost the apostolic spirit; and that want has been felt ever since the rise of the Papacy, by all believers who have gone back to the apostolic records that they might drink in the spirit of the New Testament Church. Consequently, ever since the thirteenth century, there have been in Europe a series of reformations, or attempted reformations, all in the direction of inward personal loyalty to Christ in contradistinction to outward loyalty to church organization. And it should be carefully noted, that the New Testament itself has been the fount of inspiration for all those consecutive movements which date back to Peter Waldo in Italy, to John Wickliffe in England, to John Huss in Bohemia, to the Brethren of the Common Life (of which Thomas à Kempis was a member) in Holland, and to the Mystics in Germany. The invention of printing about A. D. 1450, and the widespread circulation and knowledge of the Holy Scriptures which followed, prepared the way for the Protestant Reformation, about seventy years later, when these different movements were all brought together under the leadership of Martin Luther. "Justification by Faith," the inspiring watchword of the Reformation, was the expression of a great spiritual want. It was a great catholic cry of human nature which had been smothered for centuries by the so-called Catholic Church. The Reformation was a protest in behalf of the inward which had been ignored for the outward; a protest in behalf of the sacredness of human personality, of the rights of the individual and of the freedom of conscience, all of which had been sacrificed for outward forms, outward professions of belief and the preservation of church organization. And the fact that the Protestant Reformation has held its own for nearly four hundred years, uniting so many widely different sects under one name and in one common cause, is not only a sign of the extent of the spiritual disease which God raised it up to cure, but also a lesson from God, imprinted on the pages of church history for all future time, that the inward is never hereafter to be sacrificed for the outward, in the Church of Christ. It is also a fact never to be forgotten, that Protestantism, through the inward guidance of the Spirit of Truth, became Catholic enough to hold to the Scriptures, the Catholic Creeds, and the two Sacraments ordained by Christ Himself.

But if the Roman Church has gone too far in one direction, Protestantism, not even excepting the Anglican Communion, has gone too far in the other. The Roman Church gradually lost the Spirit of apostolic truth, while she preserved the letter of formal orthodoxy. Losing the spirit, she lost, also, those things which are especially revealed by the Spirit of God; and then followed, naturally, the corruption of those truths which were unspiritually held. The Protestants, on the other hand, in their intense desire to recover the spiritual, lost the true meaning of the outward in relation to the inward, and then fell into the error of making their own subjective impressions the ultimate criterion of the objective truths of Revelation. In this way, the Continental Reformers were unconsciously led into the error of protesting, not only against the corruptions of Rome, but also against the Scripture truths which had been thus corrupted.

The English reformers were held back from making the same mistake through national and religious causes, the majority of which had been influencing the life of the people ever since the days of Stephen Langton and the Magna Charta. Not the least of these was a national reverence for the Holy Scriptures, which had been growing for centuries, and which was immeasurably deepened by Wickliffe's English translation of the Bible. Yet, while the independent attitude of the English Church was unique in Western Europe, and while, by preserving the balance between the outward and inward elements of Christ's religion, she approached more nearly the standard of the New Testament Church than any other religious body, even the English reformers themselves could not altogether emancipate themselves from the influences which had dominated the thought of Western Christendom in the centuries that preceded the reformation. In the sixteenth century, through the power of the Papacy, the whole conception of the Church of Christ had gradually, insensibly, fallen more and more below the New Testament level. In St. Paul's Epistles the Church is held up as the Body of Christ, connected indissolubly with its head in Heaven; and to the minds of New Testament Christians there was no possibility of any separation between Christ and His Church. Whatever Christ was His Church was. But in the Middle

Ages, through the persistent teachings of the Papacy, the idea of a vicarious ministry became prevalent: a mediatorial priesthood was interjected between God and believers; and the logical and inevitable consequence of this interjection was a separation between Christ and His Church. Protestantism was not responsible for having an imperfect conception of the Church, when the true idea had been thus distorted; it can hardly be expected, therefore, that Protestant theology, after negatively protesting against the corruptions of Rome, should have been able to go further, and do the positive work of restoring the original Faith as it was before it had been corrupted. In the violence of the reaction against Rome, and especially against those doctrines of the Primitive Church which Rome had most grossly perverted, Protestantism overlooked the fact that the Church is called in the New Testament itself the Body of Christ, and went to the opposite extreme of undervaluing Sacraments, Apostolic Order, Apostolic Authority, and everything connected with the Church. This one-sidedness of Protestantism, in overemphasizing the subjective and ignoring the objective side of Christianity, was imperfectly recognized, until it was followed by its own inevitable consequences in Church history; and then, slowly but surely, those Scriptures which had been ignored began to reassert their influence, until, at last, that same authority which was appealed to three hundred years ago as supporting the sacredness of private judgement, is now being appealed to as supporting the sacredness of church principles against individualism and an exaggeration of private judgement. Indeed, it may be said that the New Testament itself, which caused the Protestant Reformation, is now causing the reformation of Protestantism.

In view of these facts, the writer has felt no hesitation in adopting for the title of this book the name of "New Testament Churchmanship."

As a glance at the Table of Contents will show, it is an humble attempt to differentiate between church principles as set forth in the New Testament itself, and church principles as they appeared at the time of the Reformation, in the mediæval setting and interpretation of the Church of Rome. As this contrast cannot be fully realized in all its bearings unless the correlation between the natural and spiritual, which is the central truth of the doctrine of the Incarnation, is kept constantly in mind, the author in the first three chapters has first emphasized this truth itself, as it stands revealed in the Incarnation and Resurrection of Christ, before passing more directly to the Church, which is an extension of the Incarnation, and to the consideration of New Testament Churchmanship which was founded on the doctrine of the Incarnation.

Though the author has not hesitated to criticise Protestant Theology frankly and fearlessly, his words have been dictated by no unfriendly spirit, but, on the contrary, by a deep and loving sympathy. Would that the same kind of sympathy might flow toward the Church of Rome, for she commands our deepest reverence on account of her apostolic origin. Two of Christ's own Apostles were associated together as her founders; an Epistle in the New Testament itself was addressed to her first members; in the early Church she was the bulwark of orthodoxy and the protector of the weak; and to-day she preserves, in outward form, not only the ancient Faith, but hallowed heritages and Catholic usages sanctified by the Christian ages, which Protestantism has thoughtlessly thrown away. If the modern Church of Rome could return to what she herself was in the ancient days, she might take a leading part in the coming reunion of Christendom, but she is paralyzed by a power that stands outside of her real life. While the Papacy dominates her destinies, and so long as the Roman Curia usurps control over her, she will keep clinging to the letter, and "the letter killeth." The only change which can ever come to her, until she shakes off this yoke of bondage, is the change of decay. But "the spirit giveth life," and Protestantism, with all its crudeness, its one-sidedness, its lack of Apostolic Order and organization, is instinct with life and energy and hope for the future.

It has been the aim of the author, throughout this book, to avoid controversy; to show that Church doctrines, apart from those exaggerations which challenge controversy, are really Bible truth; and to keep the unity of the spirit in the bond of peace. In the chapters on "Apostolic Succession" and "Christian Sacerdotalism," he has followed, sometimes quite closely, the line of thought marked out by Canon Moberly in his valuable and most helpful work on "Ministerial Priesthood." When the *representative* character of the ordained Priesthood of the Christian Church is clearly seen and understood, in its true light, the plane of cleavage will be found between a true and a false sacerdotalism, and no room will be left for suspicion or prejudice.

The author would take this opportunity of expressing his indebtedness to Dr. William C. Rives for kindly and painstaking aid in correcting the proofsheets; and to the Editor of the "Independent" for his courtesy in consenting to the reprint, as portions of chapters, of two papers by the writer which have appeared in that journal.

There is to-day an ever increasing number of earnest Christian men and women who, in their longings for the coming of Christ's Kingdom on earth, desire above all else to follow that high ideal of the Church which inspired the first believers, to aim for that kind of unity which Christ set forth in His high-priestly prayer the night before His Crucifixion, and to be filled with the New Testament spirit in doing Christ's work.

It was the privilege of the author, while in charge of Calvary Parish, New York, to be helped and cheered by a band of church workers who were inspired by such aims; to instruct them, at the monthly meetings of the Communicants' Union, regarding the principles of New Testament Churchmanship; and to study with them how rector and people might co-operate in applying these same principles to the conditions of our modern church life. And it was at the request of those communicants, made one memorable Christmastide, that this book has been written.

HENRY Y. SATTERLEE.

CHRISTMAS EVE, 1898.

CONTENTS

CHAPTER I

THE VIRGIN BIRTH OF CHRIST

I

	PAGE
Unique significance of the Birth of Christ in History and Revelation	1-2
Present day tendency to doubt the fact of the Virgin Birth . .	2

It is objected:
    (*a*) that only two of the Gospels record the fact;
    (*b*) that there is only one reference to it in Prophecy;
    (*c*) that there is no mention of it in the Epistles;
    (*d*) that it is an unnecessary miracle of no theological importance 3

In answer to such objections it must be considered:
    that if the account of the Nativity is dropped from the records, the integrity of the Gospel History is destroyed;
    that the same objections apply with equal force to the narratives of the Resurrection and Ascension 3-4

Evidences of Genuineness in the Records themselves:
    Simplicity and conciseness of style.
    The narratives of St. Matthew and St. Luke.
    Marked absence of the miraculous in the Story, apart from the angelic visions and messages 5-9

St. John's Gospel:
    It contains no record of the fact, but the Miraculous Birth necessarily implied in chap. i. 14.
    St. John also silent regarding the institution of Baptism and the Eucharist but refers to both by implication (chap. iii. 4, and vi.) 9-12

II

But it is objected: PAGE
 that the authenticity of the Gospels themselves is doubtful;
 that the canon was formed in an uncritical age·
 that ancient Gospels may be discovered in which the narrative of the Virgin Birth is wanting.
Such objections the result of ignorance of the real facts.
 Modern methods of criticism different, but scholarship equally exact and conscientious in the first three centuries   14–16
Results of critical research in the last twenty-five years all tend to establish authenticity and early date of the Gospels.
 Latest criticism fixes the date of the three synoptic Gospels within forty years after the Ascension   17
 Witness of Irenæus; the Muratorian Fragment; the Diatessaron of Tatian 18–19
Evidences that belief in the Virgin Birth of our Lord was general in this early period.
 Ignatius; Justin Martyr; Denial of the fact by the Ebionites   21

III

Mythic theory of the Virgin Birth
 Cannot be sustained by the facts   23
Theory that it was a legend equally untenable;
It must therefore be accepted as historic fact 24–25

CHAPTER II

THE VIRGIN BIRTH AND THE NEW ADAM

The real nature of the Incarnation cannot be interpreted apart from the Virgin Birth of Christ   26

I

Fundamental principal of the Incarnation — the perfect union of the Divine and human in Jesus Christ
 Inconceivable that the Godhead could assume imperfect or sinful manhood   27
 The first Adam free from the taint of hereditary sin.
 The human nature of Christ was also sinless.
 In both the will was free from bias toward sin   28
 If Christ had inherited a sinful nature, the presence of

	PAGE
a superhuman moral power in His Manhood would have been necessary to counteract the bias toward sin; but this would have destroyed His freedom of will and the reality of His temptations	29
Therefore the Virgin birth of Christ is not an unnecessary miracle, — Christ, the Second Adam, the Progenitor of a new race, must have been Himself a New Creation	30

II

Christ, the Word made Flesh, brought Heaven and earth together in His own Person 31
Therefore life in Christ includes both the physical and spiritual.
    The New Testament teaches that the sanctification of the body is inseparable from that of the soul.
Contrast between the First and Second Adam:
    First Adam and his descendants "of the earth, earthy."
    Different meaning of "sons of God" in the Old and New Testaments 32
    New principle of life imparted to humanity through the Incarnation 34
    First Adam before the fall, possessed an uncorrupted body.
    Physical corruption, one result of the fall.
    The human nature of the Second Adam made incorruptible by His conquest over sin.
    Belief of St. Peter and St. Paul that Christ's Body could not see corruption.
    Therefore it must have been created uncorrupt through the conception by the Holy Ghost 35–36

III

Mystery of personality:
    Each *human* personality separate and distinct from all others 37
    If Christ had a human father He would have had a human personality
Christ is one Divine Person, — He has a human body, soul, and will, but no human personality.
Controversies in the Nicene, and post-Nicene periods, in regard to the Personality of Christ 38–39
The fact of Christ's Divine Selfhood as it interprets His consciousness 40

PAGE

Christ was Man, not *a* man; the Elder Brother of the whole human race; His love not limited to mother and brethren, but embraced all who did the will of God.
   Because He was a Divine Person His Love was free from the limitations of human love 41–43
Christ's Self-assertion attracts, instead of antagonizing us,— because He is a Divine Person; His Personality not outside of our own 44
Importance of this truth as interpreting the Atonement, the Resurrection, the Ascension 44–46

CHAPTER III

THE GOSPEL OF IMMORTALITY

I

Universality of belief in a future life 47
   Religion of the ancient Egyptians:
      their ideas of immortality: the myth of Osiris 48
The Children of Israel uninfluenced by this Egyptian belief
Silence of the Old Testament regarding Immortality
   Explanation of this fact 49–50

II

Immortality found only in Christ 51–52

III

God's revelation of Himself to Moses 53
   Our Lord's answer to the Sadducees 54
   God revealed to the Hebrews as the Source of Life and immortality
      Their hopes for the future centred in the promised Messiah   55

IV

Our Lord's revelation of Himself as *the Life* 55–58
   No ground for the belief that immortality is inherent in human nature
   Christ alone the Way, the Truth, and the Life 59

V

The Resurrection establishes this truth forever
   Influence of the Resurrection on the lives of the early Christians 59–60

VI

Realization of the oneness of the present and future life in Christ 61

VII

The resurrection of the body 62
Immortality of soul and body inseparable 63
The twofold effects of sin 64

VIII

Prevalence of false views of the relation between physical and spiritual 64
Spiritual knowledge not comprehended by the natural man . 65
    Union of the natural and spiritual through the Incarnation 66
The Incarnation and the Resurrection 67

CHAPTER IV

HOLY BAPTISM AND THE RISEN LIFE

I

The life lost by Adam in Paradise, — restored by Christ . . 68
    Story of Adam's fall unveils a universal spiritual truth . . 69
Nature of Adam's sin:
    Man created with a free will; this involves freedom to sin 70
    Sin might have been prevented:
    (1) by creating man without a free will, (2) by removing all temptation to sin; (3) by forcibly restraining man from sin; but the moral life would thus have been made impossible for man 71
    Suggestion to sin came from an outer source.
    St. John's definition: *"Sin is lawlessness."*
    Independence of God the root sin. True freedom comes from obedience to law, whether physical or spiritual.
    Spirit of lawlessness isolates us from God 72
Results of Adam's sin:
    (1) Separation from God; (2) Doubt: of God's Law, — of God's Love; (3) Ignorance: knowledge of evil shuts out real knowledge of good, — ignorance of goodness means ignorance of God 73–77

If knowledge of God is eternal life, then ignorance of God means death.
Therefore the setting up of self-will against God's will, necessarily entails death.

II

Promise regarding "the seed of the woman" fulfilled in Christ 78
Consciousness of separation from God removed only through the Cross 79
Dependence on God the beginning of the religious life . 80

III

The Atonement not completed at the Cross 81
Exclusive attention directed to the Death of Christ by both Roman and Protestant Theology 82
Consequences of this teaching. (1) The Cross is made a symbol not only of death to sin, but of new birth to righteousness. (2) An austere and one-sided aspect of Christianity is presented. (3) Failure to realize the meaning of the Resurrection and Ascension, and consequently, of the creation of the Church, the Mission of the Holy Ghost, the efficacy of the Sacraments. (4) A divorce between faith and works. (5) Revival of the old Dualism . . 83–85

IV

Contrast in the attitude of the New Testament Church . 85
Early Christians lived in the thought of their risen Lord.
Joyousness of the New Testament 87
Power of the Resurrection to quicken both body and soul
Sanctification of the body a ruling thought in the Christian life 88

V

The Great Commission:
   (1) Christ speaks as King
   (2) He *therefore* sends His Apostles forth into all the world.
   (3) They are to make members of His Kingdom through Baptism 89–90
Baptism not instituted till after the Resurrection
Both body and soul must be born from above.
Baptism by "water" and "the Spirit."

Christ seals union of believer with Himself in Baptism, wherein, (1) the natural and spiritual are joined together; (2) we are made partakers of Christ's risen Life; (3) and members of His everlasting Kingdom 91
St. Paul's teaching regarding Baptism 92
If Baptism is undervalued it is because real meaning of the Resurrection is forgotten.
Simplicity of outward sign in Baptism:
but stupendous pledge accompanies it: the *word* of the Word of God 94
Both Baptism and the Lord's Supper depend for their efficacy on the Word of Christ 96

CHAPTER V

THE HOLY EUCHARIST AND THE ASCENSION

Christ's work of Redemption not completed on the Cross, but continued by Him as Prophet, Priest, and King in Heaven 97
Relation between Christ's Heavenly Priesthood and the Holy Eucharist 98-99
Meaning of "blood" in the Old and New Testaments.
"The Blood of Christ" means not the *Death*, but the Life of Christ 100
Doctrine of Transubstantiation inconceivable to St. Paul or St John 101
The Blood of Christ meant to them the Life of the Risen and Ascended Lord.
False impression conveyed by the substitution of the crucifix for the cross upon the altars of the Roman Church . . . 102
Christ's sacrifice continues in the offering of His life in Heaven:—therefore there can be no renewal or repetition of the Sacrifice 104
Sacrifice of intercession and thanksgiving for men part of Christ's Heavenly Offering 105
Heavenly significance of the Holy Eucharist.
The Lord's Supper was *anticipatory* 106
Christ offered Himself *in will*, before He offered Himself on the Cross.
(1) It was instituted beforehand in remembrance of His Death and Passion. (2) It sets before us the Body and Blood of the Living and Glorified Christ. (3) It looked 108

forward to the fulfillment of the Prophecy, "Whoso eateth my Flesh and drinketh my Blood hath eternal Life. (4) It anticipates the time when Christ would become an inward Presence to His disciples. (5) It was distinctively eucharistic: though instituted on the sad night of the Betrayal, yet full of the joyous spirit of thanksgiving . . 106–112
Henceforth the Sacrifice of Christ was continuous, — the unending Sacrifice of Divine Love 113

Through union with Christ His disciples join with Him in the Eucharist of Heaven.

Distinction between Christ's part and man's part in the Eucharist.

Christ alone is the Priest Who offers, and the Lamb Who is offered in Heaven 114

While Christ offers His Body and Blood in Heaven, we offer bread and wine on earth.

Christ unites our offering to His Offering, and makes our bread the Bread of Life 115

This is a truth of Heaven, and therefore a mystery to us on earth.

While Christ is present with us on earth, we, through union with Him, are lifted up into the Heavenly Places, and join in the Worship of Heaven itself 116–118

CHAPTER VI

THE CHURCH THE BODY OF CHRIST

Progressive teaching of our Lord regarding the Kingdom of Heaven 119

Many called, but not all choose to do God's Will.

Therefore the Kingdom of Heaven on earth includes both saints and sinners. From this it follows that it is outward and visible as well as invisible 120

The Kingdom is centred in the Person of Christ: it has no existence apart from Him. — Figure of the Vine and the branches 121

Christ's teaching cannot be understood apart from the facts of His Life: — these also inseparable one from another 122

Pentecost the Birthday of the Church

The Church an organism, not an organization 123

Its life centred in Christ in Heaven.

	PAGE
It is inspired by the Mind of Christ controlled by the Will of Christ: through its members Christ continues His work on earth.	124
Organic life and unity of the Church inspired St. Paul to call it the "Body of Christ"	125
Emphasis laid by St. Paul on this analogy	126
Contrast between this conception of the Church and the ordinary Protestant idea	127
Abnormal development of the Church idea in the Middle Ages. Modern reaction upholding the sacredness of personality and the individual life	128
This idea in turn has been unduly emphasized; sins of heresy and schism ignored	129
Divergence of views arises from different conceptions, not of the Church, but of Christ Himself.	
All difficulties regarding the visible Church solved by a right understanding of the Incarnation	130
Brotherhood and co-operation in the Church of Christ	132
The Body of Christ visible as well as invisible.	
"By one Spirit we are all baptized into one Body"	133

CHAPTER VII

THE VICAR OF CHRIST ON EARTH

Importance of this subject, and our Lord's anticipation of the Church's need	134

I

The Comforter to take the place of Christ's earthly Presence.	135
Our Lord, after His Ascension, not separated from His Apostles, but they from Him	135
Hence the need of a Vicar of Christ on earth	136
Our Lord's promise to the Apostles fulfilled at Pentecost Significance of the word "Paraclete"	138
Belief of the Fathers.	
Doctrine substituted in the Middle Ages.	

II

The Vicar of Christ to be invisible	
The reasons for this	138–139

III

	PAGE
The Vicar of Christ not to speak of Himself .	140
No further outward Revelation.	
Office of the Vicar of Christ to interpret Christ's Words .	141
Progress in comprehension of the Faith, but not in the Faith itself	142
The Holy Scriptures contain all necessary doctrines . .	142
Contrast between the human and Divine Vicar . . .	143

IV

Influence of the Vicar of Christ upon the outside world.	
Christianity and Civilization	144
Possibility of Salvation outside the visible Church not to be denied	145

V

The Vicar of Christ to bring Christ to remembrance . .	145-146
This effected through the Scriptures	
Neglect of the Scriptures, as history shows, always due to some abnormal disturbing influence	147
Effect of the invention of printing in hastening the Reformation	148
The doctrine of verbal inspiration substituted by Protestants for Roman Catholic teaching regarding an infallible Vicar of Christ	148
Both Romanist and Protestant forgetful of the higher truth	149

VI

The Vicar of Christ to glorify Christ	150
Teaching of the Epistles regarding Christ's glorified Humanity.—Their triumphant joyous character in consequence of this	152
This conception of the glorified Christ imperfectly recognized by both Romanists and Protestants	153
Consequent erroneous doctrines	154

VII

The Vicar of Christ, the Spirit of Truth	154
(1) Truth in the individual	
(2) in the history of the Church . .	155
The Papacy and truthfulness	156
Human craving for infallible authority	157

	PAGE
Attraction of the kind of authority the Church of Rome offers. — Positive truth in essentials not dependent on a human vicar	158
The Holy Spirit the infallible Guide.	
This doctrine not inconsistent with regard for Church authority.	

VIII

The Vicar of Christ the Comforter.	
Meaning of the word "comfort" as used by Christ . . .	160
Distinctive type of character developed by constant dependence on an unseen Spirit of Truth and Fortitude	161

IX

The Vicar of Christ the Spirit of Unity	162
Christ Himself the centre of unity between God and man. Christ's oneness with the Father: — and with His disciples. — Through union with Him they are made one with each other	163
Basis of Christian unity lies in the Incarnation.	
It must be both natural and spiritual.	
Unscriptural idea of spiritual as opposed to organic unity	163
St. Paul's teaching regarding the oneness of the Church .	164
Essentials of unity in the Church all centre, through the power of the Spirit, in the Ascended Christ	166

CHAPTER VIII

THE APOSTOLIC SUCCESSION

I

Indications in the New Testament of an Apostolic Ministry .	167
Institution of the order of Deacons.	
Further extension of the ministry in the order of Elders or Priests	169
St. James the Lord's brother and his office in the Church . .	170
Evidence that he was not one of the Twelve Apostles . .	171
St. James, the first Bishop of Jerusalem	174
Answers to objections: — (1) that he only exercised the same authority as the other Apostles; (2) that he was merely a presiding Elder	176
Conclusive evidence of the Fathers upon the subject . .	177

CONTENTS

	PAGE
Influence of St. John and his disciples upon the organization of the Churches of Asia Minor	177-178
The Episcopate not a later development of the Ministry	179
Episcopal supervision exercised by St. Paul	180

II

New Testament teaching on the transmission of authority	181
Illustrated in the choice of St. Matthias	182
The principle of transmission of authority not questioned for fifteen hundred years	183
Objections raised against it:— these not warranted by Scripture	184
Teaching of the Anglican Prayer Book	185

III

Moral and spiritual force derived from belief in the Apostolic Succession	186
Higher ideals: (1) of the Ministry itself; (2) of Ministerial responsibility; (3) of responsibility in teaching	189
Belief in the Historic Episcopate essential to Church unity. Meaning of the term	191

IV

Subordinate offices in the early Church not involving transmission of authority	192
Many unmistakably called to do individual work without ministerial authority to transmit their functions	193
Difference between Churchmen and other Christian Bodies in their views of ministerial functions and authority. How these may be harmonized	194

CHAPTER IX

CHRISTIAN SACERDOTALISM

Prejudice existing against the term Sacerdotalism	195
Common objections, — from history; from the absence of the term in the New Testament	196
Is there a true Christian Sacerdotalism?	197
Origin and universality of the idea of Priesthood and Sacrifice. Perversions of the idea of Sacerdotalism no argument against a true conception of it	198-199

II

The Jewish Priesthood ordained by God 199
Jews taught that the blood of the prescribed sacrifices represented *life* 200
Imperfect and temporary character of these sacrifices.
Fulfilment of the Priestly ideal in Christ 201

III

Christ the ideal Priest: (1) because His Priesthood was inherent (thus differing from that of the Jewish priests); (2) It was revealed in His Life; (3) in His ideal Sacrifice; (4) in the exercise of His Heavenly Priesthood; (5) in the power of Divine self-sacrifice 201–204
Self-sacrifice the law of Love 205

IV

The union of Christ and His Church 206
    The Church the Body of Christ 207
    Hence if Christ is Priest the Church is priestly 207
    Testimony of St. Peter and St. John to this truth . . . 208
    The priesthood of the laity; its responsibilities and privileges 208

V

Priesthood of the clergy in the Apostolic Ministry 209
The Christian Priesthood representative, not Mediatorial . . 210
Canon Moberly on the true idea of the Priesthood.

VI

Teaching of the New Testament regarding Christian Priesthood 216
    Why the term "priest" was not applied to Christian Ministers in the New Testament 217
    The doctrine of Priesthood and Sacrifice emphatically taught 218

VII

The real power of the Priesthood is Self-Sacrifice 221

CHAPTER X

THE BIBLE IN THE CHURCH

The Bible and the Church inseparable as standards of appeal . 223
    The Apostles charged by our Lord both to minister the

Word, and to make members of the Church through
Baptism 225
The Gospels perpetuate the witness of the Apostles to
Christ, — the Epistles perpetuate the message of the
Ascended Christ to His Church.
Consequent interdependence of the Church and the New
Testament 226
The New Testament the Witness for the Faith of the early
Apostolic Church. — Use and influence of the Bible in the
early Church 227
Suspension of certain Church activities in the Middle Ages
in consequence of the Barbarian invasions 229
Historical sketch of the English Bible 230–232
Recognition of the Authority of Holy Scripture one of the
essential conditions for the reunion of Christendom . . . 233
The teaching of the Prayer Book regarding the Bible:
(1) It enjoins continuous reading of Old and New Testaments, both in public and private; (2) the teaching of the Ordination offices; (3) the Ministry of the Word in Preaching; (4) special admonition of the Clergy on this point. — Knowledge of the Bible necessary for faithful preaching 234–238
The Anglican Church the chief present Defender of the Bible
in Western Christendom 240

CHAPTER XI

PUBLIC WORSHIP IN NEW TESTAMENT DAYS

Reasons for comparative silence of the New Testament regarding the accessories of public worship and the external ordinances of Christianity 242
Certain definite customs of the early Apostolic Church are, however, disclosed.
Prayer, and the "Breaking of Bread" 243

I

The Worship of the Temple.
The ideal of a House of Prayer for all Nations as set forth
by Christ Himself 245
Need of the Church at the present day to strive more
earnestly after this ideal 246

Prayer the one thing needful to sanctify Christian Worship
Influence of real prayer in the Church 247

II

The " Breaking of Bread " the distinctive Christian service . 248
The only service of public worship ordained by Christ
Himself 249
Names of the Holy Communion . . . .
Meaning of the service; its power 250
Early Christian Liturgies: — their agreement in essential
details regarding the Celebration of the Holy Eucharist . 251
The Lambeth declaration in regard to the conditions for
its valid administration 252

III

The Holy Eucharist in the early Apostolic Church.
Celebrated on every Lord's Day 253-255

IV

Since the Reformation the Eucharist no longer made the chief
service on the Lord's Day 257
Consequences of this change from primitive practice.
(1) Spiritual education of communicants neglected. . . . 258
(2) Non-communicants rendered careless and indifferent
to sacramental doctrine 259
(3) Lowering of the Church's standards 261

V

The Church cannot convert the world by compromising
with it 262
Present need not so much increase in *numbers*, as in spiritual power among the few 263
Influence of the Eucharist on the lives of communicants . . . 264
Communions of the Primitive Church compared with those
of the present day 265
Similarity between Anglican and Primitive precedent.
Communion office of the Prayer Book and Eucharistic
Celebrations of the Early Church 266
The test of true worship:
it must combine the moral, spiritual, and intellectual
faculties 267

VI

Balance preserved in the Anglican Church between the Ministry of the Word and of the Sacraments 268
High ideal of the Prayer Book violated by separating the Ante-Communion and sermon from the Communion itself
Eucharistic service for Communicants should be again made the chief service of the Lord's Day 269
This would be a witness to non-communicants of a higher life from which they wilfully exclude themselves . . . .
Inspiring effect of such a service on the Communicants themselves 270

New Testament Churchmanship

CHAPTER I

THE VIRGIN BIRTH OF CHRIST

ALL visions of earthly empires and all the memorable events of the historic past sink into the dim background, when we stand before the manger of Bethlehem and hear angels from Heaven proclaiming the glad tidings of a Saviour's birth.

By a gravitation of human thought, which seems to have been irresistible, the leading nations of the earth have accepted that event as the dividing point between ancient and modern history; as regulating the chronology of the civilized world; as marking an epoch to which the whole ancient world, desiring the Desire of Nations, looked forward; and to which the whole modern world, beholding the mysterious, irresistible power of Jesus Christ over the nations, looks back.

The Birth of Christ marks also, most significantly, the division between the Old and New Testaments, those two revelations of Jehovah to man, wherein "God, having of old time spoken to the fathers in the prophets in many parts and in many modes, spake unto us in the end of these days in His Son."[1] And as the Old Testament began with God's story of that first Adam, who became "a living soul," so the New Testament commences with the Gospel of the Second Adam, Who became "a life-giving spirit." As the former book discloses to us how the first man is "of the earth, earthy," and how from him are born, by natural generation, a race of earthly descendants who are bone of his bone, flesh of his flesh, and blood of his blood; so the latter reveals how the Second Man is from Heaven, and how all who, through Him, become children of God, are descended from Him by supernatural generation, being born again, "not of blood, nor of the will of the flesh, nor of the will of man, but of God."

Later on we shall endeavor to show how this scriptural contrast between the first and second Adam interprets the meaning of the Incarnation, but as this cannot be rightly understood apart from belief in the Virgin Birth of Christ it will be necessary first to fix our attention upon His Nativity; for probably since the Christian era began there has never been a time when the disposition and tendency to doubt the scriptural fact of Christ's miraculous birth has been so strong as it is to-day.

The objections raised are, to many of us, twice-told tales. It is said that the event is recorded in only two of the four Gospels; that it is referred to in but one prophecy of the Old Testament and that this one is of very uncertain interpretation; that there is no mention of it whatever in the Epistles of the New Testament, or even in the Gospels themselves, after

---

[1] Westcott on Heb. i. 1.

the opening chapters of St. Matthew and St. Luke; and that therefore it must have been a later addition to the Gospel history, which arose either as a myth or a legend. It is, furthermore, objected that the Virgin Birth of Christ is a wholly unnecessary miracle, which, so far from strengthening the Gospel narrative, really weakens its force; and that, even if the fact is accepted by believers, it is of no theological importance whatever, adding nothing to the sublime truths that are emphasized elsewhere in the Gospels and Epistles of the New Testament; and some even go so far as to maintain and believe that they can omit this part of the Gospel story without detriment to the rest, or without altering their attitude as orthodox believers in the Christian religion.

I

In answer to these objections we must, first of all, remember that the account of Christ's miraculous birth cannot be dropped from the inspired records without destroying the integrity of the whole Gospel history as it has been handed down to us. If it be said that this account appears in only two of the Gospels, let us remember that only two of the Gospels record the Ascension. If it be argued that the passages regarding Christ's Nativity can be left out of St. Matthew and St. Luke without impairing the harmony of the rest of their narratives, we would point out that, by the same arbitrary criticism, the account of the Ascension, given by St. Mark and St. Luke, can be eliminated without doing violence to the context; for the intervening portions are equally silent regarding both events. Nay, we might go a step farther even than this. With the exception of a few prophecies from the lips of Christ, there is no reference to the Resurrection itself in the three Synoptic Gospels, before its actual occurrence. Strike out these detached prophecies, which might, with equal plausibility, be regarded as subsequent additions, and, on the same principle on which the account of the Nativity is dropped from the beginning of the Gospel history, that of the Resurrection, as well as of the Ascension, could be omitted from its end. As a matter of fact, the narrative of the miraculous birth of Christ (including that of the visit of the Magi and of the nativity of St. John the Baptist, with which it is inseparably interwoven) occupies almost as large a place in the Gospel as the combined records of His Resurrection and Ascension; while all three together — the Nativity, Resurrection, and Ascension — are less than a third as long as the account of Christ's Passion and Crucifixion. If it be answered here that the Resurrection and Ascension were miraculous events, so wholly unexpected in human history that there could be no direct reference to them before their actual occurrence, we would ask the objectors to face the bearings of this same argument on the other side. The miraculous birth of Christ was, likewise, an event so wholly unexpected in human history, that, *after* its actual occurrence, the Christians of New Testament times were held back by an awe-inspiring consciousness of mystery and the delicacy of a sacred reserve from communicating the whole truth of Christ's Virgin Birth in their preaching of the Gospel to their Jewish contemporaries and adversaries in the outside world. Indeed, it was not until after Christ rose from the dead and ascended to Heaven that the real reason and necessity for His miraculous birth could be fully appreciated even by His disciples themselves.

The Gospels, of course, were written after this date; written by men who were overshadowed by the consciousness that He Whose earthly life they were portraying was not only their reigning King in Heaven, but that He was 'Ἀλήθεια, — Ideal Truth. Dominated and inspired by this consciousness, the authors of the four Gospels have written their records with a conciseness, a straightforward artlessness, a transparent truthfulness and simplicity of style, a conspicuous absence of praise or censure, of comment or attempt at amplification, which is unique in the annals of all literature. And the same characteristics which mark the other parts of the Gospel narratives are to be observed in the accounts of Christ's miraculous birth. Though these were written after He had ascended to Heaven, it was providentially ordered by God that the event itself should be inscribed on the Gospel page before the first generation of Christians had passed away, for St. Matthew was one of Christ's own chosen apostles, in the days of His Ministry, while St. Luke carries us back even further still, to the very commencement of the Gospel times, for he says that he gained his information from those who "*from the beginning were eye-witnesses, and ministers of the word.*"[1] He does not mention who these persons were. Whether they were Zacharias and Elizabeth, or those of their neighbors who dwelt " in

---

[1] St. Luke i. 2.

the hill-country of Judæa,"[1] or the shepherds of Bethlehem, or the Virgin Mary herself, he does not say; but certainly, if they were not these they must have been "eye-witnesses and ministers of the word," who "from the beginning" were intimately acquainted, not only with the events preceding Christ's birth, but with that little circle of God's saints whose names appear in the first two chapters of St. Luke's Gospel; for the narrative lifts us up above the level of mere tradition or legend. Though it has the poetic fervor of the ancient Jewish prophets, it soars higher than poetry. It has that severe brevity which characterizes the rest of the Gospel history. It breathes that atmosphere of simplicity and truthfulness, of fervent praise and lowly humility, of Christ-like purity and refinement of thought, which belongs only to those unworldly and pure-hearted men and women who know God. These characteristics of the sacred record have scarcely received the attention that they deserve, at the hands of Biblical scholars. If the narrative of Christ's Nativity is dropped from the Gospel page, a vision of exquisite purity, which has enthralled the hearts and refined the souls of men all through the Christian era, will be gone, and the world will be the poorer forever after.

The record begins with the message of an angel to Zacharias regarding a son to be born unto him, who shall go before the coming Messiah, "in the spirit and power of Elijah;" then follows the annunciation of the same angel, Gabriel, to the Virgin Mary herself, foretelling both the miraculous birth of the Son of God, and also the nativity of St. John

[1] St. Luke i. 65.

the Baptist. After the departure of the angel, Mary, following a natural, spontaneous, and womanly impulse, arose with haste, went into the hill-country of Judæa, and entered into the house of the aged Elizabeth, her saintly and revered cousin. The narrative tells how, on the very threshold, Elizabeth, moved alike by the inspiration of the Holy Ghost and the intuitions of womanly sympathy, greeted her with the words, "Blessed art thou among women, and blessed is the fruit of thy womb. And whence is this to me, that the mother of my Lord should come unto me?"[1] and then records that the young Virgin Mary abode in the house of Zacharias and Elizabeth about three months, when she returned to her own home at Nazareth. Supplementing this history with St. Matthew's entirely separate and distinct account of the angel that appeared unto Joseph in a dream, announcing unto him the conception of a Son of Mary "Who should save His people from their sins," we discover that there were, at least, four saintly persons who expected the miraculous birth of Christ before His actual Nativity, — Zacharias and Joseph, Elizabeth, and the Virgin Mary herself.

Then follows a description of the Birth of Christ at Bethlehem, which is as remarkable for what it does not record as for that which it narrates. For if there were any prepossession or predisposition in the Jewish mind regarding their coming Messiah, it was the fixed idea that He was to appear as a temporal monarch, whose glory should eclipse that of Solomon and whose power should exceed that of the Roman empire. When we contrast the reality itself with all

[1] St. Luke i. 42, 43.

these fervent anticipations, we cannot discover one point of correspondence. We read, indeed, of a vision of angels, singing in the starlit skies, "Glory to God in the Highest, and on earth, peace, good-will toward men," but in all other respects the Nativity of Jesus Christ is a commonplace scene, the counterpart of which, in general details, has been witnessed a thousand times over in peasant life and homes of poverty, especially in oriental countries. When we apply to the narrative the searching tests of nineteenth century thought and try it by the principles of modern criticism, we are struck not so much by the appearance of the angels, as by the fact that, side by side with this vision, there should not have been other miraculous signs, which, if the record is not a plain report of actual fact, human imagination would have been far more apt to insert; converting the commonplace scene into one of earthly splendor, and changing the stable into a palace or church, the village inn into traditional holy ground, the manger into an altar of Heaven, and the speechless, helpless Babe into a transfigured, miracle-working Prince of Peace. If the angels with their messages from Heaven, preceding and following Christ's birth and bearing witness to His Virgin Birth are fictions, created by the devout imaginations of the faithful, then the same imaginative tendencies which conjured up these visions would have led on, inevitably and irresistibly, to the invention of these other miraculous signs; and if, in turn, such other signs had been superadded, then the reality of Christ's human condition, of His sufferings and temptations — yes, of His very manhood itself — would have been abrogated; and thus the story of His Nativity, like those of the childhood of Christ that are told in the spurious gospels, would have been utterly inconsistent with the other parts of the New Testament narrative, and the integrity of the Gospels would have been destroyed. As a matter of fact, the absence of the miraculous is a marked feature of the story itself. The herald angel announces to the shepherds: "*This* shall be a *sign* unto you. Ye shall find the Babe wrapped in swaddling clothes, lying in a manger.[1] The only miraculous part is the angel's own words. And if the angelic visions and messages themselves are objected to, it is to be noted that such appearances are in perfect harmony with all the rest of the Gospel history, in which it is recorded that angels appeared also after Christ's Temptation, on the day of His Resurrection, and at the time of His Ascension.

Leaving the synoptics, let us now turn to the record of St. John. It is often said that the fourth Gospel is absolutely silent regarding the Nativity of Christ: if so, it is no less silent concerning His Ascension, His institution of the Eucharist, His commission to the Apostles regarding Baptism and other important events that the synoptics record. Indeed, this is St. John's method; and it is an indication of the later origin of his Gospel. Yet the omission is, in almost every instance, supplied and compensated for by indirect references of the strongest kind.

So also is it with regard to the Nativity. Though St. John's narrative, unlike those of St. Matthew and St. Luke, has at its beginning no account of the miraculous birth of Christ, yet there is a passage in the

[1] St. Luke ii. 12.

first chapter of the fourth Gospel which cannot be interpreted as setting forth the full and complete meaning of the Incarnation, unless it be taken as referring directly to Christ's Virgin Birth. Of Christ, the Light of the world, the Apostle writes: "He was in the world, and the world was made by Him, and the world knew Him not. He came unto His own, and His own received Him not; but as many as received Him, to them gave He the right (δύναμις) to become the sons of God, even to them which believe on His name: *which were born, not of blood, nor of the will of the flesh, nor of the will of man, but of God*.[1] Then he adds, in closest juxtaposition: "And the Word was made flesh, and dwelt among us, and we beheld His glory (the glory as of the only begotten of the Father), full of grace and truth."[2] The doctrine here set forth by St. John is that Christ, the Word of God, " by Whom all things were made, and without Whom was not anything made that was made," at last, in the fulness of time, came into the world and became the Head of a new race of men. Taking the thirteenth and fourteenth verses of the first chapter of his Gospel together (as we are obliged, by the context, to do), St. John tells us that it was not before but *after* Christ, the Word of God, became flesh, that He, as the Second Adam, gave the power or right to those who received Him to become immortal children of God. If, therefore, the only begotten Son of God, *through His Incarnation*, regenerates believers in body and soul and makes them sons of God by a new birth from above, then it follows, inevitably, that He, the Progenitor, "the Word

[1] St. John i. 10-13. [2] St. John i. 14.

made flesh," as well as those to whom He gives power to become sons, must be born, "not of blood, nor of the will of the flesh, nor of the will of man, but of God." Nay, it is absolutely inconceivable to any theologian, who has a right understanding of the meaning and purpose of the Incarnation of Christ, that St. John could have written words like these, had he believed that Christ was the earthborn offspring of human parents. It must have been nothing less than the consciousness of the miraculous birth of Christ, — "not of the will of the flesh, nor of the will of man, but of God," — and the illumination which his mind had received regarding the profound meaning of that event, which inspired him to place this passage in the forefront of his Gospel. As Bishop Westcott well says: "The fact of the miraculous conception, though not stated, is necessarily implied by the Evangelist. The coming of the Word into flesh is presented as a creative act in the same way as the coming of all things into being was.[1]

Again, Joseph and the Virgin Mary, we read, were themselves dwellers in Nazareth both before and after Christ's birth.[2] The visit to Bethlehem was only temporary. They returned to Nazareth very shortly after Christ's birth, and we all know that when our Lord's public ministry began, thirty years later, He was universally regarded by the Jews as a native of Nazareth; nor is there anything in the synoptic Gospels, after the account of his Nativity and the visit of the Magi, to show that He was not so. Indeed, so prevalent was the belief, that Pilate affixed

---

[1] Westcott's Commentary on St. John i. 14.
[2] See St. Luke i. 26, 56; ii. 4, etc.

to the cross itself the title: "Jesus of Nazareth, the King of the Jews." In view of this fact, it is noteworthy that the single reference to the real place of Christ's birth, in those after years, is to be found not in St. Matthew or St. Luke, who record His Nativity, but in the Fourth Gospel, which omits it. It is St. John alone who tells us that those Jews who were disposed to accept Jesus as the Christ found a stumbling-block in the fact that he was a Nazarene;[1] it is in St. John's Gospel alone that we read of those stormy discussions among the Jews themselves, in the last year of Christ's life, in which while some said "Is not this the Christ?" others answered: "Shall Christ come out of Galilee? Hath not the Scripture said that Christ cometh of the Seed of David, and out of the town of Bethlehem, where David was?"[2] Here we find the Scribes and Pharisees, after a lapse of thirty years, quoting the same ancient prophecy regarding the birthplace of the Messiah to which the doctors of the law had pointed when the Magi came to Herod, asking where Christ should be born.[3] This indicates how prominent a place the words of the Prophet Micah occupied in the Jewish mind, in the time of Christ; and it is scarcely possible that when this same prophecy was adduced by Scribes and Pharisees as a proof that Jesus of Nazareth was not the Christ, St. John should have recorded the incident, without note or explanation, had it not been a recognized and well-known fact among the Christians of that day that Christ was born in Bethlehem.[4]

[1] St. John i. 46.   [2] St. John vii. 41, 42.   [3] St. Matt. i. 6.
[4] It may seem strange, at first sight, that St. John, of all the

Time fails to pursue this branch of our subject any further; but enough, we trust, has been adduced to show how fully one Gospel supplies that which the others take for granted, and how all stand or fall together as a whole. If we apply any of the tests of the Higher Criticism which are now regarded as so searching, we find that in authenticity, in credibility, in integrity and style, the account of the Nativity of Christ stands upon the same high level with the other parts of the Gospel narrative. The same prepossession and bias of mind against the miraculous which would throw doubt upon the Virgin Birth of Christ bring equally under suspicion the whole miraculous element in New Testament history and every other passage where it occurs. Those who, yielding to this prepossession, dismiss the first chapters of St. Matthew and St. Luke as spurious, will sooner or later, if they are logical and consistent, be obliged, on the same principles, to treat all the other great events of Christ's life in the same way. And thus

Apostles, should have failed to hand down to us, in place of such indirect references, a detailed narrative of Christ's Nativity itself, for, in his own Gospel, he tells us that, by the dying charge of Christ on the cross the blessed Virgin was left to the care of "the disciple whom Jesus loved," and that, "from that hour, that disciple took her unto his own home" (St. John xix. 27); but when we think of the bond of union that had been cemented between them by Christ Himself in those words, "Behold thy son, — Behold thy mother;" when we reflect upon that sacred companionship and upon the mutual influence of the Virgin Mary and the disciple whom Jesus loved upon each other's life and thought; when, above all, we remember those characteristics of silent pondering, of quiet self-control and self-sacrifice, of delicate reserve and sacred humility, which appear, from the Gospel narratives, to have belonged to the blessed Virgin, we can see reason enough why her name and her connection with Christ appear so rarely in St. John's Gospel.

the whole Gospel history must inevitably, in the end, lose its hold upon their consciences as an authoritative testimony regarding the supernatural facts in the life of the incarnate Son of God.

II

But here some objector will answer: "I am compelled to follow truth, wherever it leads, whatever it costs, and however holy and revered the authority may be that holds me back. There is no proof that the Gospels were actually written by those whose names they bear. Even granting that they were, there is no evidence that they have come down to us in the form in which they were originally transcribed. The Christians in the first and second centuries lived in an uncritical age, and two hundred years is a period long enough for the insertion of any number of additions to the original four Gospels, while other Gospels, quite as trustworthy, may have been lost, which may yet come to light. What if copies of St. Matthew's or St. Luke's Gospels, more ancient than those we possess, should be recovered in which the first chapters should be wanting? Or an additional Gospel should be found, which gives an entirely different and a non-miraculous account of Christ's birth?"[1]

Objections like these would scarcely deserve consideration, and we would not venture on this digression, were they not made in such a spirit of

---

[1] The writer has, time and again, heard these very objections made, not only by intelligent and well-educated men, but also by some who are prominent ministers in various Christian bodies.

sincerity and honesty, by men who have neither the time to investigate and see for themselves how little foundation there is for their objections, nor the opportunity for learning the real facts. Such criticisms arise, of course, from the trend of popular thought and the bias it unconsciously creates in men's minds, but they are, nevertheless, an illustration of how the human imagination can be as uncritical and undisciplined on the side of scepticism as on that of credulity. For none could speak thus except objectors unacquainted with the history of the formation of the Canon of the New Testament in the first three centuries; or critics like Baur and the author of "Supernatural Religion," who are so biassed by their desire to prove an hypothesis contrary to facts, that they give to the facts themselves an unnatural interpretation. It is true that the Christian Church, in the first three centuries, had not the training in that *kind* of criticism which characterizes the biblical scholars of the nineteenth century. It would be an anachronism to expect this even of the most learned and exact scholars of that day, for our modern method of criticism is the result of an evolutionary process which has been going on for centuries. But this does not justify us in stigmatizing the first three centuries as "an uncritical age;" for the scholars of the early church were just as exact in following their own methods of criticism as we are in prosecuting ours. And, as they lived so much nearer than we do to the date when the original documents were written, their advantages for arriving at the truth, and for distinguishing the difference between true and spurious documents, were correspondingly greater than our own. In addition to this, the Church of God has always felt the tremendous responsibility, to use the language of St. Paul, of being "the Keeper of Holy Writ," and one has but to read the writings of the early Fathers and the records of the early Councils to see with what earnest solicitude, careful examination and sacred caution the inspired records of the New Testament were preserved and separated from other contemporaneous Christian writings. Any one who is familiar with the ecclesiastical history of that period will see at a glance that, in those days of the gradual formation of the Canon of the New Testament, the feeling of responsibility in the Church concerning Holy Writ was far greater and more pressing than it is, or can possibly be, now, when that Canon has been already formed and accepted. Yet the Christians of the present day are often charged with assuming an attitude of ultra conservatism regarding the Canon of the Bible; this is instructive; it is an outward indication of the feeling of grave responsibility shared by all believers in common, as to the necessity of protecting and guarding the Word of God. If it is so strong in these days, we can realize what its development must have been in those more crucial times when that Canon was in the process of formation.

Finally, whatever may have been said fifty years ago as to the additions made to the original documents in the second century, the work of the English and American Revisers of the New Testament in comparing the manuscripts and versions which have come down to us; the advance that has been made in New Testament criticism itself since the days of Ferdinand Baur; the recent vindication of the authenticity of patristic writings like the Epistles of Ignatius that were once regarded as spurious; and last but not least, the additional patristic documents that have been discovered within the past twenty-five years, have all gone to prove the genuineness of the Gospels in the form in which we possess them.

While few of us have the time or the training to enter into this subject with that accuracy of thought, that sufficiency of knowledge, and that cultivated power of judgement which those New Testament critics possess who devote their whole lives to its study, our interest in the authenticity of the Gospels is just as real and vital as theirs; and there are some facts whose weight it needs no expert training to understand and appreciate.

The latest criticism accepts the three synoptic Gospels as having been written within forty years after the Ascension. Listen to what Dr. Sanday, one of the greatest living authorities on the New Testament, says:

"On this point, however, I can speak with great confidence . . . that the great mass of the narrative in the first three Gospels took its shape before the destruction of Jerusalem, *i. e.* within less than forty years of the events" (Bampton Lectures, page 283).

"But indeed, all three Gospels, not only the older documents out of which they are composed, but our present Gospels as we have them, lie under the shadow of the fall of Jerusalem. . . . Of this I think that we may rest assured that the whole process of the composition of our first three Gospels, a process no doubt highly complicated and in its details obscure, must be comprised within limits of which the least is not later than the year 80 A. D." (Bampton Lectures, p. 293).

Irenæus, who was a follower of Polycarp, a disciple of St. John, and who lived through the greater part of the second century (A. D. 130-190), writes as follows : —

" So firm is the ground on which these three Gospels rest that the very heretics themselves bear witness to them, and starting from these [documents] each one of them endeavors to establish his peculiar doctrine. For the Ebionites, who use Matthew's Gospel only, are confuted out of this very same, making false suppositions with regard to the Lord. But Marcion, mutilating that according to St. Luke, is proved to be a blasphemer of the only existing God by that which he still retains. Those again who separate Jesus from Christ, alleging that Christ remained impassible but that it was Jesus who suffered, preferring the Gospel of St. Mark, if they read it with a love of the truth, may have their errors rectified. Those, moreover, who follow Valentinus, making copious use of that according to John, shall be proved to be totally in error by means of this very Gospel.

" It is not possible that the Gospels can be more or fewer in number than they are. For, since there are four zones of the world in which we live, and four principal winds, while the Church is scattered throughout all the world, and the 'pillar and ground' of the Church is the Gospel and the spirit of life, it is fitting that she should have four pillars, breathing out immortality on every side."

Again, the Muratorian Fragment was written A. D. 160-220. It contains a canon of the New Testament and is so mutilated that it commences at the middle of the second Gospel; but the other books are there. If, as Bishop Lightfoot thinks, this was composed by Hippolytus, Bishop of Portus (A. D. 160-226), a writer whose position and influence were unique among the Roman Christians of his day, then its importance is even more strongly emphasized. And Hippolytus himself supplies the missing portion by having written a commentary on St. Matthew's Gospel.

Again, the Fathers of the primitive Church often spoke in their writings of a very early Harmony of the four Gospels, called the Diatessaron of Tatian, in which were woven into one continuous narrative the combined accounts of St. Matthew and St. Luke regarding the Nativity of our Lord; and for centuries it was a subject of deepest regret that a work quoted with such approval by the early Fathers and written in the second century by a Christian of such marked ability, should have been lost. Tatian was an Assyrian, born about 110 A. D. At Rome he became the pupil of Justin Martyr, and after the martyrdom of the latter (155-166), became his successor. The period of Tatian's literary activity is placed by Lightfoot between A. D. 155-170; by Westcott, A. D. 150-175; by Harnack, 152-3. In 1886 the long lost, long sought Diatessaron, or Harmony of the Four Gospels, was suddenly discovered, and it has become of immense value, directly and indirectly, in proving their early origin.[1]

---

[1] The Diatessaron of Tatian. "Tatian the Assyrian, a pupil of Justin Martyr wrote a harmony of the four Gospels, called the "Diatessaron," about, or a little after, the middle of the second century. (*i. e.* A. D. 150-175.) This work, and also a Commentary upon it,

So far, we have adduced only Irenæus, Hippolytus and Tatian as authorities, because they relate to all four Gospels. Our space will not permit us to go back from author to author in whose writings the words of the Gospels are quoted. In instances of this kind, the writings of heretics, like Marcion and the Gnostics, are even more valuable than those of orthodox believers, for they reveal in what reverent estimation the Gospels were held at that early day even by those who were in the position of doubters. It is by bringing all these proofs together that Dr. Sanday has felt justified in stating that all four Gospels were written before the fall of Jerusalem; and Professor Harnack, in his most recent work, says: "The oldest literature of the Church, in all main points, and in most details, from the point of view of literary criticism, is genuine and trustworthy. In the whole New Testament there is, in all probability, only a single writing which can be looked upon as pseudonymous in the strictest sense of the word,— namely, the Second Epistle of St. Peter."

written later by Ephraem the Syrian, are referred to by ancient writers, but no manuscripts of either of the writings were discovered, until in 1876 a Latin translation of the Commentary was made from an Armenian version found in Venice,— and in 1888 an Arabic translation of the Diatessaron itself was discovered in the Vatican library.
Only thirteen years ago the evidence which could be alleged in support of the traditional theory that Tatian's Diatessaron was composed of our four Gospels, though in my judgment sufficient, was scanty. The recovery of Ephraem's Lectures, and of the Arabic translation of the Diatessaron, has wholly changed the conditions of the controversy. That Tatian, the friend of Justin Martyr, knew our four Gospels, and that in his Diatessaron he worked them into a continuous narrative, is now finally demonstrated."— *The Living Christ and the Four Gospels*, Dale, p. 170.

All through this period the miraculous birth of Christ was undoubtedly accepted as an historic fact by the Church of Christ. Before A. D. 117, or within twenty-five years of the death of St. John, Ignatius, his disciple, in one of the seven epistles which the late Bishop Lightfoot proved conclusively to be genuine, wrote to the Ephesians: "Hidden from the prince of this world were the virginity of Mary, and her child-bearing, and likewise, also, the death of the Lord, — three mysteries to be cried aloud, the which were wrought in the silence of God. How then were they made manifest to the ages? A star shone forth in the heavens above all the stars: and its light was unutterable, and its strangeness caused amazement" (Ignatius, Epistle to Ephesians, cap. 19).

The following passages from Justin Martyr, written not more than forty years after Ignatius, are also unmistakable in their import: —

"The angel of God who was sent to the same virgin at that time brought her good news, saying, 'Behold, thou shalt conceive of the Holy Ghost, and shalt bear a Son, and He shall be called the Son of the Highest' . . . as they *who have recorded* all that concerns our Saviour Jesus Christ here taught."—*First Apology*, cap. 33.

"And since we find it recorded in the Memoirs of the Apostles, that He [JESUS] is the Son of God; and since we call Him the Son, we have understood that He proceeded before all creatures from the Father by His power and will, and that He became man by the Virgin." — *Dialogue with Trypho*, cap. 100.

"I have already proved that He was the only begotten in a peculiar manner, Word and Power by Him, and having afterwards become man through the Virgin, as we have learned from the Memoirs." — *Ibid*. cap. 105.

One more fact is to be borne in mind as we look back to those early centuries, which, in accordance with the principle that every denial presupposes an anterior affirmation, is conclusive that these writers were expressing the ordinary belief of the Christians of their day. In the beginning of the second century the sect of the Ebionites denied outright that Christ had ever been conceived of the Holy Ghost and born of the Virgin Mary; and the very existence of this emphatic denial on their part, as Dr. Dorner well says, throws out with great emphasis the fact that the miraculous conception of our Lord must have been, previously, the common and accepted Creed of the Church.

III

But the methods of modern criticism justify us in assuming a still stronger position. As Professor Weiss of Berlin has recently shown in his Life of Christ, the miraculous birth of our Lord stands out as an historic fact, which, by its own inherent force, refutes every hypothesis as to its mythic or legendary origin. For what is a myth and what is a legend? The two are diametrically opposite to one another. A myth is an idea for which a fact is, in process of time, invented by the fervent imaginations of the faithful; while, on the contrary, a legend is a fact which becomes, by and by, the basis for an idea. Now it so happens, that both of these hypotheses regarding the whole miraculous history of the New Testament have been discussed in Germany and elsewhere by some of the most brilliant minds of the nineteenth century. Fifty years ago the mythic theory was broached by Strauss and prosecuted by his adherents; and this, in turn, was followed by the legend theory of Ferdinand Baur and his school of critics.

The first, or mythic theory, necessitates a predisposition and tendency toward a certain belief, which gradually grows stronger and stronger until, at last, a fact is imagined to express the fixed preconceived ideas. According to the laws of history and human thought, therefore, a myth cannot arise without such a prepossession in the minds of believers. Applying this test to the mythic theory of Christ's supernatural birth, we fail to find in the Rabbinical literature of the Jews before Christ, and even in the Old Testament itself, the slightest trace of any expectation that Christ should be born of a virgin. On the contrary, the whole trend of Hebrew thought was in the opposite direction, for among the Jews married life was always considered a higher state than single life. It was not until a later age that the idea of the superior sanctity of the virgin state became prevalent; and it is a gross anachronism to imagine that the ancient Jews were influenced or governed by it. Certainly, we can discover no trace of such influence in the writings of the Jewish prophets, for the only passage in the whole Old Testament which refers directly to the miraculous birth of Christ is that verse in the prophecy of Isaiah which foretells that a virgin shall conceive and bring forth a child, and shall call His name Immanuel (Isaiah vii. 14). But, as the word "virgin" was often used among the Jews before Christ, in the general sense of any young woman, this prophecy of Isaiah, wonderful as it is, was entirely passed over and forgotten by the Rabbis and Doctors of the Law, until, at last, it was interpreted by the fact. The fact was not invented, like a myth, to meet the prophecy, but the prophecy was sought out by St. Matthew, and discovered by him to meet a fact which had already taken place. As Dr. Weiss well says, the silence of the Old Testament itself regarding any prepossession or feeling of expectation of Christ's miraculous birth of a virgin, disposes forever of the mythic hypothesis of His Nativity.

Let us now pass from the theory of myth to that of legend, and from the Old to the New Testament. In a similar way, a legend takes time to grow, and the gradual development of its growth can be traced in the literature of the times, showing how a natural fact slowly becomes, in the imaginations of the faithful, a supernatural one, to which the idea of a divine significance becomes attached. But, in the New Testament, which hands down to us the earliest of all Christian writings, there is not the slightest trace of the development of the legend theory. After the record of the Nativity itself, in the first chapters of St. Matthew and St. Luke, and the allusion to it in the beginning of St. John's record, the Gospels make no further allusion to it. What is even more remarkable, in the Epistles of the New Testament, where we can trace, in other ways, a very distinct development of Christian doctrine, there is no direct allusion to the Nativity whatever. In several passages, we shall show later on, it is taken for granted, and in one verse of the Epistle to the Galatians, where St. Paul speaks of God, in the fulness of time, sending forth His Son, "made of a woman"[1] the emphasis laid upon the last sentence may show that the Apostle had the Virgin Birth of Christ in mind; but this is very different from the development of a fact into a legend. After the narrative of the Nativity itself, the New Testament is as silent as the Old regarding the miraculous birth of our Lord. And when we turn to the post-apostolic writings the same story repeats itself. While enough is recorded, in detached sayings of the Fathers, and sentences of the early symbols of faith, to show that the Church of Christ held firmly to the belief that He was conceived by the Holy Ghost, born of the Virgin Mary, there is none of that continuous emphasis laid upon the fact, none of that imaginative language, none of that gradual expansion of the supernatural side, that the legend theory requires. Testing the scriptural record of Christ's Nativity by those very laws of history and human thought which govern the formation of legends, we are compelled to the conclusion that the Gospel narrative of Christ's birth cannot possibly be legendary. If, therefore, that record is neither myth on the one hand, nor legend on the other, there is only one alternative left, — it must be historic fact.

[1] Gal. iv. 4.

CHAPTER II

THE VIRGIN BIRTH AND THE NEW ADAM

IN the last chapter, we spoke of the scriptural contrast between the First and the Second Adam, and showed that the reference to the Virgin Birth of Christ, as the New Adam and the Founder of a new race, appears by necessary implication, and as a truth that is taken for granted by St. John, on the very first page of the fourth Gospel. Indeed, without that fact, St. John's words, both in this passage and also in the third and sixth chapters of his Gospel, which implicitly refer to Baptism and the Holy Communion, are left without the key to their true interpretation and stand unrelated to one another. For never can we comprehend the wonderful nature of the Incarnate Life of Jesus Christ, and the way in which it not only solves the conflicting problems of human existence but interprets His own sacramental teaching, until we fix our attention closely upon the beginning of His Incarnation as it is revealed in the New Testament records.

I

The fundamental principle underlying the Incarnation of Jesus Christ is the perfect union in Him of the Divine and human life.

From time immemorial, philosophers and seekers after God in every age have felt that there were insoluble difficulties uprising before them whenever they faced the great problems of Divine and human existence and endeavoured to reconcile them.

There was the relation between the infinite and the finite, between the subjective and the objective, between the spiritual and the material, and so on. Nor was the world ever able to reach satisfaction in all its age-long attempts to reconcile these difficulties until the birth of Christ. The first page of the Gospel of St. John proclaims that Christ was the Light of the world, that in Him was life, and that the Life was the light of men. It was so because It was both Divine and Human; God and all that belongs to the Godhead; manhood, and all that pertains to our humanity in its perfection, found their perfect union in Jesus Christ.

Let us fix our attention upon this fundamental truth. It is inconceivable that the Godhead could have become enshrined in an *imperfect* or sinful manhood. The body prepared for Christ, when He said, "Lo, I come to do Thy will, O God," must have been a perfect human body, for He was to be the Lamb of God, without spot or blemish or any such thing. He was to be the Ideal Man, and the absolutely Sinless Man. Therefore He assumed all that pertains to human nature, imperfection only excepted. He was tempted in all points like as we are, yet without sin. This absolute necessity of sinlessness in the Saviour of the world, from every Christian point of view, is fundamental; without it the

Crucifixion and the Atonement, the Resurrection and Ascension, are robbed of their profound depth of meaning; nay, the Incarnation itself becomes an impossibility. And here let us anticipate any question which may arise as to the nature of sin by saying that sin is not an entity in itself. It is a *spirit* of lawlessness within us which is always rebelling against God. Sin, however, does not arise only from a lawless will which refuses to do the will of God; it comes also from a weak will which is *powerless* to do the will of God. And this enervation of will power within us arises from a hereditary bias toward lawlessness, or, if you will, a moral defect, which has been handed down to us by a long line of sinful ancestors.

The first Adam was unlike us, in that he was free from this taint of heredity. His will, before his fall, was in a state of equilibrium. If he sinned, it was through his own individual choice, and not because, like ourselves, he had any predisposition or bias toward sin, that weakened his power of resistance. So was it with Christ, the Second Adam. It is of great importance to our understanding of this whole subject, that we should bear this distinction in mind. If Christ had been created *like us*, He would not have been like the first Adam; and conversely, if he was created like the first Adam, He was unlike us in one respect, His human nature was perfect. His will power was not warped and weakened by the sinful will power of a long line of ancestors, handing down, by heredity, the moral defects that resulted from their sinfulness. Christ's human nature was like that of Adam in Paradise before sinning.

It was unlike ours, not in being a different kind of nature, but only in the one respect in which the First Adam's was unlike ours. Both the First and Second Adam were free from the taint of hereditary sin.

Yet this very unlikeness, so far from separating Christ from us, unites Him more closely to us. For if Christ, with a human will in a perfect state of equilibrium between right and wrong, was tempted in all points like as we are, yet kept Himself sinless by His own freedom of choice, and simply and only by His personal resistance to every temptation, then we are united to Him in the closest bonds of sympathy and by every tie of a common manhood. But if, instead of being like the first Adam, Christ had been created like us, and had that weakness of will power, that moral defect, which comes through the sinful entail of human heredity, then, notwithstanding His personal willingness to resist every temptation and to do God's will on earth as it is done in Heaven, the force of these sinful hereditary influences would, in Him as in us, have overcome His power of resistance, unless it were counteracted by a superhuman moral force infused into His manhood, enabling Him to live on a superhuman level of sinlessness. And the possession of this mysterious superhuman moral power, so different from anything that we have ever found in humanity, would not only have destroyed the reality of His human temptations, but also have separated Him from us by a gulf that is far wider and deeper than that which intervenes between us and the First Adam, or a Second Adam, Who was like the First. And this is our answer to the objection that the Virgin Birth of our Lord is an unnecessary miracle, which, so far from strengthening the Gospel narrative, really weakens its force. Christ must have been distinctly a new creation if He is the Second Adam and the Progenitor of a new race of men, who are born again into the Kingdom of Heaven. For these also are a new creation.

"Some modern theologians, accepting the moral miracle of sinlessness, reject the physical miracle, which, according to the Gospels, was its actual, if not necessary presupposition; or at least, treat it as a thing of no religious importance so long as the moral miracle is believed in. The element of truth in these views is that the supernatural birth is not an end in itself, but only a means to an end. It is the symbol, the sinlessness being the substance. A sinless Christ is the proper object of faith. Under what conditions such a Christ is possible is a very important question, but it belongs to theology rather than to religion. Yet it has to be remembered that faith is ever in a state of unstable equilibrium, while the supernatural is dealt with eclectically,— admitted in the moral and spiritual sphere, denied in the physical. With belief in the virgin birth is apt to go belief in the virgin life, as not less than the other a part of the veil that must be taken away that the true Jesus may be seen as He was — a morally defective man, better than most, but not perfectly good. . . . A sinless man is as much a miracle in the moral world as a virgin birth is a miracle in the physical world." [1]

II

And this brings before us another important truth regarding Christ's physical nature.

The doctrine of the Incarnation, as it has always been held by the Catholic Church, teaches us that

[1] "Apologetics," Bruce, p. 409.

when the Logos, or Word of God, was made flesh, He brought Heaven and earth together in His Own Person, and that in the dispensation of the fulness of times, God will gather together in one all things in Christ, both which are in Heaven and which are on earth.

If this interpretation of the meaning of Christ's Incarnation is correct, then it follows that life in Christ, which is not only the highest, but the broadest and most comprehensive life of which our human nature is capable, is not to be reached by pursuing and dwelling upon the spiritual to the exclusion of the material side of existence. The highest life comes from the combination of spiritual with physical forces, and develops itself out of their union.

This is a truth so plainly and distinctly set forth in the Epistles of the New Testament, and so necessary to a right understanding of their contents, that it is not only to be ceaselessly borne in mind whenever we think of the Incarnation, but is to stand as a fundamental principle, by which we test the truthfulness and accuracy of different theological propositions; for, from time immemorial, the tendency of religious thought has been to emphasize the separation of the physical from the spiritual, and to believe that spirituality is to be found on the spiritual side alone. Indeed, it is not too much to say that this unscriptural idea has been the cause of most of the sects and divisions in the Church.

The New Testament writers everywhere teach us that the sanctification of the body, with the physical conditions of existence connected with it, is as necessary to growth in grace as the sanctification of the soul. The body is "the Temple of the Holy Ghost;" the body is, in fact, the organ of the soul, for the two are inseparable in the preparation for immortal life. And if we look for the origin and source of that immortal life, it is to be found only in Christ Himself.

And here comes out, in sharp contrast, the distinction between the First and Second Adam. The First Adam "is of the earth, earthy." And all his descendants, who derive their life from him by natural generation, are likewise "of the earth, earthy." As he was made "a living soul," so are they living souls, made in the image of God. As Adam was called "the son of God," so are all his descendants, likewise, sons of God; only we must carefully bear in mind the fact that there is a wide difference in the meaning of this term, as it is used in the Old and New Testaments. As is well known, the doctrine of immortality and belief in immortal life do not appear, in any distinct form, in the Old Testament.

Adam and his descendants were simply called children of God for this life, and all the promises made to him and to them related to this life only. There was no promise of life hereafter. On the contrary, there is, at the end of the third chapter of Genesis, a very mysterious and significant passage, which tells us that, although Adam and Eve were allowed to live on in this lower world, yet God, when He drove out the man, "placed in the east of the Garden of Eden, Cherubim and a flaming sword, which turned every way to keep the way of the tree of *life*."[1] Here we see the limitations of the life of

---

[1] Gen. iii. 24.

Adam and his descendants. They are under the covenant mercies of God; but there is no *promise* of life beyond the grave; only, as sons of God, they have a right to look to Him and call upon Him as their Father in Heaven, and, also, a right to expect from Him a heavenly Father's protection and care here and hereafter.

In the same chapter in which St. Paul, an Apostle of Jesus Christ, tells us that the first man is "of the earth, earthy," he also tells us that "flesh and blood cannot inherit the Kingdom of Heaven, neither doth corruption inherit incorruption;" and that, before the dead can be raised, "this corruption must *put on* incorruption, and this mortal must *put on* immortality."[1] Some new power of life, therefore, which we do not derive by natural generation from Adam, must "change" us;[2] must be "put on," or infused into our nature, before it can be raised to immortal life. And it is New Testament teaching that this power comes through the Incarnation. All the promises of God regarding immortal life in Heaven are made only in and through Jesus Christ. The Gospels and Epistles ring with the message, now in this form and now in that, that he that hath the Son hath life, and he that hath not the Son of God hath not life.

The Incarnation of Christ, therefore, must be the basis and starting point of our thinking, if we would understand New Testament teaching. Both soul and body are corruptible: in the one we see the spiritual, in the other the physical effects of sin; and neither can be raised to life immortal in Heaven

[1] 1 Cor. xv. 53. [2] 1 Cor. xv. 51.

without the impartation of a new principle of life, through Christ.

As Christ Himself assures us, it needs something more than to be born of flesh and blood for us to become possessors of immortal life. Flesh and blood cannot inherit the Kingdom of Heaven. A man must be born again — that is, born from above — before he can enter the Kingdom of God. And it must be, both materially and spiritually, a birth from above, for not only the soul but the body are to be raised from mortal to immortal life.

This new birth, as we have said before, comes only through the Incarnation of Jesus Christ. "To as many as received Him," writes St. John, "gave He power to become the sons of God, even to them which believe in His name: which were born, not of blood, nor of the will of the flesh, nor of the will of man, but of God."

The First Adam was made "a living soul," the Last Adam "became a life-giving spirit;" the First Adam is of the earth, earthy, the New Adam is "from Heaven," or, in the language of St. John, "the Word made flesh;" the First Adam, after his fall, had that sentence pronounced against him, "Dust thou art, and unto dust shalt thou return," the Last Adam pronounced *His* sentence against death itself, and declared His power over death in those words: "I am the Resurrection and the Life"[1] "No man taketh [My life] from Me, but I lay it down of Myself. I have power to lay it down of Myself and I have power to take it again."[2] The First Adam after the fall was imperfect man; the Second

[1] St. John xi. 25.   [2] St. John x. 18.

Adam was perfect man, not only in soul but in body. In the Old Adam, we behold our human nature dwarfed, stunted, corrupted, and in a fallen condition; in the New Adam, we behold our human nature revealing its boundless capacities for good, purified, glorified, immortalized.

To comprehend how this difference affected the physical nature of Christ, we must go back to the condition of Adam before his fall, and remember that he possessed then not only an uncorrupted soul, but also an uncorrupted body. The very fact that *after* his fall the sentence was pronounced against him, "Dust thou art and unto dust shalt thou return," indicates that he had not been under this sentence before, and that his fall had brought about a change not only in his spiritual and psychical, but also in his physical condition. When our Lord came into this lower world as the Second Adam, though human and like ourselves in every respect but that of sinfulness, the very perfection of His Manhood freed Him from these effects of sin, and from the attendant changes in these spiritual, psychical, and physical conditions of man that it wrought.

His uncorrupted soul was wedded to an uncorrupted body. His conquest over sin, at last, made that body incorruptible. And this was undoubtedly what St. Peter meant when in his Pentecostal sermon he first spoke of the risen Christ as One "Whom God hath raised up, having loosed the pains of death, for it was not *possible* that He should be holden of it;" and then, quoting the words of the patriarch David in the Sixteenth Psalm, added, "He [David] seeing this before, spake of the Resurrection of Christ, that His soul was not left in hell, neither did His flesh see corruption.[1] The reference becomes still more important when we remember that St. Paul, years afterward, pointed back to this same psalm as a prophecy of Christ's Resurrection, saying: "David, after he had served his own generation by the will of God, fell on sleep, and was laid unto his fathers, and saw corruption, but He, whom God raised up, saw no corruption."[2] The chief point to be observed here is that both Apostles evidently held the belief that when Christ died, His body not only did not, but *could* not, see corruption; or, in other words, it was not only sinless, but incorruptible.

The Transfiguration of Christ before His death is also a fact to be remembered in this connection, for our Lord Himself, then and there, expressly charged those who had witnessed it, "to tell the vision to no man, until the Son of Man be risen again from the dead."[3]

The bearing of all this upon the miraculous birth of Christ is evident. For if Christ's body was incorruptible in death, through His doing the will of God on earth as it is done in Heaven, it must have been created uncorrupt at His birth, through the conception by the Holy Ghost, as is recorded in St. Matthew's and St. Luke's Gospels.

Our flesh is imperfect. It is diseased, and it must be "changed" before it can "put on" incorruption

---

[1] Acts ii. 23-32. [2] Acts xiii. 36, 37.
[3] St. Matt. xvii. 9. Dr. Godet has a striking commentary on the Transfiguration of Christ, in which he suggests that Christ's body was then and there immortalized, but that Christ refused immortality apart from the salvation of mankind.

and immortality; but the body of Jesus Christ was perfect. In it we behold our physical manhood perfected, just as in His moral and spiritual life we behold the ethical and divine lineaments of our manhood perfected. He was on the natural, as well as the spiritual side, the Ideal Man; and we must bear both in mind, if we would understand His Incarnation in its varied aspects.

If we deny this truth, then we become involved in all those grave difficulties which fifteen hundred years ago beset Apollinaris and his followers. The only answer to Apollinarianism is the immaculate conception of Christ.

III

We come now, in considering the Incarnation, to the question of personality. This is, perhaps, the greatest mystery of our human existence. Descartes believed that he had reached a final definition, when he uttered that famous maxim, "I think, therefore I am;" but thought is only one attribute of personality. Another celebrated philosopher has said, "I act, therefore I am," but will power is only a second attribute. Love is, again, a third, and so on. These are signs, indications, proofs to us of our own personality, but the personality itself lies back of them all. It is one selfhood, combining inseparably in one human consciousness, intellect, will power, and love. Now, taking our human nature as it is, we discover that each man is a different personality from every other man. It is a simple fact of nature that the child of every human father is a separate and distinct person, living outside of, and apart from, his own parent and every other human person. This law is universal. If, therefore, Christ had a human father, according to this universal law of nature, He would have had, not only a human body and a human soul, but, also, a human personality. There would have been, under such conditions, two personalities, two separate and distinct *selves* in Christ,—a human self and a Divine self. This is utterly impossible, nay, it is unthinkable, for there cannot be two separate selves in the same individual self, because each person, each self, is forever outside of and distinct from every other self; in addition to this, the complete union of the human and Divine in Christ would thus have been thwarted. Christ had, indeed, a human body, a human soul, a human will, but He had no human personality. The self that was in Him, the Ego, was Divine.

There was once a time in the history of the Church when great confusion of thought prevailed upon this subject. During the Ante-Nicene and Nicene periods Christ's relation to God the Father was gradually thought out in the light of Holy Scripture, by the early Fathers, and found, at last, expression, satisfaction, and rest in the Doctrine of Three Persons in One God; then came the Post-Nicene period, in which the attention of the Church was directed to Christ's relation to man. Apollinaris, filled with the spirit of Trinitarianism, began the discussion by denying that Christ had a human soul. When it was proved and became manifest that he was in error, Nestorius, reacting to the other side and identifying — or rather confusing — a human soul with a human personality, proclaimed that there must be two persons in the one Christ. When Nestorius, in turn, was proved to be in the wrong, then, Eutyches affirmed that if Christ were but one Person, He must have, essentially, but one nature, or, rather, that His human nature must be merged in the Divine, as a drop of water is lost in the ocean; while the Monothelites, also reacting in the same direction, taught that as personality reveals itself in will power (or that will power and personality are one and the same), therefore there must have been, of necessity, in Christ, not two wills, but one Divine will.[1]

When this truth of Christ's Divine Selfhood is

[1] All this while, the underlying truth, that a human soul and a human will power were not the same as personality itself, kept growing clearer and clearer to the mind of the Church. The skill, the intellectual force, the subtle power of analysis displayed by the Fathers of the Church, lifts them up to the first rank, not only of the theologians, but of the men of genius that the Christian era has produced. And to-day, when the whole drift of modern thought is in the direction of the study of Divine and human personality, we shall sooner or later discover how widely and exhaustively the field has been already covered in the writings of those early Fathers.

There may, in some ways, be an advance upon their thought and a clearer comprehension of the subject, after the same field has been traversed once more, under the increased knowledge of these nineteenth century times: the advances made in the study of psychology will lend their aid, and the new science of physiology will probably contribute, from a different side, additional truths to those already apprehended, but the ultimate result will be only to enforce, and bring out with greater emphasis, the conclusions to which those ancient Fathers came. For the first effort to understand this whole subject of human personality originated in the study of the human character of Christ, the Light that lighteth every man that cometh into the world. Christ Himself, however, was different from all other men. Christ took His human nature, in its full perfection, from the substance of the Virgin Mary, but it was a human nature *without* a human selfhood.

firmly grasped it explains many things in the Gospels, lightens up many mysterious passages, and solves difficulties which, without it, would be inexplicable.

For example, it interprets for us in many ways the consciousness of Christ. In general there is implanted in the human breast a consciousness, first of the overshadowing life of human parents, and then, behind this, of a Father in Heaven; but with Christ the greater consciousness of the Divine Father's love, protection, and care, seems to have obliterated and taken the place of the ordinary human love for an earthly parent. To Him, the love of God the Father was not only just as vividly realized and as immediate, as that of a human father is to us, but far more so. Out of the fulness of that consciousness and that affectionate confidence in His Father's love, He was not only able to say: " If ye, being evil, know how to give good gifts to your children, how much *more* shall your Father in Heaven give good things to those that love Him?" "Not a sparrow shall fall to the ground without your Father;" "By Him the very hairs of your head are all numbered;" but by the spontaneous, involuntary way in which He keeps reiterating that expression "My Father," we can see for ourselves that His Father's love was the familiar, most natural and ever present thought of His mind. And, in this connection, it is to be observed that we never find Him, in the Gospel, referring to His human parents or betraying those instinctive feelings with which a younger generation looks up to the generation which precedes it. Filial obedience and affectionate reverence appear in those passages where Joseph and Mary are mentioned, and during the period of His youth and early manhood, our Lord has set an example of filial duty to every child of human parents. Indeed, all through the years that followed His visit to Jerusalem, when He was twelve years of age, we read that He went down to Nazareth and was subject unto them; and even up to the time when, at the age of thirty, He began His public ministry, He appears to have been an inmate of that home at Nazareth; but where in the whole Gospels do we find Him revealing, by a single word, the ordinary human consciousness of being the son of a human parent?

In several places, it is true, Joseph and Mary are spoken of by others as His parents; and one of these passages, it is noteworthy, is to be found in the very chapter of St. Luke's Gospel which records His miraculous birth; but throughout the whole Gospel narrative our Lord never is recorded as addressing, or even referring to Joseph. At the close of that visit to Jerusalem to which we have already referred, the child Jesus was lost. When, after three days, Mary found Him in the Temple, and said, "Son, why hast thou thus dealt with us? behold Thy father and I have sought Thee sorrowing," His immediate reply was, "Wist ye not that I must be about My Father's business?" It was as though there were something in the Virgin's words that had a false ring in His ears and jarred painfully with His personal consciousness. His response came, almost in the form of a gentle rebuke; when she spoke of a human father, He, in his reply, referred instantly to a Divine Father.

Thus was it on one other occasion, even with His mother herself. When the Virgin with His brethren stood without the door, unable to reach Him in the crowd, and a messenger came, saying, "Thy mother and Thy brethren stand without, desiring to speak with Thee," He instantly — and, as it were, instinctively — replied: "Who is My mother? and who are My brethren? And He stretched forth His hand toward His disciples and said, Behold My mother and My brethren! for whosoever shall do the will of My Father which is in Heaven, the same is My brother, and sister, and mother."[1] Does not the same gentle, instinctive protest appear here, against those who claimed to have a nearer relationship to Him than He in the power of His Divine Personality recognized? Again, when a certain woman in a crowd cried out, "Blessed is the womb that bare Thee and the paps that Thou hast sucked," His immediate reply was, "Yea, rather blessed are they that hear the word of God and keep it."[2] The only other occasions, recorded in the Gospels, where Christ addresses the Virgin directly are, first, at the marriage of Cana of Galilee, when, in response to the Virgin's exclamation, "They have no wine," our Lord said, "Woman, what have I to do with thee?" and second, when on the Cross He committed her to the care of St. John with those words, "Woman, behold thy son."

If Christ had no human personality all this becomes plain. He possessed our human nature in all the perfection of its powers, but it was a human nature without a human selfhood, without the separations

[1] St. Matt. xii. 48–50.   [2] St. Luke xi. 27, 28.

that human individuality necessitates, without the egoisms that condition human personalities, without the limitations which belong to a human self.

Christ was Man, not *a* man. He was the Son of man, the Universal Man, the Elder Brother of the whole human race. And it was for this reason that He so instinctively resisted the claim of His human relatives to be nearer to Him than others were. It was not that He was destitute of filial or fraternal affection, or even that there was an absence of individuality in His love; but it was because He lavished upon all who did the will of God that same kind of love which, with ordinary men, would be *confined* to mother and brethren and blood relatives.

It needs but a short experience of Christian work in Christ's name to discover that we cannot possibly love the world, and the men of this world, as Christ Himself loved them. *Our* love has its limitations. We may have, in some faint degree smouldering in our hearts, Christ's passion to save the lost, but our personal attachments are confined to a few. Our Lord's love for souls was Divine as well as human. He claimed all men as His brothers, not only in the way in which we love those who are nearest and dearest to us, but in a far deeper and wider sense. And He could manifest this kind of personal love for all who do the will of God, simply because He was a Divine Person, Who did not feel those separations and limitations which fetter the love of every human personality.

Keeping in mind this thought of Christ's Divine Selfhood, we have the clue to the real meaning of words and events in Christ's life which would otherwise be very difficult to comprehend. Take, for example, the self-assertion of Christ as it is manifested in such passages as these: "Heaven and earth shall pass away, but My words shall not pass away;"[1] "I am the door;"[2] "I am the Good Shepherd;"[3] "I am the Way, the Truth, and the Life;"[4] "I am the Resurrection and the Life;"[5] "No man cometh unto the Father but by Me;"[6] "I am the Vine, ye are the branches . . . without Me ye can do nothing."[7] If any human master, however great, spoke words like these, they would offend and antagonize us as the utterances of an egoist. Why? Just because our human personalities are outside of and separate from one another. Christ, on the contrary, does not offend us; He *attracts* us when He thus speaks, because we feel instinctively that the Being Who speaks is not a human person but a Divine Person. It is not a personality that is outside of our own, but a Personality which overshadows us from above; a Personality in Whom all men are drawn together and united.

So it is with the Atonement. No one man can die, and by dying blot out the sins of another man, because our human personalities are separate and outside of one another; but if the Being Who dies is not a man, but universal Manhood, not a human person, but the God in Whom we live and move and have our being, — then we can understand how the blood of Jesus Christ cleanseth us from all sin.

---

[1] St. Matt. xxiv. 35.
[2] St. John x. 9.
[3] St. John x. 11, 14.
[4] St. John xiv. 6.
[5] St. John xi. 25.
[6] St. John xiv. 6.
[7] St. John xv. 5.

Half of men's perplexities about the Atonement arise from the fact that they always think of Christ as having a human personality.

The same is true of the Resurrection. When Christ says, "because I live ye shall live also," we at once begin to think of the limitations of human life. How can one man's rising from the grave affect our destinies after death? what possible connection can there be between his life and our life? But the moment we remember Who it is that rises, — the Person by Whom all things were made, and without Whom was not anything made that was made; the Person Who is Himself the Resurrection and the Life, — all becomes plain.

So also with the Ascension. It is utterly inconceivable, however holy any human person might be, that all power should be given him in Heaven and on earth. It is utterly inconceivable, likewise, that any human father should be able to claim a parental relationship to the Being sitting on the throne of the Heaven of heavens as Lord of lords and King of kings." The very thought itself appears blasphemous. But all seems right when we think of Christ, the Son of God, descending to this earth to become the Son of man, that the sons of men might become sons of God, and then "ascending up where He was before."

At the beginning of God's revelation to man, and as a promise given to Eve at the very time of the curse, stands the Protevangelion, the first prophecy of the Bible, "The seed of the woman shall bruise the head of the serpent." However men may treat this mysterious promise and explain away its meaning, it is remarkable that, in the fulness of times, the exact and literal fulfilment came when God sent His only Son into the world, and Jesus Christ was "conceived of the Holy Ghost, born of the Virgin Mary."

CHAPTER III

THE GOSPEL OF IMMORTALITY

IS there a life to come? Wherever one travels, the wide world over, one finds Christians, Mohammedans, Buddhists, Indians, even South Sea Islanders, believing, either definitely or vaguely, in a life to come. And when we gaze back into the past, we discover that as it is now, so it has always been. The human race seems impelled, as by a divine instinct, to believe in a life to come.

This belief in the immortality of the soul has been described by some modern thinkers as the result of a slow evolution of religious thought that has been going on for ages, but the annals of the past tell a different story. As we look back into antiquity, — back to the time when all Europe was a wilderness of woods; back to those forgotten centuries before Brahmanism or Buddhism were ever heard of in India, or Zoroastrianism in Persia, or Confucianism in China; back of the time of Moses and even of Abraham, the father of the faithful; back to the days when the whole race of Israel and the Jewish religion were yet in the unborn future; we come at last to the religion of Ancient Egypt. We need no Egyptologist or skilled oriental scholar to tell us what that Egyptian religion was like, for every modern traveller sees the monuments of its belief, many of them built more than three or four thousand years ago, rising upon every side, as he journeys up the Nile; and those monuments proclaim, in almost every line, the doctrine of immortality.

I

Whatever changes took place in the national religion, as dynasty followed dynasty and new names for old deities were adopted, that one intense, passionate, all-mastering desire for the life to come dominated and assimilated all variations of religious belief.

It expressed itself in their very buildings, for eternity was the ruling idea of all Egyptian architecture; and their structures, from the Great Pyramid to the obelisks that meet the eye on every hand, were raised to stand forever. It expressed itself in their magnificent tombs, which were veritable cities of the dead; it expressed itself in their desire, as far as possible, to immortalize the perishable body by embalming it; it expressed itself in those painted hieroglyphics that covered the sarcophagus, wherein the winged soul appears hovering over the heart of the dead, as though escaping from the body; it expressed itself in the pictured representations of the dead man, appearing in the presence of the gods to be judged by them, according to the life he had lived in this world of probation; it expressed itself, most vividly of all, in the remarkable myth of Osiris.

As far as that myth has as yet been deciphered it reads as follows: —

Osiris descends to earth and appears here as a man. He comes in conflict with Typhon, the power of darkness, by whom he is slain. After his death, he becomes the judge of the dead, and is recognized among the gods by the mummied cerements, the symbol of having passed through death, which enclose his lower limbs. Before him the dead are brought, when they enter the other world, to be judged according to the deeds done in the flesh. They are weighed in the balances, and if they are found worthy of immortal life, they are allowed, after a certain period, to return for the embalmed body, which thereupon becomes immortalized also.[1] What happens to the disembodied soul, if judged unworthy, is uncertain, for, at this point, the myth becomes obscure, owing to the varying religious beliefs held in different parts of Egypt. Here was a creed, held by a civilized people before the days of Moses, that almost anticipated Christianity itself, in its intimations of a life to come.

And this was the atmosphere of religious thought and belief in which the children of Israel lived, through the four hundred years of their sojourn in the land of Egypt. All of them must have been indoctrinated from earliest childhood in the details of this belief; many of them must have helped to embalm the dead, and assisted as slaves in the painting of those sarcophagi on which this whole story of Osiris was delineated.

Yet, when we turn to the Old Testament, the

---

[1] There appear to have been various beliefs, in different parts of Egypt, as to the exact relation between the ethereal Ka and the embalmed body.

doctrine of human immortality is conspicuous by its absence. Moses, we read, was brought up as the son of Pharaoh's daughter in the reign of Rameses II., the greatest of all the Pharaohs and the one whose monuments are most numerous; Moses was, moreover, "skilled in all the wisdom of the Egyptians." Jewish tradition even goes so far as to tell us that he was educated as an Egyptian priest; yet Moses utters not one word in all his writings about the immortality of the soul. Many are the references in the Pentateuch to Egyptian life and manners and customs. It is a fact, undisputed by the Higher Criticism, even in its extreme forms, that Israel came out of Egypt. It is granted by every biblical scholar that the Exodus itself is an event which forms the basis of Old Testament theology; yet nowhere is there any reference to the religious belief of Egypt or to the doctrine of immortality.

What is the explanation of this strange silence? Was it because the depised Hebrew slaves were treated by their task-masters as an inferior race, who had no share in the hope or the immortality of the more favored Egyptian? or was it because the Hebrews felt that the Egyptians dishonored their high belief by the low moral level of their daily lives? There is nothing that antagonizes and alienates the mass of men more surely than unreality in religion. In the religious history of the past, we behold, after every reformation, an intense and violent dislike, on the part of the reformers, to the particular doctrines, rites, and practices which were the most flagrant examples of such unreality. We certainly detect unmistakable traces in the Hebrew writings of such repugnance to Egyptian life, and it may well have been that here was one cause for the absence of all allusion on the pages of the Old Testament to the Egyptian doctrine of immortality. But it does not explain the studied omission of the doctrine itself, apart from its Egyptian associations, for centuries after the Exodus. There was a spiritual as well as a natural reason for the omission. In this complete historic break with the past, we behold an undoubted proof of the inspiration of the Old Testament.

II

In the very beginning of God's revelation to man appears the statement that when God drove Adam from Paradise with the sentence of death, He placed "at the east of the garden" Cherubim and a flaming sword, to keep the way of the tree of *life*.

The human race might long for the life to come. Men might take it for granted, and, following a divine instinct, might create beautiful myths of a resurrection from the dead, until, as in the case of ancient Egypt, this became the ruling idea of a nation's life. But the Egyptian immortality had no power to hold the nation up to its high moral ideal or influence its ethical and spiritual development; and the children of Israel, who had become for centuries familiar with the religion of Egypt, had to be educated, by centuries of training, *out* of the false idea of immortality which the Egyptians held. Viewed in this light, the silence of the Old Testament becomes more eloquent, more expressive than words. For while the argument from silence may generally be received with caution, here its teaching is as plain as day. It applies equally to the myths of ancient Egypt and to the speculations about the immortality of the soul that are so prevalent at the present day. The silence of the Old Testament stands side by side with the silence of Nature itself. Neither give anything more than vague, mysterious intimations of the life to come. Everything in the way of proof or evidence is carefully held back and hidden from all human eyes. The purpose of God our Father is here made so plain that we cannot possibly misread it. Before the Jews were prepared to receive true ideas of immortality, they needed to have true ideas of God Himself, from Whom all immortal life proceeds.

III

All this is strikingly brought out in the way in which God dealt with their future leader, in the vision of the burning bush, before the Exodus took place. Moses, it will be remembered, filled with a sense of the burning wrongs of his people, had slain an Egyptian; and when Pharaoh threatened his life in consequence, he fled to the wilderness of Mount Sinai, there to pour out his heart to God, and to be trained by God, amid the solitudes of a shepherd's life, for his future work. Moses was born with the heart and instincts of a reformer. Trained in the wisdom of the Egyptians, he now had time to ponder, and realize how utterly imperfect all wisdom was that was not founded upon right ideas of God

and true spiritual conceptions of God's service; how
artificial that Egyptian belief in a resurrection must
be which had no power to elevate the actual moral
life of the people; how unreal were all ideas of a
life to come, in which shallow sentiment or poetic
myths were substituted for the ethical instincts of
human souls made in God's image and longing for
His Presence; and how immeasurably superior his
own despised nation were, with their simple moral
belief in the God of Abraham, Isaac, and Jacob, to
their highly cultivated but corrupt Egyptian oppres-
sors, with all their mythological gods and their
beautiful visions of a future life. In our study of
holy Scripture, we find that God never sends a
revelation to one of his chosen servants until he
is thus prepared beforehand for it, and until,
through prayer and silent pondering, his mind is
ripe for the message that comes from on high. And
so it was with Moses when God met him at the
burning bush, and revealed Himself first as the God
of Abraham, of Isaac, and of Jacob, and then as
"I AM," the Self-Existent One.

We should never have known or realized the profound ethical meaning of this revelation or its won-
drous adaptation to the religious experience through
which the Hebrews had been passing in Egypt, had
it not been for Christ. A few days before our Lord's
crucifixion, the Sadducees — who denied that there
was any life after death, or any trace of a belief in
immortality in the five books of Moses — came to
Christ and virtually asked Him to point to a single
passage of the Pentateuch where that doctrine was
taught. Our Lord's memorable answer was: "Ye

do err, not knowing the Scriptures, nor the power of God. . . . As touching the resurrection of the dead, have ye not read that which was spoken to you by God, saying, I am the God of Abraham, the God of Isaac, and the God of Jacob? God is not the God of the dead, but of the living."[1]

Thus it was, then, that God had met the troubled religious thought and deep moral misgivings of Moses and the Hebrews regarding the kind of immortality which the Egyptians preached and believed. Immortal life begins, not at man, but at God. It does not exist separate from the life of God Himself. Even the patriarchs, Abraham, Isaac, and Jacob, had no independent life of their own apart from God. Those who knew God and obeyed Him could unreservedly commit the keeping of their souls to Him as to a faithful Creator. The children of Israel were prepared to receive the revelation of this truth, for it met and answered their own unspoken thoughts, and it would come as a word of power appealing to their deepest religious instincts; therefore when Moses said to God, "Behold, when I come to the children of Israel what shall I say unto them?" the answer God put into his mouth was: "Thus shalt thou say unto the children of Israel, I AM hath sent me unto you." . . . "The Lord God of your fathers, the God of Abraham, the God of Isaac, and the God of Jacob hath sent me unto you: this is My Name forever, and this is My Memorial unto all generations."[2] Henceforth, that revelation that God was I AM, the Ever-Living One, was enough for the Hebrews.

---

[1] St. Matt. xxii. 29, 31, 32.   [2] Exod. iii. 14, 15.

If He were the Fountain of all Life, they might leave all visions of the life to come with Him. This explains the reason why the doctrine of immortality does not specifically appear on the pages of the Old Testament, — the Jews were satisfied in leaving the future to God. They were all the more content to do so, because the dominating influence or characteristic of their whole religious history was the expectation of the promised Messiah, — the promised Seed of the woman, Who should bruise the head of the serpent;[1] the promised Prophet, Whom the Lord should raise up like unto Moses;[2] the promised Priest, Who should be made a priest forever after the order of Melchizedek;[3] the promised King, Who should sit as David's Son on David's throne, and be known as Wonderful, Counsellor, the Almighty God, the Everlasting Father, the Prince of Peace.[4] Every succeeding prophet added to the glowing promises of those who had gone before regarding the golden age of this King Messiah, of the increase of Whose government there should be no end, and Who would establish it with judgment and justice forever; and this vision of future glory so lightened up, with hope and anticipation, the whole horizon surrounding the children of Israel, that all other considerations were lost sight of; they paused not to think, like other nations, of the problems of existence, the mysteries of mind and matter, of good and evil, of life and death, or of the immortality of the soul.

There are, indeed, a few passages where life after

[1] Gen. iii. 15.
[2] Deut. xviii. 18.
[3] Psalm cx. 4.
[4] Isaiah ix. 6, 7.

death is, or seems to be, set forth, especially after the Babylonian Captivity had blotted out from the mind Egypt and the former house of bondage; but these passages only appear after the Hebrews had been educated out of the false immortality of the Egyptians, and, without an exception, they refer to the coming Messiah and the immortal life He will bring with Him.

IV

By and by that promised Messiah came, bringing life and immortality to light with a fulness and completeness that revealed how much more God means in His promises than the heart of man ever anticipates. God had commanded Moses to tell the children of Israel that I AM had sent him, and that He was the God of Abraham, of Isaac, and of Jacob. We have seen how Christ illumined the whole history of the Old Testament when He unfolded to the Sadducees the inner meaning of those words. Let us now note how He completes that revelation.

Our Lord's ministry was drawing to its close; He was in the Temple teaching, and as His custom was, He was leading his hearers on step by step. He had been telling the Jews that many who rejoiced to be reckoned as the children of Abraham, Isaac, and Jacob were really, unlike their father Abraham himself, the servants and slaves of sin, and therefore were separated from the God of Abraham, Isaac, and Jacob. When they responded, "We be Abraham's seed and were never in bondage to any man, Abraham is our Father," our Lord replied that

Abraham would never, like them, have sought to kill a prophet from God who told them God's truth; and then added solemnly: "Amen, amen, I say unto you. If a man keep My saying, he shall never see death."

The words produced the very effect that Christ intended they should, and the Jews answered: "Abraham is dead and the prophets are dead, and Thou sayest if a man keep My saying he shall never taste of death. Art Thou greater than Abraham and the prophets? Whom makest Thou, Thyself?" Still leading them on, our Lord replied: "Your father Abraham rejoiced to see My day, and he saw it and was glad." Then, when the Jews in bewilderment and astonished indignation cried out, "Thou art not yet fifty years old and hast *Thou* seen Abraham?" came the tremendous revelation for which Christ had gradually been preparing their minds: "Amen, Amen, I say unto you before Abraham was I AM."[1]

Christ Himself was the Speaker at the burning bush, Who had revealed Himself to Moses as the God of Abraham, Isaac, and Jacob. That incommunicable Name "I AM," which betokened that He was the Fountain of all life to the quick and the dead, and which He of old time had declared to be "His Name forever and His Memorial unto all generation," was now once more declared. The light of Heaven had broken in this lower world; the revelation had reached its climax and completion in His incarnate Life, Who was both Son of God and Son of Man. And now, when Christ stood self-disclosed, as the Self-Existent One, Who was the Light of the

[1] St. John viii. 33-58.

world and the Life of Men, that revelation of immortality in Him became daily more clear and explicit. "I am come that they might have life, and that they might have it more abundantly."[1] "My sheep hear My voice and they follow Me, and I give unto them eternal life; and they shall never perish, neither shall any man pluck them out of My hand. My Father, which gave them Me, is greater than all, and no man is able to pluck them out of My Father's hand. I and My Father are One."[2] "I am the Resurrection and the Life. He that believeth in Me, though he were dead, yet shall he live. And he that liveth and believeth in Me shall *never die.*"[3] "This is Life Eternal, that they might know Thee, the only True God, and Jesus Christ whom Thou hast sent."[4] And St. John, the disciple whom Jesus loved, adds: "He that hath the Son hath Life, and he that hath not the Son of God hath not life."[5]

Nothing could be plainer than these declarations. The Christless immortality of the Egyptians, as well as the Christless immortality that is believed and preached by so many at the present day, is contrary to the Word of God. The New Testament brings out the teaching of the Old. There is from beginning to end no reference to any eternal life save life in Christ.

The assumption, so often taken for granted that such blessed immortality is inherent in human nature and that it belongs to every man as a birth-

---

[1] St. John x. 10.   [3] St. John xi. 25, 26.
[2] St. John x. 27–30.   [4] St. John xvii. 3.
[5] 1 John v. 12.

right, by virtue of his having been made in the image of God, is not only an hypothesis unsupported by any fact of Scripture, but a theory for which there is not a particle of proof or vestige of evidence in Nature itself. The God of Nature and the Bible has carefully shut out all kind of proof in order that we might be compelled to go to Christ, in Whom alone the promise of a life to come is centred. We have heard Christ's own direct and corroborative statements of this truth. He, and He alone, is the Resurrection and the Life; the Way, the Truth, and the Life. No man cometh unto the Father but by Him.

V

But Christ did not stop here, leaving us to rest upon His word alone. The Jews in His day wanted something more than words; they were constantly craving and asking for "a *sign.*" The *one* sign upon which He kept concentrating their attention, and to which He persistently pointed forward, as the proof positive which would establish for all time the fact that He was indeed the Resurrection and the Life, was His own rising again from the dead.[1] And it is strange, but perfectly natural from a psychological point of view, that while His own disciples forgot these predictions until after the Resurrection, His enemies remembered them so distinctly that they endeavored to make one of them,[2] uttered in Jerusalem, at the very beginning of His ministry,

[1] St. Matt. xii. 39, 40; xvi. 21; xvii. 9; xx. 19; xxvi. 32, 61; St. Mark ix. 9; x. 34; xiv. 28; xvi. 7; St. Luke xviii. 33.
[2] St. John ii. 19-22.

the charge upon which the great Sanhedrim should condemn Him to death;[1] and afterwards quoted another to Pilate, the Roman Governor, saying: "Sir, we remember that that deceiver said, while He was yet alive, after three days I will rise again."[2]

The Resurrection of Christ came home to the hearts of the Apostles and the Christians of New Testament days, after their first strong impulse to doubt was overpast, with all the tremendous, overwhelming force of an historical fact that brought certainty to their eyesight and physical senses, certainty to their common sense and reasoning powers, certainty to their conscience and sense of right, certainty to those spiritual instincts regarding a life to come in union with God, and an answer to those longings for the Presence of God which they felt that God Himself, had planted in their breasts.

VI

And when this reposeful certainty and assurance of Christ's Resurrection became a part of their life, it raised them out of and above their former selves to think and reason and live on a higher level. To express it in their own words, they knew that they were "risen with Christ" to a higher kind of existence than they had ever known or experienced before. It had brought to them an absolutely new revelation of the meaning of that word "Life" as it had been so frequently used by Christ. "Life"

---

[1] St. Matt. xxvi. 61 ; St. Mark xiv. 58. Compare St. Matt. xxvii. 40, St. Mark xv. 29.

[2] St. Matt. xxvii. 63.

was no longer limited and circumscribed by earthly conditions, nor was it terminated by death. As they stood in the presence of the risen Christ and felt the reality of the life to come, — the life that was on the other side of the grave, — that consciousness gave a new meaning to the life on *this* side of the grave; they realized the continuity of life here and hereafter, and the oneness of the life of earth and the life of Heaven. They felt the power of an endless life stirring within them, making spiritual things more natural and natural things more spiritual. They were risen with Christ to newness of life and freshness of being.

VII

And this feeling — this consciousness of oneness with Christ in His risen life — was intensified by the fact that Christ had arisen from the dead in body as well as soul. Though His former physical nature was changed and immortalized; though His human body was different from what it had been before and possessed new powers,[1] yet it was still the same body, the same voice, the same face, the same pierced hands and wounded side. As He rose, so one day they too should rise.

It is instructive to observe how near the ancient religion of Egypt came to this resurrection truth, and yet how utterly that religion failed because it did not, and could not, discern that the higher life was hid with Christ in God.

[1] St. Mark xvi. 12; St. Luke xxiv. 16, 31, 36; St. John xx. 15, 19, etc.

The Egyptians believed, not in the immortality of the soul, but of soul and body together. They held that the dead, as long as they remained disembodied spirits, were excluded from Heaven and could not have fulness of life, except in the perfection of their human powers. And this was the reason why the Egyptians expended such enormous cost upon their tombs; why they embalmed and took such scrupulous care of the bodies of their dead; and why this ruling idea survived all changes, as dynasty followed dynasty, and different forms of religion swept over the land.

The very persistence of the belief is a proof how vividly it expressed a divine instinct of human nature. And it was, indeed, a marvellous approximation to Christian truth. Never has the human mind, in following its own intuitions, come nearer to divine reality. For Christianity itself nowhere teaches the doctrine of the immortality of the soul — at least in the way commonly supposed.

The people of God had to wait patiently for ages, until they were sufficiently educated to know the truth. Then Jesus Christ "brought life and immortality to light;" and when at last the full revelation came, it came *through His Resurrection.* It was not a revelation of the immortality of the soul alone, but of soul and body together. And it must be constantly borne in mind that in the New Testament the one revelation does not antedate the other; they not only synchronize, but are inseparable; there is no promise of the life of the soul in Heaven apart from that of the body. Indeed, when we once grasp the profound meaning of the Incarnation, as it is set forth in the New Testament, we cannot imagine how there can be any separation between them. The two are correlated in the same way that speech is wedded to thought. While it is conceivable that the soul, existing apart from the body, in a perfectly passive condition, yet without losing self-consciousness, may be in a receptive state to divine impressions and inspirations, and thus grow in spirituality and knowledge, it is unimaginable to us that it could *exert* itself in any way known to us; for without the body the soul is not only powerless to express itself, but paralyzed in every effort. It needs a mortal body for life on this earth, and an immortal body for life in Heaven. For if the body is the organ of the soul, then, in whatever state we are, there is, and must be, a complete conformity and correspondence between the two, and an adaptation of the former to the condition of the latter. No question has been more closely studied in modern times than the connection between soul and body. Yet physiologists and scientific men have been utterly baffled in all their attempts to discover where the one ends and the other begins. And the more knowledge increases and facts accumulate the more hopeless the inquiry becomes.

Now, while we have no means of ascertaining whether, if Adam had continued sinless, the body would have been immortalized, without the Incarnation of Christ, we have very distinct intimations in the Bible that the cause of a corruptible body is a corruptible and corrupted soul. Sin is a disease, whose effects are both spiritual and physical. We cannot see the spiritual effects in the same visible, tangible way in which we behold the physical effects; and therefore the physical effects impress themselves the more strongly upon our imaginations. Our thoughts become unconsciously tinctured in this way with an exaggerated materialism to such a degree, that we associate the idea of death and corruption exclusively with our physical nature. Another difficulty, producing similar doubt, is that we do not, and often cannot, distinguish the difference between a sinful body and a sanctified body. We imagine that a soul may become incorrupt, while a body may not. And this is the chief reason why it is so much harder to believe in the resurrection of the body than in the immortality of the soul. If our minds were perfectly unbiassed, we Christians should experience no difficulties in the one belief that do not equally encompass the other. It is simply because we have not become so familiar with the thought of a *sanctified body* as with that of a sanctified soul, that we find it so hard to believe in a physical resurrection.

VIII

But there is another and a deeper cause in the background of human thought for this proneness to accept the half truth of the immortality of the soul instead of the whole truth of the resurrection of soul and body. It is that men have wrong ideas regarding the relation of the physical to the spiritual. A half truth is oftentimes the parent of the most dangerous of errors. The error here is the old gnostic supposition that the kingdom of nature and

THE GOSPEL OF IMMORTALITY

the Kingdom of Heaven are necessarily and essentially separate from one another; the cause of the error is that "the natural man receiveth not the things of the Spirit of God, neither can he know them, because they are spiritually discerned;" and the very way in which this ancient gnostic idea obstinately holds its own from age to age, from the time of Zoroaster down to this nineteenth century, is, in itself, one of the strongest proofs of the limitation of natural thought. From the natural, — which is, of course, the *unspiritual* point of view, — the kingdom of nature and the Kingdom of Heaven will always appear separate simply because the real relation of the two can never be seen, or the right perspective gained, from this wrong standpoint.

When St. Paul uttered those memorable words which we have just quoted, "The natural man receiveth not the things of the Spirit of God," he added, "But he that is spiritual *judgeth all things.*" The Apostle expressed here a fundamental truth of life brought to light by the Christian religion. For though the natural can never rise to the spiritual, the spiritual can assimilate the natural. The secular man never rises above the secular consciousness, and the reason for this is truly given by Hegel, when he says that no one is aware of a limit or defect until he is lifted above it. The natural belongs to the natural alone. The spiritual comprehends both the natural and the spiritual. The Kingdom of Heaven can sanctify and spiritualize the kingdom of nature, but the natural can never spiritualize itself.

Now the Kingdom of Heaven on this earth begins

in the life of Him Who was the Word made flesh, or in the Incarnation of Jesus Christ. When the Son of God came down into this lower world, He not only brought the life of Heaven into the life of nature, but He made the Kingdom of God and the kingdom of nature one. This truth is set forth and emphasized in the opening chapter of St. John's Gospel. Henceforth, there was to be no separation between the two, — between the Kingdom of God above and the kingdom of nature below; between human life here and human life hereafter. The Son of God became the Son of Man, with a perfect human nature, that the sons of men, through Him, might become the immortal sons of God, with a perfected human nature. And, just as Christ rose from the dead in body and soul, and afterward ascended in body and soul to the right hand of God, so we too shall rise. As the highest Christian life, here on earth, lies neither in the physical alone nor in the spiritual alone, but in the union of both with all their combined powers, so life in Christ hereafter must continue to be a development or higher evolution of both. If it be not so, then, after the hour of death, human nature will be shorn of half of its powers, and life hereafter will become more one-sided and less comprehensive than life here.

This is the teaching of the Gospels themselves. This is one of the fundamental principles of New Testament life, and this is the reason why the Apostles preached with such persistence the resurrection of the dead. We must not read into their words a thought that was never in their minds. They did not differentiate, as we do, between the immortality of the soul and the resurrection of the body, and we shall lose the completeness of conception if we thus misinterpret their inspired message. It was the resurrection of the whole man, in body, soul, and spirit, that they preached; it was the resurrection of our human nature in its completeness that they set forth. And this whole Christian doctrine of the Resurrection, as it was held by the Apostles and the New Testament Church, was a necessary consequent of the Incarnation of Christ, in which Heaven and earth, spiritual and material, are brought together in perfect union.

CHAPTER IV

HOLY BAPTISM AND THE RISEN LIFE

AT the beginning of the Bible we read the mysterious statement that, as the result of Adam's sin, God said to him, "*Dust thou art and unto dust shalt thou return*," and then sent him forth from the Garden of Eden, placing at the east end of the garden "Cherubim and a flaming sword . . . to keep the way of the tree of *life*."[1] At the beginning of the Gospel of St. John we have that other mysterious statement regarding Christ, "As many as received Him, to them gave He power to become the sons of God, even to them which believe on His Name: which were born, not of the will of the flesh, nor of the will of man, but of God."[2]

The life which Adam lost in Paradise was restored, when Christ rose from the dead, to those that believe on His name.

I

Before we can realize fully what this restoration means, we must comprehend *the real nature of Adam's sin, and why the penalty visited upon that sin was death*. For the narrative with which the Bible begins, however we may explain its origin, possesses for each one of us far more than a mere historical, literary, or

[1] Gen. iii. 19, 24.   [2] St. John i. 12, 13.

even religious interest. It is profound in its psychological as well as its theological import. It is the unveiling of a universal spiritual truth that applies not only to Adam but to every human soul.

We men do not have to go back to the Fall of Adam to know that we are fallen creatures. Even if we had never heard of Adam in the Garden of Eden, we have a life experience of our own which, for us, anticipates the Bible story. Somehow, we were born with a conscience. That conscience was strong even in the earliest days of our childhood, while our intellect was as yet dormant. When we came into this world fresh from the hand of God, conscience itself told us that God was our Father, prompted us to cry, "Abba, Father," and then bore witness that we, ourselves, were *evil*, unworthy of our Father. One of the first lessons we learned about ourselves was our unfaithfulness to the ideal of conscience. We wanted to be true, but inwardly felt we were untrue. The good that we would, we did not, but the evil which we would not, that we did. As we grew older and self-knowledge increased, we discovered that the good was there, within us, but that it had become distorted, dwarfed, perverted. Every vice within us was a distorted virtue; our generous human sympathy had degenerated into selfish love of popularity; our firmness of character into obstinacy; our self-respect into conceit; our tact into deceitfulness; our humble-mindedness into cowardice; and so on.

The story of Adam in Paradise is, therefore, a kind of mirror in which we see ourselves reflected. It is a wonderful corroboration and explanation of our own inward life experience. And whatever men's ideas about Old Testament history may be, those first chapters of Genesis will never, to the end of time, lose their hold upon human hearts as a revelation, first, of God, second, of self and the presence of evil in self. Whether it be a parable or not, the fact remains that in this narrative a strange and remarkable light is thrown upon the nature of human sin.

This is the scene which meets us on the threshold of human existence. After the evolution of untold ages, a being appears on the earth who is dissimilar to all that preceded him. He is not, like the rest, the possessor of a mere animal existence. He is a *responsible* being; that is, he has the ability to respond to a voice calling to him from another world. He is created, we are told, "in the image of God;" this means, of course, that man is endowed with a distinct personality of his own, and one of the essential attributes of human personality is will power. If a man loses his will power and his freedom of choice, then, as Dorner well says somewhere, "he is no longer a *human* being."

And now go a step further. If such a being, made in the image of God, is really free, he is free to commit sin.

There are only three ways in which such sin might have been prevented. First, God might have created a being with no free-will of his own, but in that case he would have been an automaton, *not* a human being made in God's image. Or, secondly, God might have placed the beings He created in a garden of Eden, with no tree of the knowledge of Good and Evil in the midst of it, and where, consequently, they would be kept safe from all *temptation* to sin. Or, thirdly, He might have placed the same Cherubim which guarded the way of the tree of life before this other tree of the knowledge of Good and Evil, and thus forcibly *restrained* them from sin. But, in each of these cases, the result would have been the same. Adam and Eve would not have been free agents. They would have had no opportunity of exercising their will power: the *moral* life would have been beyond their reach.

As long as they were left to themselves they seemed to have had no inclination to disobey God. Their wills were free indeed, but they exercised their freedom by willing to do God's will. But, by and by, a suggestion of evil came to them. Whether the serpent was fact or metaphor is a secondary consideration. The point is that the suggestion came from an outer source. And perhaps this is the reason why that dark problem of evil so completely baffles us: it originates outside of our cosmogony. Evil begins and evil ends in the "outer darkness." "And the serpent said, . . . ye shall not surely die [if ye eat of the tree of knowledge of Good and Evil], for God doth know that in the day ye eat thereof, then your eyes shall be open, and ye shall be as God, knowing Good and Evil."[1]

Observe the concluding words. "Ye shall be *as God*," as God Himself, "knowing Good and Evil." There, covered up in those words lies the root sin of all the world. For what is sin?

Sin is not a sentiment, or a mere theological term. It is a moral disease, a moral defect, which, by and

[1] Gen. iii. 4, 5.

by, when yielded to, produces also a physical defect. The most profound definition of sin ever set forth was given by St. John in the third chapter of his First Epistle, and he gives it in three words: "*Sin is lawlessness.*"[1] When a man holds aloof from God, determines that he shall be a God to himself, in choosing what he shall do or not do, and substitutes his own knowledge for *God's* knowledge of Good and Evil, that is the root sin. He is setting self-will above God's will in a spirit of lawlessness. In this feeling of independence of God, we have the first fertilizing germ of sin, the first microbe, so to speak, of an awful disease, which soon spreads itself through the system.

On every side we behold all sorts and conditions of men who rejoice to consider themselves "independent" men. Because they take upon themselves no Christian vows, they think that they are as free as air. But *are* they free as air? The air obeys the laws of nature. The scientific man obeys the laws of God in nature. Science never became free until the days of Lord Bacon, when it first learned to obey. And, to-day, the greatest sin which science itself knows is a spirit of lawlessness or reckless disobedience to the laws of nature. Yet physical science deals with but one tract or region of the knowledge of Good and Evil. God is the Maker of the rock, the tree, the animal, but he is *our Father.* We men are made in His Image. The royal blood of Heaven itself is in our veins; and to be worthy of our birthright and lineage we must do the will of God on earth as it is done in Heaven. We have *a personal relationship* with

[1] 1 John iii. 4, R. V.

our Father, and therefore above the physical laws of nature stand the higher spiritual laws of personal relationship and intercourse. If a spirit of lawlessness in social life cuts us off from personal intercourse, personal intimacy, personal union with the noblest and most refined of men, much more does that same spirit of lawlessness or sin isolate us from God our Father and the society of Heaven. Sin is the separator. And this is the heavy penalty that one pays for taking an "independent" stand and holding aloof from God. Down to the depths of his soul he knows and feels that he is separate from God, isolated from God. Lawlessness or sin erects a barrier between him and God, and before he can be at one with God or free from the consciousness of separation, that spirit of lawlessness must be judged at the bar of conscience and crucified. See how that inward feeling of separation, of guilt, of being *uncovered*, unprotected by a Father's love, at once followed upon Adam's sin. When he heard the voice of the Lord God calling "Where art thou?" he went and hid himself because he was naked. "Who *told* thee thou wast uncovered, — naked," was God's searching question. This lonely, awful feeling of separation was the first result of lawlessness.

The second result was *doubt*. If Adam and Eve, the instant the suggestion was made, had fallen back upon their confidence in God; if they had taken refuge in the thought that the God who created them in His own image could not be false or untrue to them, or the kind of being that the serpent pictured Him, they would have been safe. But they harbored the doubt, they allowed themselves to look at God out of Satan's eyes. Then they lost their hold on God and were helplessly swept away by temptation. The teaching of the narrative here tallies so closely with our own inward experience of life that the resemblance is startling. It shows us that unbelief always manifests the same characteristics and approaches human hearts in the same way.

It first manifested itself in doubt of God's Law. "Hath God said ye shall die, if ye eat? Ye shall *not* surely die," the tempter said. "God has no power over nature. The laws governing physical life are fixed; the laws of spiritual life, set forth in the Word of God, are words only; they cannot be proved." Even when Christ says, "Heaven and earth shall pass away, but My words shall not pass away," this solemn statement means nothing to those who doubt. And who of us is there who does not know what this kind of doubt means?

But it manifests itself even more strongly in the doubt of God's Love. "God *doth know* that in the day ye eat thereof, then your eyes shall be opened," the tempter insinuated. God, then, had deceived them; He was holding back a part of His truth from the minds of His children. After having made them, He was deliberately keeping them in ignorance of that which they ought to know and had a right to know. That was what the insinuation really meant. The world was bigger than He had represented it to them, and the time had come for them to rebel against such unjust restraints.[1]

---

[1] This threefold temptation of Adam and Eve in Paradise is so comprehensive that it covers the whole field of subsequent human temptation. This was forcibly expressed by St. John when he

Is not this the very temptation which comes to us all in the days of our youth, when we stand on the threshold of manhood? We distrust God's love, God's wisdom; the religious life seems tame and insipid compared with worldly life : we think we know better than God what is best for us. Having no being higher than ourselves to look to, self-love soon crowds out the consciousness of God's love from our hearts, and God Himself becomes an unreality in our self-centred life. Then, as the stream cannot rise higher than its fountainhead, and as self sees only this present world, we lavish on a passing world — which is but a carnal copy of heavenly things — the wealth of a heart that is bigger than the world, only to find in the end that this world can never satisfy a soul that was made for Heaven.

The third result of sin, or the spirit of lawlessness, is ignorance.

"Disobey God," the tempter said, " and your eyes will be opened to the knowledge of Good and Evil.

The only way to know the difference between good and evil, according to the Gospel of Satan, is to taste the forbidden fruit of sin; in other words, to gain knowledge by yielding to temptation.

There was a half truth here. There is a kind of knowledge of the world which comes from yielding to sin, and therefore the tempter skilfuly insinuated,

wrote: "If any man love the world, the love of the Father is not in him. For *all* that is in the world, the lust of the flesh, the lust of the eyes, and the pride of life, is not of the Father, but is of the world. And the world passeth away and the lust thereof, but he that doeth the will of God abideth forever" (1 John ii. 15-17). In the same way it covers the ordinary threefold division of the World, the Flesh, and the Devil, or, the Evil of Others, the Evil of Self, and the Evil One.

"God doth know that in the day ye eat thereof, your eyes shall be opened." But a half truth is the worst of all lies. And when Satan went on to add: "In the day ye eat thereof ye shall be *as God*, knowing good and evil," he was uttering the lie which has led the whole human race astray, and to which Christ Himself plainly referred when he said that Satan was a "liar from the beginning." It is the lie which is ever confusing those who think that to know good and evil one must first *yield* to evil. The truth is the exact reverse. To know sin it is necessary to be tempted, but not necessary to yield.

The positive reveals the negative by contrast; good reveals evil, as light reveals darkness.

But the negative can never reveal the positive. Knowledge of evil can never create a corresponding knowledge of good. On the contrary, as all experience of life shows, it only distorts and brings false ideas of goodness. We do not thus learn to know goodness as *God* knows it, but as Satan knows it — from the outside. You must *believe* in a virtue, *experience* a virtue, to realize its power.

All knowledge is power, goodness is moral power, faith in goodness is spiritual power, and the will of God is life power. All through the Bible, God's will and God's law are set forth as the expression of God's life.

We must will to do God's will if we would know moral and spiritual truth;[1] we must will to do God's will if we would live. God and morality are as inseparably linked together, in the Bible, as God and Love. The Prophet's name for Christ was "The

[1] St. John vii. 17.

Lord our Righteousness." The very name "God" itself means the Good One.

The man therefore who has false ideas of goodness — virtue — must inevitably have false ideas of God.

And this ignorance is the last and most awful penalty visited upon Adam's sin. "This is life eternal," said our Lord, "to know Thee, the only True God, and Jesus Christ whom thou hast sent."

If knowledge of the will of God is knowledge of God Himself; if knowledge of God Himself is eternal life, then ignorance of God can only mean *death*.

For the setting up of self-will against God's will leads to the gradual destruction of life. And this is what St. John meant when he wrote: "If any man love the world, the love of the Father is not in him. For all that is in the world, the lust of the flesh, and the lust of the eyes, and the pride of life, is not of the Father, but is of the world. And the world *passeth away*, and the lust thereof: but he that doeth the will of God *abideth forever*."[1]

And death is the most awful penalty visited upon sin or lawlessness. How appalling in its profound depth of meaning is the conclusion of the description of the fall of Adam! "The Lord God said, Behold, the man is become as one of us, to know good and evil; and now, lest he put forth his hand, and take also of the tree of life, and eat, and live forever: therefore, the Lord God sent him forth from the garden of Eden. So He drove out the man; and He placed at the east of the Garden of Eden, the Cherubim

---

[1] 1 John ii. 15–17.

and the flame of a sword which turned every way to keep the way of the tree of life."[1]

This sentence of death and exclusion from the tree of life was no arbitrary decree of God. It was the result of a cause. The setting up of self will against God's will necessarily entails death. The feeling of separation or isolation that every sinner experiences, whether he will or not, is an unerring voice, proclaiming, as it were, by instinct, his real condition in this life; and it is a premonition of his future condition after this life is over. All the religions of this world have striven to overcome this consciousness of separation, and consequently of condemnation, some in one way, some in another, but it persistently remains, in all real seekers after God, and until Christ came it was ineradicable.

II

Let us now turn to Christ Himself.

Just before the curtain fell upon that scene with which the Bible opens, it will be remembered that the mysterious promise was given that the seed of the woman should bruise the head of the serpent; and it was given in such a way as to imply most distinctly a terrible conflict, in which the seed of the woman, through suffering, should gain the victory over evil. No Jew could understand the meaning of that promise, as it is now unfolded to us Christians, when we gaze upon Christ, the Virgin Born, who suffered for our transgressions and was bruised for our iniquities. This first prophecy of the Bible was fulfilled when

[1] Gen. iii. 22–24, R. V.

Christ, Who did God's will on earth as it is done in Heaven, laid down His holy, sinless life as a ransom for sinners, and thus opened once more the gate of Paradise and the way of the tree of life.

Men may theorize about this redemption as they will, and have their different explanations of the Atonement, but there stands the fact; the only practical way in which any one has ever been able to rid himself of the consciousness of separation from God is by first of all coming to the cross of Christ as a *repentant sinner*. The whole New Testament lays the greatest emphasis upon the necessity of repentance. The first message, not only of St. John the Baptist, but of Christ Himself, was, "Repent, for the kingdom of Heaven is at hand." And the reason for this becomes evident when we remember that repentance means the absolute renunciation of that spirit of self-will — or independence, or lawlessness — of which we have spoken so often in this chapter. But repentance is only the first step. After repentance, must come faith that Jesus Christ can save us from our sins. We may keep on repenting to our dying day, without being able to get rid of the burden of sin and separation from God, for this only comes through faith in Christ. Our Lord himself dwelt with a living earnestness on this fact in His teachings to the Jews. "If ye believe not that I am He," He said to them, "ye shall die in your sins;" and the way in which He kept on reiterating that sentence, "ye shall die *in* your sins," as though He would brand it upon their memories, is most significant.[1] Then, He told them

---

[1] St. John viii. 21, 24.

that they could never by any possibility be freed from the slavery of sin, and the inward consciousness of its bondage, except through Him. "Whosoever committeth sin is the servant literally *slave*) of sin. . . If the Son shall make you free, ye shall be free indeed."[1] And the reason why such faith in Christ is absolutely essential to entrance into the Kingdom of Heaven is just as evident as the reason for repentance. The spirit of lawlessness must be crucified before we can become at one with God. The last refuge that self-will takes is in the plausible moral attitude, that every man must bear the full burden and responsibility of his own sins, and cannot therefore throw them upon any other, even if that other be Jesus, the Son of God. When analyzed, it will be found that this is still the old spirit of independence of God in disguise, and the very obstinacy in which it takes and clings to this last stand is a sign of the terrible strength of sin. As long as that spirit remains, the life of God is impossible. It is only where self ends that God begins. One must die to live. The old man must die before the new man can be raised up in us, the old sinful nature must be crucified with Christ; independence of God must give place to complete dependence on God. There must be an absolute self-surrender of one's life into the hands of Jesus Christ. And this is the profound truth which underlies faith and the acceptance of Jesus Christ as a Saviour.

The beginning of all religious life lies in this inward consciousness of implicit dependence on God. And therefore the first beatitude of the Gospels was,

[1] St. John viii. 31-36.

"Blessed are the poor in spirit, for theirs is the Kingdom of Heaven." If sin is the separator, there is only one way in which that state of separation can cease to exist; only one way in which the consciousness of separation can be blotted out; only one way in which we can become at one with God, with the realization that we are completely forgiven; and that is through the cross of Christ. There is one practical way and one only in which the Christian believer can possibly succeed. He must work, not *to* the cross, but *from* the cross, with the unceasing prayer in his heart: —

"Look, Father, look on His Anointed Face,
And only look on us, as found in Him;
Look not on our misusings of Thy Grace,
Our prayer so languid and our faith so dim;
For lo! between our sins and their reward
We set the Passion of Thy Son, our Lord."

III

But we must not stop with the Crucifixion, as so many are prone to do in these days. From a variety of causes familiar to every student of church history, and some of which will be pointed out hereafter, the vision of the cross has so completely enthralled and monopolized both Roman and Protestant thought as to obscure all that came after; [1] and the result is that

[1] "This is no unfair or exaggerated representation of Christian sentiment in every age of the Church's history. The minds of men have been directed to the cross, and to the cross alone." — *The Ascension of our Lord*, by Dr. William Milligan, p. 129.

"The Roman Church has practically expelled the Resurrection by making the Mass the centre of her worship. The Protestants have done the same by directing almost exclusive attention to the death of Christ." — *The Resurrection of our Lord*, by Dr. William Milligan.

among Protestants the cross has been made the centre of a theological system, in which, while some Gospel truths have been disproportionately exaggerated, others equally important have been correspondingly undervalued, until at last only those principles and doctrines are accepted which can be logically subordinated to the supreme doctrine of justification by faith in Christ crucified; while those which cannot be thus subordinated, become either ignored or practically denied. An anti-climax has been thus created, in which the Resurrection appears to be little more than a corroborative seal of Christ's Divinity; while the Ascension only marks the departure of Christ to His former home in Heaven after His work on earth is ended. All this stands out in such marked contrast to the faith of New Testament Christians that we pause a moment to dwell upon those consequences which have followed this modern conception of Christian truth.

(1) This doctrine teaches, that the cross of Christ becomes to all believers, both a death unto sin and a new birth unto righteousness. Both results, it is believed, follow the one act of accepting the crucified Christ as our Saviour; and hence arises inextricable confusion of religious thought. For the cross is the symbol and sign of *death*, not of life. A believer can comprehend at once how we are crucified with Christ in His death; but it is hard to believe that newness of life comes from the dead Christ. And if this difficulty is felt regarding the sanctification of the soul, it becomes almost insuperable when we consider the santification of the body.

(2) If the Atonement begins and ends at the cross, and if a supreme act of faith in that Atonement is

all that is required of the believer to be forever "at one" with God, then there necessarily follows a divorce between faith and works. There is oneness with Christ in His death through faith in His death; but not necessarily oneness with Christ in works, if Christ ceased working for our redemption when He died upon the cross. If, then and there, He completed the work of our salvation, in every particular, leaving nothing more to be done either by Him or by ourselves, then our works are works of self wrought apart from Christ, and if we invest them even with the slightest importance as religious acts, we are just so far subtracting from the fulness and completeness of Christ's perfect work of redemption that was finished on the cross. Yet no man can deny altogether the value of Christian service and rest on Faith alone, for we thereby paralyze the sense of Christian responsibility, undervalue the necessity of holiness, and ignore some of the plainest injunctions of the New Testament regarding the necessity of continuous effort and growth in grace.

This, perhaps, has been of all others the greatest source of perplexity to many thinking minds, for it seems to separate religious faith from religious effort; and in recent years it has undoubtedly been the chief cause why so many have first doubted the doctrine of the Atonement and then rejected it altogether.

(3) By connecting the whole religious life of the soul with Christ's death upon the cross, Protestantism, with all its robust faith and its splendid virtues, has always presented an austere, and consequently a one-sided, aspect of Christianity. The cross is the symbol of death, and if the victory that Christ won

for us over the power of sin and darkness was won by His death alone, then the Christian religion, of necessity, becomes mournful and sad in tone.

(4) Those who hold that the work of Redemption was completed at the cross, fail to grasp and realize the meaning of the Resurrection and Ascension; and with this follows, of course, a corresponding failure to comprehend the meaning of those facts of Christianity which are the consequence of the Resurrection and Ascension: the Creation of the Church as Christ's Body on earth, the Mission of the Holy Ghost to unite Christ's visible Body on earth with its Glorified Head in Heaven, and the efficacy of the Sacraments instituted by Christ as means of grace for the development of the life of that Church. Hence, Protestant denominations, as a rule, are antagonistic to the doctrines of a visible Church and of sacramental grace in Baptism and the Holy Communion. Whatever other explanations may be given for this characteristic attitude, the real underlying cause is that there is no place for these doctrines logically in their theological system.

(5) Very vague and confused ideas have become prevalent regarding not only the resurrection of the body, but its vital connection with our own future life, and some have even gone so far as to hold that the doctrine of the resurrection of the body is a mere matter of speculation, which is an unimportant and unnecessary addition to the really vital truth of the immortality of the soul. Whereas, in the Bible itself, as we have shown in a previous chapter, there is no revelation of the immortality of the soul apart from that of the body.

(6) Protestant Theology has thus unconsciously revived the old dualism of the ages, which, from time immemorial, has divorced the spiritual from the natural, teaching that the highest life is in the spiritual alone; whereas the Incarnation of Christ reveals that the highest life is in the union of the spiritual and natural.

IV

In vivid contrast to this modern phase of Christian thought stands the equally characteristic attitude of the New Testament Church, as it is so clearly portrayed in the Book of Acts and the Apostolic Epistles. Christ's death upon the cross was to the first Christians only the first link in that marvellous chain of events that culminated in His Ascension, or rather, that will not be completed until He comes again in the glory of His Incarnation to judge the quick and the dead. It is a noteworthy fact that all the Gospels which were written by them terminate abruptly, and convey the idea of incompleteness; as though, on account of some unexpected interruption, they were suddenly broken off before the writers had really reached the end. Yet we know they were all written after Pentecost. This abruptness, which characterizes all four alike, is a striking proof how overwhelming was the consciousness of the Resurrection and of the continuity of Christ's life after the Crucifixion, in the minds of the writers. They reached the end of the earthly narrative but not of the life itself. They could describe all that preceded the Crucifixion, but no earthly language could rise to the height of portraying adequately what *followed* the Crucifixion;

yet, in their religious consciousness these tremendous after developments in the life of Christ were the key which unlocked the meaning of all that had gone before; the light from Heaven interpreting the meaning of the previous Gospel history; the glorious and triumphant consummation of that strange story of a suffering Christ which the Gospels record.

All this is clearly, unmistakably shown, first, in the Acts of the Apostles, which give us the external, and, secondly, in the Epistles of the New Testament, which record the internal history of the early Church. The cross of Christ was to the first Christians but the beginning of that Atonement in which believers were made at one with God. Nowhere in the Apostolic Epistles do we find that isolated prominence given to the Crucifixion apart from the Resurrection which appears in post-reformation times. And it has doubtless been a source of silent surprise to an untold number of Christian men, when they discovered for the first time how different the language of the New Testament itself is from the doctrine that was preached to them from earliest childhood. When we go back to the words and lives of the apostles — back from the atmosphere of post-reformation thought to the clearer and purer atmosphere of first century thought, all those difficulties about the Atonement to which we have referred, disappear as mists before the rising sun; for in the New Testament the power to live a Christian life is connected, not with the Crucifixion, but always with the Resurrection of Christ. Our Lord had not only plainly declared "I am the Resurrection and the Life: he that believeth in Me, though he were dead, yet shall he live: and whosoever liveth and believeth in Me shall never die;"[1] but He had reiterated that truth again and again. Filled with the triumphant conviction that as He rose so they too were risen, and that as the old man in them was dead and crucified with Christ on the cross, so the "new man" in them was raised up with Christ from the death of sin, Christians of New Testament times actually felt the power of Christ's Resurrection as a daily influence in their lives.

In their own personal experience they realized what this newness of life and freshness of being meant, and they manifested in consequence a joyousness, a consciousness of victory over sin, and a power to overcome sin, which stands out in conspicuous contrast to that sad and austere type of religion which characterizes modern Protestantism. There is no book in the whole world, no history or biography or poem, so joyous in tone, so triumphant in the conviction that all things work together for good to them that love God, as the New Testament itself. A noteworthy illustration of this consciousness of power is found in the fact that they regarded the whole world, which to them meant the Roman Empire, as already conquered by Christ, — and this, at the very time when they were being martyred for Christ's sake.

Never will that old-time joyousness and triumphant consciousness of victory return, until the Resurrection of Christ means to us what it meant to St. John and St. Paul.

Again, as the Apostles never separated soul and body except for the sake of differentiation, and as they knew of no Christian doctrine of the immor-

[1] St. John xi. 25, 26.

tality of the soul apart from the resurrection of the body, they taught that the power of that resurrection, passing into them, quickened them in *body* as well as in soul. The Church cannot lose sight of that truth without losing also some part of that high ideal of the Christian life which inspired the first Christians. If she does, it will not be long, as the generations pass by, before the direct and indirect influences of that loss begin to manifest themselves, and as they *have* most plainly manifested themselves in recent times. When we hold firmly to the belief that the bodies as well as the souls of Christians are mysteriously connected with that risen life which Christ imparts to His followers as He Himself rises in body and soul from the grave, a new, more definite, and more blessed signification is given to all Christ's promises regarding the power of His Resurrection. Not only is this in accordance with the whole doctrine of the Incarnation, not only does it save us from that bias toward dualism which secretly and unconsciously dominates the religious thought of so many Protestants at the present day, but it brings home, both to our hearts and consciences, a vivid realization of what our union with the risen Christ actually means. He unites, not merely a portion of our human nature, but our whole manhood unto Himself. Henceforth, the sanctification of the body becomes a ruling thought in our Christian lives. It evokes a new and deeper sense of responsibility within us, and it infuses a new strength into our being to resist the sins of the flesh; for the body as well as the soul is to be prepared and kept sacred for immortal life in Heaven.

And with this thought, or rather this conviction, in mind we comprehend, now as never before, the profound truth to which St. Paul referred when he wrote: "If ye then be risen with Christ, seek those things which are above, where Christ sitteth on the right hand of God. . . . For ye are dead, and your life is hid with Christ in God. When Christ, Who is our life, shall appear, then shall ye also appear with Him in glory. *Mortify, therefore, your members which are upon the earth;* fornication, uncleanness, inordinate affection, evil concupiscence, and covetousness, which is idolatry.[1]

V

And this leads up to the great Commission which Christ gave to His Apostles after He rose from the dead. During those forty days when He remained on earth before His Ascension, He met the Apostles in a mountain of Galilee, which He had previously appointed, and said: "All power is given unto Me in Heaven and on earth. Go ye, therefore, and make disciples of all nations, baptizing them in the name of the Father, and of the Son, and of the Holy Ghost; teaching them to observe all things whatsoever I have commanded you: and lo, I am with you alway, even unto the end of the world."[2]

The following particulars will be observed in this great Commission: (1) Christ here speaks as the King of the Kingdom of Heaven. Because He, Who was in the form of God, had emptied Himself and taken the form of a servant, doing God's will as Man, on earth as it is done in Heaven; and had become

[1] Col. iii. 1–5.   [2] St. Matt. xxviii. 18–20

obedient unto death, even the death of the cross; therefore, when He rose, in body and soul, from the dead, God highly exalted Him, and gave Him a Name which is above every name, that at the human name of Jesus every knee should bow, of things in Heaven and things on earth.[1] Because, in this way, His manhood had been taken up to God, Jesus now proclaims as King that all power is given to Him in Heaven and on earth. (2) Immediately following this announcement, comes His kingly charge to His Apostles to go throughout the earth and bring men into His Kingdom of Heaven on earth. "Go ye, *therefore*, into all the world, and make disciples of all nations." (3) The Apostles are thus to make men of all nations members of His Kingdom, by baptizing them in the name of the Father, and of the Son, and of the Holy Ghost.

This baptism is, as Christ had previously explained, a new birth, by water and the Spirit, into Christ's Kingdom of Heaven on earth.[2] It is a baptism by water, "an earthly thing,"[3] because the Kingdom of Christ is of Heaven and earth, united in His Incarnation; and because the body which is "an earthly thing" is through Christ to be immortalized. It is also baptism by the Spirit, a Power sent down from above, by Christ, after He reached His throne in Heaven, to regenerate the Christian world and consecrate our human nature, in its entirety, to Him.

Bearing all these facts in mind, we find that there is the most intimate connection between this outward ordinance and all that has gone before. Baptism was not instituted by Christ in the days of His

[1] Phil. ii. 6–10.   [2] St. John iii. 5.   [3] St. John iii. 12.

flesh, and before His Crucifixion; He waited until *after* His Resurrection,—until He was able to stand forth in the power of His risen life, as King, before He commissioned His disciples to go and baptize all nations. The importance of Baptism, when we remember all this, can scarcely be over-estimated. It is not enough for a follower of Christ simply to believe inwardly, he must also be baptized outwardly; for the union with Christ, which began at the cross, and which was continued in the Resurrection, is sealed and cemented by Christ Himself in this sacrament of Baptism, wherein (1) the things of earth and the things of Heaven, outward and inward, natural and spiritual, are joined together; (2) we are made to share in Christ's risen life: and (3) are initiated as members of the everlasting Kingdom of Heaven while we are yet on the earth. All this is most clearly set forth, and especially the sanctification of both body and soul in Baptism, by St. Paul when he wrote to the Romans: "Know ye not that so many of us as were baptized into Jesus Christ were baptized into His death? Therefore, we are buried with Him by baptism into death, that like as Christ was raised up from the dead by the glory of the Father, even so we also should walk in newness of life. For if we have been planted together in the likeness of His death, we shall be also in the likeness of His Resurrection: knowing this, that our old man is crucified with Him, that the *body of sin* might be destroyed, that henceforth we should not serve sin. For he that is dead is freed from sin. Now if we be dead with Christ, we believe that we shall also live with Him: knowing that Christ, being raised from the dead, dieth no more; death hath no more dominion over Him. For in that He died, He died unto sin once: but in that He liveth, He liveth unto God. Likewise reckon ye also yourselves to be dead indeed unto sin, but alive unto God through Jesus Christ our Lord. Let not sin therefore reign *in your mortal body*, that ye should obey it in the lusts thereof."[1]

"If Christ be in you, the body is dead because of sin; but the Spirit is life because of righteousness. But if the Spirit of Him that raised up Jesus from the dead dwell in you, He that raised up Christ from the dead shall also quicken *your mortal bodies* by His Spirit that dwelleth in you."[2] And again, when he wrote to the Colossians: "Buried with Him in baptism, wherein also ye are risen with Him, through the faith of the operation of God, Who hath raised Him from the dead."[3]

When Christ told Nicodemus that we must be born from above, of water and the Spirit, before we can enter the Kingdom of Heaven, He meant exactly the same thing, and was setting forth the self-same truth which St. Paul emphasized when he said, "Therefore we are buried with Him by baptism into death, that, like as Christ was raised up from the dead by the glory of the Father, even so we also should walk in newness of life."

And if, notwithstanding these plain statements in the New Testament itself, there is a tendency among modern Christians to undervalue the importance of Baptism, the true, underlying reason is that they have lost the realization of what the Resurrection of Christ means, together with the relation which that

[1] Rom. vi. 3-12.   [2] Rom. viii. 10, 11.   [3] Col. ii. 12.

fact of our Lord's life bears to the life of the Church. No man can be expected to comprehend Christian Baptism who does not previously comprehend the meaning of Christ's Resurrection, and this our Lord Himself intimated when He first spoke of the new birth by water and the Spirit; for when Nicodemus demurred and said, "How can these things be?" Christ plainly indicated that these things would not be understood until after the Resurrection and Ascension.[1]

Thus, through Baptism, are we mysteriously united, in body and soul, to our risen Lord in Heaven. He it is Who was the Life, and the Life was the light of men.[2] He it is, therefore, Who was the Lord of nature and the Power behind nature, by Whom all things were created that are in Heaven and in earth, and by Whom all things consist.[3] He it is Who, at last, in the fulness of times, appeared *in nature* as the Word made flesh, dwelling among us, full of grace and truth, as the Son of Man.[4] He it is Who proclaimed, "I am the Resurrection and the Life; he that believeth in Me, though he were dead, yet shall he live, and whosoever liveth and believeth in Me shall never die."[5] "Because I live, ye shall live also."[6] He it is (let us be careful not to lose the connection), Who gave power to as many as received Him to become the sons of God, which were born, not of blood, nor of the will of the flesh, nor

---

[1] "If I have told you earthly things and ye believe not, how shall ye believe if I tell you of heavenly things? And no man hath ascended up to Heaven but He that came down from Heaven, even the Son of Man which is in Heaven" (St. John iii. 12, 13).

[2] St. John i. 1-4.   [4] St. John i. 14.   [6] St. John xiv. 19.
[3] Col. i. 16, 17.   [5] St. John xi. 25, 26.

of the will of man, but of God.[1] He it is Who explained that to be thus born from above into the Kingdom of Heaven one must be born of water and of the Spirit.[2] And He it is Who, as King of Heaven and earth, therefore commissioned His disciples to go and make disciples of all nations, baptizing them in the name of the Father, and of the Son, and of the Holy Ghost.[3]

If Baptism means all this — a new birth into the Kingdom of Heaven on earth after the old man is dead, and a beginning of a new life through the power of Christ's Resurrection — why is not such a stupendous change in the condition of Christ's followers marked by a sign that is more powerful, more convincing than the simple act of baptizing with water in the Name of the Father, and of the Son, and of the Holy Ghost? That question has often been asked, and, more often still, silently pondered in perplexity and doubt. The answer is that, in reality, the greatest and most stupendous of all pledges accompanies Baptism. Greater than prophecies, greater than miracles, greater than any seal of truthfulness that the human heart can imagine, is the word of that Word of God by Whom all things were made, and without Whom was not anything made that was made. It is never to be forgotten that both the sacraments of Baptism and the Lord's Supper are dependent for their efficacy on the *word* of the Divine Speaker. To the outer world, with whom the word of Christ means less than many other things in Heaven and earth, they may be meaningless rites; but in the eyes of the Church they bring to all true believers oneness

---

[1] St. John i. 12, 13.   [2] St. John iii. 3-5.   [3] St. Matt. xxviii. 19.

of Life with Him Who is the Way, the Truth, and the Life, because He who ordained these two Sacraments of His own Life by His own word is the same Who has solemnly assured us: "Heaven and earth shall pass away, but My words shall not pass away."[1]

He Himself has said, "The words that I speak unto you, they are spirit and they are life."[2] If

---

[1] Many shrink from receiving and believing all that the Gospel itself thus teaches regarding Holy Baptism, because if they accept the whole truth, they think they would be committed to the belief that all unbaptized persons will be excluded from the Kingdom of Heaven. They say that such a belief seems contrary both to the Love of God and the Justice of God, because there are myriads of upright men and women in Christian as well as heathen lands, myriads also of little, innocent children who die unbaptized. But surely, this is a want of faith in Christ and Christ's word. It is not that kind of faith which Abraham, who lived so many centuries before Christ, manifested when, as the mysterious judgment upon Sodom and Gomorrah was revealed to him, he cried, "Shall not the Judge of all the earth do right?" (Gen. xviii. 25).

Christ the Judge of Quick and Dead, Who said, "Except a man be born of water and the Spirit he cannot enter the Kingdom of God" (St. John iii. 5), said also, to the repentant but unbaptized thief on the cross, "To-day shalt thou be with Me in Paradise" (St. Luke xxiii. 43); and to His disciples about the Roman centurion · "Verily I say unto you, I have not found so great faith, no, not in Israel. And I say unto you, that many shall come from the east and west, and shall sit down with Abraham and Isaac and Jacob in the Kingdom of God: but the children of the Kingdom shall be cast out into outer darkness" (St. Matt. viii. 10, 11, 12). If even under human governments it is customary to allow the king or chief magistrate to pardon malefactors condemned under the law of the land, is it inconsistent to suppose that a King to Whom all power is given in Heaven and on earth is not bound Himself by the laws of life that bind us? or that He can save to the uttermost and supply every need to those who lack the spiritual opportunities in this life which the children of the Kingdom enjoy?

[2] St. John vi. 63.

our own natural life is a mystery which no human mind has ever been able to fathom, how can we ever hope to penetrate that greater mystery of the risen life upon which those believers enter who are born again of water and of the Spirit into the Kingdom of Heaven? We only know that the Word of God, Who is at once the source of all physical and all spiritual life, unites them, through the power of His Resurrection, to Himself; and that, henceforth, the life that believers live on this earth, the life of the body as well as the life of the soul, is hid with Christ in God.

CHAPTER V

THE HOLY EUCHARIST AND THE ASCENSION

THE union of the Christian believer with Christ, which was begun at the cross, is continued in the Resurrection and Ascension. We are "one" with Christ in His death on the cross; "one" with Him as He rises from the grave, and "one" with Him when He ascends to Heaven. This was the fixed conviction of the New Testament Christians; without this conviction, we circumscribe the meaning of the Atonement, and our belief is separated just so far from that of the early Church.

As the Crucifixion leads up to the Resurrection, so the Resurrection leads up to the Ascension. Between the last two events there was an interval of forty days, in which Christ remained on earth, to convince His disciples "by many infallible proofs," that He was indeed alive;[1] and when this work was completed, He ascended in bodily form, and with all the faculties of His human nature spiritualized and perfected, to His throne in Heaven, there to continue the work of that redemption which He had begun in this lower world, and to wield "all power in Heaven and on earth." Ten days afterward, from the invisible heavens, He sent down the Holy

---
[1] Acts i. 3.

Ghost to perfect His union with His Church on earth, as an abiding Presence, lo, alway, unto the end of the world. Henceforth, therefore, to the New Testament Christians, as all the apostolic writings show, He was not a past, but an ever-living Leader; not an absent, but an ever-present Christ; a human Head of the Church in Heaven, Whom God had exalted to His own right hand, Whose Manhood had been taken up into God, and Who henceforth was to be to His Church on earth the ever-speaking Prophet, the ever-officiating Priest, and the ever-reigning King.

As Prophet, He revealed through the Holy Ghost the profound depth of meaning in the past events of His earthly life, in His holy Incarnation, and His Cross and Passion; in His precious Death and Burial, in His glorious Resurrection and Ascension. And if the Gospels are a record of His life on earth, the Epistles are a revelation of His life in Heaven, and contain the messages He sends down to His Church below.

As King, Christ is shaping the course of earthly history and ruling by those same principles He set forth in the Gospels, until the day dawns when God's Kingdom shall come, and His will be done on earth as it is in Heaven. And the civilization which we behold to-day is the sign of the growing power of that Kingdom, as the ruling ideas of Christianity become more and more the dominant forces in the life of the nations.

But it is to the work of Christ as Priest in Heaven that we would chiefly draw attention, because of its close and intimate relation to the doctrine of the

Holy Eucharist. From the time of the institution of the Passover, the Jews understood that without the shedding of blood there was and could be no remission of sins, and this truth was kept continually before them, not only by the slaying of the Passover lamb, but by the daily morning and evening sacrifice of the Jewish ritual. At the same time God's people were unceasingly reminded that the blood of the sacrifice meant "the life thereof." All these Jewish sacrifices were typical of the sacrifice of Christ, Who is called in the Scriptures "the Lamb of God, slain from the foundation of the world;" that is, the lamb prophetically offered up by these anticipatory and symbolical sacrifices of the Jewish ritual. The connection between the type and antitype is a wide one.[1]

It will suffice to dwell here upon one point. The underlying idea of all the Jewish sacrifices was that the blood of the sacrifice was the life of the sacrifice. The people were forbidden to eat blood because the blood represents the physical life *as it is*, and as such, was given upon the altar to make atonement for men's sins. The offerer of the sacrifice slew the lamb with his own hands for his own sins.

Then the blood that was released was offered by the priest upon the altar, and thus symbolically united to God. Dr. Westcott truly says: "Moreover, the blood already shed is distinctly treated as living. When it is sprinkled upon the altar it makes atonement in virtue of the life that is in

---

[1] This subject is treated more at length by the writer elsewhere, and the reader is referred to page 345 of "The Creedless Gospel and the Gospel Creed" for its fuller consideration.

it." Yet the sacrifice was really dead. In the sacrifice of Christ, the Lamb of God came to life again. Christ rose from the dead in body and soul. If His body was changed, the blood that was in His body was changed also; if His body was spiritualized and immortalized, His blood was henceforth spiritualized and immortalized also. The symbol passed into a reality; the blood that was in that mysterious human body with which Christ rose from the grave and ascended to Heaven, was henceforth the life-giving blood of Christ; it was the power of an endless life to those for whom it was shed, and to whom it should be imparted.

When we bear this Gospel truth in mind, it not only illumines with spiritual meaning all those New Testament expressions regarding the blood of Christ which we so frequently meet, but rescues us from the errors into which both Protestantism and Romanism have fallen. The prevailing Protestant idea is that the blood of Christ means exclusively the *death* of Christ, the blood that was shed upon the cross. This is wholly a modern misconception of Bible words, for to every scribe who studied the Scriptures, as well as to the whole Jewish nation, including the writers of the New Testament themselves, the blood of the sacrifice always meant not the death but the life of the sacrifice. The blood of Christ includes, of course, the death of Christ, for it was on the cross that His blood was poured out, and thus made available for others; but it signified also, and this was its inner meaning, "the life that willingly passed through death" to the power of the Resurrection.

The theological error of Romanism, on the other hand, is even more profound. When the Roman Church teaches that the bread and wine in the Eucharist are transubstantiated into the flesh and blood of Christ, the implication certainly seems to be that the body and blood of the risen and ascended Christ are to-day exactly what they were on the night before His Crucifixion, when He first instituted the Lord's Supper; whereas a great and mysterious change had taken place in both when Christ rose from the dead in the power of an endless life. The doctrine of Transubstantiation would have been utterly inconceivable to those who felt as St. Paul felt when he wrote to the Ephesians, or St. John when he wrote the Book of Revelation, or as the writer of the Epistle to the Hebrews felt; for they had the intense realization, the overwhelming consciousness, that the blood of Christ meant the Life of the risen and ascended Christ, Who is now our reigning Prophet, Priest, and King in Heaven. Nor could the Roman Church itself have ever promulgated a doctrine like this had it not lost or forgotten the meaning of Christ's Resurrection and Ascension as it was grasped and realized by the primitive Church. Romanism, in fact, like Protestantism, has been too prone to regard the Crucifixion as the culmination of Christ's redemptive work, and perhaps when we go back three centuries we will discover that the latter was really, but unconsciously, biassed by the former in this direction. Protestantism is, in this and other ways, full of Romanistic germs without knowing it. To-day, when we enter a Roman church, the most prominent object which meets our gaze is the crucifix, the representation of the dead or dying Christ on the cross. Crucifixes were not thus used in the early Church. At Ravenna, where the oldest Christian mosaics and sculptures are found, and where many of the churches date back to the fifth and sixth centuries, representations of the Crucifixion are conspicuous by their absence.

It is noteworthy that those churches upon whose altars there is a simple cross, the cross from which Christ ascended to Heaven, are far nearer the primitive Faith and the apostolic Church of the New Testament. Indeed, the placing of a crucifix, instead of a cross, upon the altar is apt to convey a false impression to the popular mind, for Christ's body is no longer on the cross, but in Heaven; and unless it becomes a daily habit, so familiar as to be almost second nature with Christian believers to think of Christ's body as in Heaven, not on earth, they will be very apt to lose or misunderstand the real meaning of the Epistles of the New Testament. There is no greater corrective to the exaggerations and abnormal developments of such Roman doctrine, in this and kindred subjects, than the teaching of the Epistle to the Hebrews.

"By His own blood Christ entered once into the holy place,"[1] because as He was, at one and the same time, Priest and Victim, — the Priest of God and the Lamb of God, — the living blood in the living Lamb was presented by the living Priest at the altar of Heaven. Christ, "because He continueth forever, hath an unchangeable priesthood;"[2] therefore He is unceasingly acting as our great

---

[1] Heb. ix. 12. [2] Heb. vii. 24.

High Priest in Heaven, "and is able also to save them to the uttermost who come unto God by Him, seeing He ever liveth to make intercession for them."[1]

The offering that He, as Priest, presents in Heaven is, of course, in no sense a renewal or repetition of that one, full, perfect, and sufficient sacrifice, oblation, and satisfaction that He made for the sins of the whole world on the cross. As the author of the Epistle to the Hebrews so earnestly and repeatedly reminds us, the offering for *sin* was completed forever when He cried on the cross, "It is finished."

But the effect of that sacrifice is perpetuated in the life of the Offerer, Who is at once the Offerer, the Lamb, and the Priest; and it is continuously present in the life that willingly passed through death. Christ in Heaven stands in the midst of the throne, and of the four living creatures, and in the midst of the elders as "a Lamb, *as it had been slain.*"[2] And at another time He declares with His own voice, "I am He that *liveth and was dead*, and behold I am alive forevermore."[3] He is not merely alive, but "alive from the dead." The idea therefore of the repetition or renewal of the sacrifice on the cross, either in a Roman Mass or in any other way, is not only unscriptural, but it is false. For the continuation of the sacrificial life and work of our great High Priest in Heaven excludes and renders impossible any repetition of the sacrifice for sins on the cross.

---

[1] Heb. vii. 25.   [2] Rev. v. 6, 9, 12.   [3] Rev. i. 18.

Nor could such an idea have ever prevailed if the theology of the middle ages had not fallen below the New Testament level. Those who argue against the continuance of the sacrifice for sins in the life of Christ Himself, stand side by side with those who believe in the repetition or renewal of that sacrifice in the Mass. Both, in their religious thinking, stop at the Crucifixion; both have lost the conception of the glorified Christ, and have thus unconsciously fallen below the level of New Testament truth.

As long as some believe in the cessation of the sacrifice of the cross, others will be stimulated into believing in the repetition of the sacrifice, for cessation carries with it the inherent idea of imperfection, and robs the sacrifice of Christ, at least in this one point, of that essential superiority over the ancient Jewish sacrifices which brought about their disuse. The consciousness of the continuance of Christ's sacrifice in Heaven was one of the chief influences that caused the cessation of the Jewish sacrifices among the early Christians. But if the idea of continuance is lost, that of repetition is no longer so completely negatived.[1]

[1] The Protestant contention, indeed, is that it negatives continuance equally with renewal and repetition. But cessation is an essential mark of imperfection, as well as renewal and repetition. If the sacrifice of the Cross ceased to be offered, it would not have that essential superiority over the sacrifices of the Old Covenant which is claimed for it by the Epistle to the Hebrews, nor would it so completely have done away with all these sacrifices. It has only done away with these sacrifices because, itself once offered, it continues to be offered, and is offered no longer on earth, but in Heaven, where it has opened the way for us also to enter. " By one offering He hath perfected forever them that are sanctified " (Heb. x. 14). These

But was the sacrifice for *sin* all the sacrifice that Christ, as our great High Priest, had to offer? Here is another error of all those whose religious thinking goes no further than the Crucifixion. Following the sacrifice for sin comes the continuous sacrifice of praise and thanksgiving for men; the continuous sacrifice of prayer and intercession for men; the continuous sacrifice of imparting His life to men. All this will be more fully treated later when we come to the subject of Priesthood.

Suffice it to say here, that our whole conception of Christianity will fall below the New Testament level if we fail to realize, as the early Christians did, that the ascended Christ in Heaven is a Priest forever after the order of Melchizedek; and that He entered the holy place not made with hands, to begin, amid the endless alleluias of those angels

very words imply the continuance, not the cessation, of the offering. The sanctification is continuous, so also the offering which sanctifies. So long as we need sanctification, so long must the sacrifice of our sanctification continue to be offered. The argument of the sacred writer is, that the perfect offering once come remains for the perfect sanctification of all who come to it, and only on this account has it superseded the previous offerings of the law, which could not "make the comers thereunto perfect" (Heb. x. 1). The previous offerings could only sanctify to the purifying of the flesh, but the perfect offering of Christ sanctifies to the purifying of the spirit.

And it is the offering itself which sanctifies, not mere faith in the fact that an offering has been made. It is to the actual offering we have to "draw near with the full assurance of faith." The very purpose of our faith is to bring us into real contact with the real offering. Moreover it is by our real participation of it that the perfect offering perfectly sanctifies. The perfect offering is that which is not only offered, but partaken of. Christ continues to offer His one offering for the purpose of our participation of it. — *Doctrine and Practice of the Eucharist,* by the Rev. J. R. Milne, pp. 72, 73.

who rejoice over every sinner that repenteth, His work as our ever-interceding and ever-officiating High Priest.

We have now arrived at a point where we should consider the heavenly significance of that Feast of His Love which Christ instituted a few hours before His death on the cross.

We should observe that the Lord's Supper was distinctly *anticipatory*. Every effort that commentators have put forth to make the institution of the Lord's Supper on Thursday night synchronize with the actual slaying of the passover lamb has failed, and every explanation they have offered, with this object in view, is strained and unsatisfactory. There was evidently a purpose in the very hour that was chosen, — an intention that it should *not* synchronize with the slaying or offering of the passover lamb. For Christ offered up His body and blood in *will* before He offered His body and blood in *deed*. In the former offering, He was one with all those of His disciples who willed to do God's will, and who, in will, would be crucified with Him. In the latter offering *no one* could unite with Him, or participate with Him, or be crucified with Him. Of the first offering He said to His disciples: "Do this in remembrance of Me." Of the second, He said: "All ye shall be offended because of Me this night, and shall leave Me alone; and yet I am not alone, because the Father is with Me."

The reasons why the Lord's Supper was anticipatory were (1) because it was instituted beforehand in "*remembrance*" of His approaching Death and Passion. The blood was in the body of the living Christ when He spoke, and both were united until the Crucifixion. When in the Lord's Supper He separated them prophetically, saying first, "This is My body," and then, "This is My blood," He plainly referred here to His future death as though it had already taken place, and was being already remembered and commemorated as an event of the past. Yet the body and blood, though thus separated, are not, and cannot be, the body and blood of the *dead* Christ. They signify the life that *willingly* passed through death; the life over which death has no power. The Communion Feast commemorates, by anticipation, not only the dead Christ Who was crucified for the sins of the whole world (although this is of course included), but also the Living Christ as He rose from the dead; it commemorates the Lamb of God Who came to life again after He was slain; it commemorates Him who said to St. John in the Apocalypse, "I am He that liveth and was dead; and behold I am alive forevermore, Amen; and have the keys of hell and of death."[1]

(2) The Lord's Supper is anticipatory because it sets before us the Body and Blood of this living, glorified Christ. Not the physical body and red blood of the living Christ, as they were before the Crucifixion, and as they are imagined by those who believe in the doctrine of Transubstantiation; not the lifeless body and blood of the *dead* Christ after the Crucifixion, and as they are imagined by those who hold the Zwinglian doctrine that the Holy Communion is a bare memorial of Christ's

[1] Rev. i. 18.

death upon the cross; but the body and blood of Christ as they became after He rose from the dead, — the immortalized, spiritualized, glorified body, and the immortalized, spiritualized, glorified blood, as they are now united once more in Him who liveth and was dead, and Who is forevermore both the Priest of God and the Lamb of God. It seems strange that so few, so very few, of Christ's disciples in these days, grasp this blessed satisfying truth; especially when it meets and resolves so many difficulties as to the choice by Christ of the elements of bread and wine to be consecrated as His body and His blood. The Lord's Supper was instituted by Christ at the season of the Passover. The Apostles of Jesus Christ, on the night before the Crucifixion, participated for the last time in the Jewish Passover, and then, immediately after, they took their first communion. They had heard Christ say most solemnly, "My flesh is meat indeed, and My blood is drink indeed."[1] And there was the flesh of the passover lamb — the lamb that typified and prefigured the Lamb of God — before them on the table. Why did not Christ choose and consecrate the flesh of this passover lamb to represent His flesh? Why, after the injunctions of the Jewish Law had been carefully observed,[2] was there only a loaf of bread and a cup of wine left on the table? Why did Christ take the bread and say of it, "This is My body;" and then the cup, saying, "This is My blood?" Clearly because the elements of bread and wine must have been more peculiarly fitted than the flesh of the passover lamb, or any other natural

---

[1] St. John vi. 55. [2] Ex. xii. 10; Numb. ix. 12; Deut. xvi. 4.

or earthly elements, to bring home to the minds of Christ's followers for all time a realization of what His immortalized, spiritualized, and glorified body and blood were, and are, in Heaven.

(3) The Lord's Supper was anticipatory because it looked forward to the time when Christ's prophecy would be fulfilled. "I am the *living* bread which came down from Heaven. If any man eat of this bread he shall live forever, and the bread that I will give is My flesh, which I will give for the life of the world. Except ye eat the flesh of the Son of Man and drink His blood, ye have no life in you. Whoso eateth My flesh and drinketh My blood hath eternal life, and I will raise him up at the last day."[1] It will be remembered that at the time when Christ first uttered this charge, the Jews were intensely and grievously offended at His words; and the reason for that strong manifestation of feeling, which is indicated in St. John's Gospel, was that their bitterest Jewish prejudices were aroused by Christ's saying. For the law of Moses had expressly and repeatedly prohibited them from drinking blood.[2] The soul that drank blood was to be cut off from God's people. There is, perhaps, no other instance in the whole Gospel where Christ's teachings ran so directly counter to the most solemn injunctions of the Jewish law; and therefore we are told by St. John that at this time even many of His own disciples went back and walked no more with Him. Nor could they have hoped so long beforehand to understand them, for

[1] St. John vi. 51, 53, 54.
[2] Lev. iii. 17; vii. 26–27; xvii. 10–14; xix. 26.

Christ's words had not as yet been interpreted by the Crucifixion, Resurrection, and Ascension. And this fact Christ Himself expressly intimated at that time. In answer to their murmurings, He told them just as plainly as He *could* tell them at that early date, that these subsequent events, especially that of the Ascension, were necessary to interpret His meaning. "Doth this offend you? What and if ye shall see the Son of Man *ascend up* where He was before? It is the Spirit that quickeneth, the flesh profiteth nothing; the words that I speak unto you they are spirit, and they are life."[1] But after the Ascension, all became so plain that even the reason for the prohibition in the law of Moses was self-evident. The Jews had been forbidden to drink the blood of the sacrifice because that blood was not really a life-giving power. It was, indeed, called life[2] because it was the nearest approximation to life itself that this world afforded; but as it was, in reality, only symbolic of the life of the true Lamb of God, they were forbidden to drink it. The prohibition was necessary to restrain them from an utterly false belief, and to keep them from idolatry. But when Christ, the Everlasting Lamb of God, rose from the dead and ascended to Heaven; when, in Him, mortality was swallowed up of Life and His body and blood became spiritualized, immortalized, glorified, then they were not a mere symbol of life, but forever, indissolubly connected with Him, Who is the Life of the world. They became, not only a part of His glorified humanity, but the channel — the

[1] St. John vi. 61-63.   [2] Lev. xvii. 11-14.

means of grace — whereby the one Mediator between God and man, now in Heaven, was able, *through His humanity*, to infuse life into the humanity of His disciples on earth. If He said to the Jews in Gospel days, "Except ye eat the flesh of the Son of Man and drink His blood, ye have no life in you," He also said, "It is the Spirit that quickeneth, the flesh profiteth nothing." Yet there is no contradiction in the two statements; on the contrary they are united in the closest interrelation. For the "flesh" and "blood" of the Son of Man, as the Jews understood His words, had to become changed, spiritualized, and glorified, before they could impart the spiritual life power of His Resurrection and glorified humanity to believers; the body of Christ which we receive in the Holy Communion is "the bread that cometh down from Heaven," and the blood of Christ which we receive is the "Life of the world." They are not, we repeat, the body and blood of Christ as they were before His Crucifixion, but as they are now in Heaven, — they are Spirit, they are Life.

(4) The Lord's Supper was anticipatory of the time when Christ should be not an external but an internal presence to His disciples. Our Lord had prophesied, "He that eateth My flesh and drinketh My blood *dwelleth in Me, and I in him.*"[1] It was not till after the Ascension that this prophecy was fulfilled. Christ could not become an inward Presence until His glorification was completed in Heaven and the Holy Ghost was sent.[2] After His Ascension this was, for the first time,

[1] St. John vi. 56. [2] St. John xiv. 17-23.

realized by His Apostles. Then it is that St. Paul is able to exclaim, "Though we have known Christ after the flesh, yet henceforth know we Him so no more;"[1] and then it is that the Epistles begin to teach us that Christ's followers are "*in Him*" and that He is "*in them.*"

(5) the Lord's Supper was anticipatory because it was so distinctively *eucharistical*. It was instituted on the sad night of the betrayal. It was immediately followed by Gethsemane, by the triumph of the sin power of the whole world over the sinless Son of Man, by the Crucifixion, by the Death and Burial of our Lord. If ever there were a night of darkness and sorrow, it was that Good Friday eve. Yet the service in the upper room breathes, from beginning to end, the joyous spirit of thanksgiving. Christ gave thanks as He took the bread; He gave thanks as He took the cup; and He said to the Apostles, "Now is the Son of Man glorified, and God is glorified in Him."[2] Clearly this Lord's Supper refers to something beyond the death of Christ; yes, it even points forward to something beyond the sacrifice for sin. It prophetically looks forward to the time when Christ is in Heaven, offering up a perpetual sacrifice of praise and thanksgiving and intercession for men.

As Melchizedek, "King of Salem" and "priest of the most high God," brought forth bread and wine in the king's dale to Abraham,[3] so Christ, the Priest forever after the order of Melchizedek, brings forth bread and wine to His disciples on earth before

[1] 2 Cor. v. 16, R. V. [2] St. John xiii. 31.
[3] Gen. xiv. 18.

He parts with them, and utters those mysterious prophetic words: "I will not drink henceforth of this fruit of the vine until that day when I drink it new *with you* in My Father's kingdom."[1]

Now, before His death, He of Heaven joins with them of earth in that service of thanksgiving, just as, by and by, after His Ascension, will they on earth, by virtue of their union with Him, be raised up into "the heavenly places,"[2] and join with Him in the Eucharist of the skies which He, our great High Priest, is perpetually offering.

As there is a mysterious timelessness in all heavenly things, so there is with this offering. Henceforth the sacrifice of Christ, our great High Priest, is continuous. It is unending, because it is the unending sacrifice of Divine Love. The one perfect and sufficient sacrifice for sin on the cross is only a part of it; the sacrifice of praise and thanksgiving, of intercession, of communion, are other parts; but through all, beneath all, above all, it is the perpetual offering of love. This brings us, in conclusion, to a very important distinction. In the Lord's Supper, in which Christ and His disciples unite and participate, there is Christ's part and man's part, and Christians should be very careful how they confuse the two together.

Christ and Christ alone offered up His body and blood, in actual fact, upon the cross. Christ and Christ alone offered His body and blood in actual fact as He rose from the dead and ascended to Heaven. Christ and Christ alone is present as the Priest who offers, and the Lamb Who was offered, in

[1] St. Matt. xxvi. 29. [2] Eph. ii. 6.

Heaven. His body and blood are *there*, for by His own blood He entered into the Holy place not made with hands, and His body and blood are perpetually being offered in Heaven, for His presence there, as our great High Priest, is in itself a perpetual intercession for us.

Realizing this truth to the uttermost, let us now turn to man's part on earth.

Every time we celebrate the Holy Communion on earth, we join with the worship of Heaven and participate in the heavenly Eucharist. It is to be carefully noted in this connection that throughout the Communion Service we are continuously addressing and praying to God the Father. While Christ, our High Priest, is praying to the Father in Heaven, we are praying to the Father on earth. While Christ offers His body and blood in Heaven, we offer, at the same time, bread and wine on earth.

We do not offer the body and blood; that is Christ's part. Man's part is to offer the bread and wine. We reach our highest act of devotion and make our highest OBLATION when we say: "Wherefore, O Lord and Heavenly Father, according to the institution of Thy dearly beloved Son, our Saviour Jesus Christ, we, Thy humble servants, do CELEBRATE and MAKE here before Thy Divine Majesty, with these Thy holy gifts which we now offer unto Thee, the memorial Thy Son hath commanded us to make; HAVING IN REMEMBRANCE His blessed Passion and precious Death, His mighty Resurrection and glorious Ascension; RENDERING UNTO THEE MOST HEARTY THANKS for the innumerable benefits procured unto us by the same."

THE HOLY EUCHARIST AND THE ASCENSION 115

"The Oblation" for us is the offering of the bread and wine, which never ceases to be bread and wine. But because we do this in accordance with Christ's own command, because we do it in remembrance and commemoration not only of what He was, but of what He *is;* because we pour out our thanksgivings to God for the innumerable blessings which Christ by His blessed Passion and precious Death, His mighty Resurrection and glorious Ascension has brought to us, therefore He, our blessed Lord, in the fulness of a love which passeth all understanding, accepts our oblation and does with it what we ourselves could never do. He unites our offering with His offering and makes our bread the Bread of Life. And because He Himself in Heaven does this, we, on earth, are able to say, through our union with Him, "Although we are unworthy, through our manifold sins, to offer any sacrifice, yet we beseech Thee to accept this, our bounden duty and service."

It is the Holy Ghost, not we, that consecrates the bread and wine. It is Christ in Heaven, the High Priest, Who says, "This is My body," "this is My blood." How, or in what way, Christ unites our offering so closely with His offering that He calls the bread His body and the wine His blood, is and will ever be a mystery to men in this lower world, because it is a truth of Heaven, not of earth. If we know not what kind of bodies we ourselves shall have after the resurrection, how can we possibly hope to comprehend the far greater and more stupendous mystery of Christ's glorified humanity when His Manhood was taken up into God?

Jesus Christ once, in the days of His flesh, when He walked this earth as the Man of Nazareth, was fettered by the limitations (sin only excepted) of our human existence. His human presence then was localized. But now that His Manhood has been taken up into God; now that Jesus is "Alpha and Omega, the beginning and the ending, which is, which was, and which is to come, the Almighty,"[1] His Presence is no longer subject to limitations of time and space, in such a way as to be conditioned by them, for it is a heavenly not an earthly presence. He who sanctifies the sacramental gifts is above and beyond those gifts themselves, in the fulness of His heavenly presence, even while He graciously and lovingly vouchsafes to make them to us, the communion of His body and blood.

Again, while it is true that Christ has promised to be present on earth wherever two or three are gathered together in His Name,[2] we should be exceedingly careful that we do not press this fact so far that it will exclude and shut out from view another important truth. For it is equally true that by virtue of our union and communion with Him, when we lift up our hearts at the time of "the Holy Eucharist," we ourselves are lifted up into the heavenly places, to join with angels and archangels and all the company of Heaven in the worship of Heaven itself, and to enter into the Presence of Christ, our great High Priest, in Heaven itself.

In other words, we must keep the *whole* truth before us as it is in Christ Jesus. If we think of the Presence of Christ with us on earth, we are still

[1] Rev. i. 8; xxi. 6; xxii. 13.   [2] St. Matt. xviii 20.

more earnestly to think, in the Eucharistic Service, of our being with Christ in the heavenly places, and knowing His Presence, as it is manifested, *there*. And when we thus rise to the height and length and breadth of New Testament truth, we begin to realize how utterly insufficient are all those sacramental theories which define the manner of Christ's Eucharistic Presence, and of all those sacramental rites and customs which localize that mysterious Presence in the bread and wine alone.

Time and space are human ideas. They are of the earth, earthly. When applied to earthly things, they help toward accuracy of thought and definition; but when applied to heavenly things, they become the expression of human ignorance. We know that the bread, while still bread, and that the wine, while still wine, are united to the body and blood of Christ in Heaven in such a heavenly, mysterious way that our offering is made by Him one with His offering, enabling Him to say: "This is My body," "This is My blood." And because *He* said it, Who has now entered within the veil as our great High Priest, we rest upon His almighty word. We can go no further than this. We can only say, in faith: —

> "Christ was the Word that spake it,
> He took the Bread and brake it,
> And what His word doth make it
> That I believe and take it."

Most of the difficulties and controversies that have disturbed the peace of the Catholic Church in the past nine hundred years are due to the fact that believers have lost sight of that vision of the ascended Christ which was so constantly and so vividly before the eyes of the New Testament Christians. As the sacrament of Baptism cannot be understood apart from the Resurrection, so the sacrament of the Holy Communion cannot be understood apart from the Ascension.

Every follower of Christ who feels the reality of those truths about the life of our ascended Lord that are emphasized so earnestly and so particularly in the Epistles to the Ephesians and the Hebrews, and who realizes what the Presence of Christ, as our great High Priest, means, will find his thought, his reasoning power, and his devotional feelings lifted up above the region of these endless eucharistic controversies, because he seeks those things which are above, where Christ sitteth, at the right hand of God.

CHAPTER VI

THE CHURCH, THE BODY OF CHRIST

THE first message both of St. John the Baptist and of Christ Himself, when they began to preach, was: "Repent ye, for the Kingdom of Heaven is at hand."[1]

And from this time onward, we find that our Lord's teachings regarding the Kingdom of Heaven were distinctly progressive, keeping pace with the development of Gospel truth, but never anticipating the sequence of events.

In the Sermon on the Mount, Christ taught His disciples to pray, "Our Father, Thy Kingdom come, Thy will be done on earth as it is in Heaven," implying plainly that the growth of the Kingdom of Heaven on earth would depend upon the way in which men prayed and tried to do God's will. And He followed up this charge by showing, in the object teaching of His own life and example, how God's will was to be done on earth as it is done in Heaven.

At a later day, Christ disclosed the fact that while many were called, all would be left free to choose, not only whether they would obey or reject God's will, but, also, what the measure of their obedience would be. And He taught that the Kingdom of

---

[1] St. Matt. iii. 2; iv. 17.

Heaven on earth would therefore include both saints and sinners, those who would be saved and even those who would ultimately be lost. This truth is strikingly brought out in the group of parables recorded in the thirteenth chapter of St. Matthew's Gospel, and logically entails the further truth that the Kingdom of Heaven on earth must be visible as well as invisible.

When the Apostles had been educated by Him for a year or more in the mystery of the Kingdom of Heaven,[1] He began to be much more explicit, for they now comprehended that Christ had brought down the Kingdom of Heaven to earth through His Incarnation, and therefore their minds were open to the truth that the Kingdom was centred in His own Person. Gradually but surely the realization grew under His teachings that it did not, and could not, exist apart from Him; that it was wholly dependent on Him and was an emanation from Him. As the Crucifixion drew near, Christ's revelations on this point became very plain. "I am the door," He said; "I am the Good Shepherd, who giveth His life for the sheep;" "I am the Resurrection and the Life;" "Because I live ye shall live also;" "I am the Way, the Truth, and the Life, no man cometh unto the Father but by Me." "If ye had known Me, ye should have known My Father also."

Yet now there appeared a strange paradox in His teachings. For, at the very time when He most solemnly assured His disciples that He was their Life and would remain with them forever, He also said that the time was at hand when He should be

---

[1] St. Mark iv. 11.

taken from them, and that "it was expedient for them that He should go away." Then, at the very end, lest they should miss the intentional paradox by a misinterpretation of His plain words, — lest, in a word, they should imagine that when He really left this earth, the *memory* of His teachings, His example, His life was to take the place of His actual personal Presence, — Christ made use of a remarkable figure which implied an objective as well as a subjective basis of union. "I am the true Vine," He said to them, a few hours before His Crucifixion. "Abide in Me, and I in you. As the branch cannot bear fruit of itself except it abide in the vine, no more can ye except ye abide in Me. I am the Vine, ye are the branches: He that abideth in Me and I in him, the same bringeth forth much fruit, for without Me, ye can do nothing."[1]

We can imagine the state of bewilderment in the minds of the Apostles as they listened to those mysterious words, in the concluding chapters of St. John's Gospel in which our Lord's progressive teachings regarding the Kingdom of Heaven on earth reached their climax. Yet He could not at that time make His meaning plainer, for He would not anticipate the *results* of events that were still in the future.

And if one asks why it was that Christ did not explain in the Gospels more definitely the truths which shine out so clearly in the Epistles of the New Testament, the answer is as significant as it is simple.

The teachings of Christ and the great doctrines of the Gospel are so closely interwoven with the facts of Christ's life that they cannot possibly be under-

[1] St. John xv. 1, 4, 5.

stood or interpreted apart from the actual events themselves.

And these events, in like manner, are so indissolubly bound together, in interrelation and interdependence, as to be inseparable one from another. The Crucifixion cannot be isolated from the Resurrection, the Resurrection is incomplete without the Ascension, the Ascension cannot possibly be comprehended without Pentecost. As we have repeatedly said, the Atonement, which began at the Cross, does not end until the Holy Ghost is sent down to regenerate humanity; nor can men on earth become so completely one with Christ in Heaven that they are *in Christ* and Christ is *in them*, unless the union is perfected by the power of the Holy Ghost.

Pentecost was, therefore, the birthday of the Church of Christ on earth; the time when the Gospel promises of Christ reached their blessed fulfilment, and when all His anticipatory teachings regarding "a Kingdom of Heaven" on earth were at last to be interpreted, realized, and fulfilled in the history of His Church. Henceforth, therefore, in the development of Christianity, the Kingdom is called by this new name, and it is a noteworthy fact that while in the Gospels the phrase "Kingdom of Heaven" occurs over a hundred times, and the word "Church" only two or three times, in the Epistles of the New Testament, written after Pentecost, the word "Church" appears over a hundred times, while the "Kingdom of God" is not used a dozen times. The explanation is that the Church of Christ became after Pentecost the *organized* Kingdom of Heaven on earth.

THE CHURCH, THE BODY OF CHRIST

Observe, however, that it was an organism, not an organization. This distinction is never to be lost sight of. An organization is a federation formed by men; an organism is a body endued with the power of life and created by God. Observe again: though the Kingdom of Heaven began in Christ's own Person when He brought Heaven to earth and came in personal contact with men, the Church, or organized Kingdom, did not begin until He went back to Heaven, and sent the Holy Ghost, enduing them with power from on high, to carry on the work which He had taught them to do, and which He had, by His life and death, His Resurrection and Ascension, made possible. After Pentecost, through the inspiration of the Holy Ghost, they understood as never before how completely the Kingdom of Heaven was centred in His own Person. For if, by His Incarnation and Nativity, He in His own Person had brought Heaven down to earth, so, by His Resurrection and Ascension, He in His own Person had raised earth to Heaven, where He was henceforth to sit on the right hand of God as the Prophet of Humanity, the Priest of His Church, and the King of the Kingdom of Heaven on earth. When, therefore, from His throne in Heaven He sent down the Holy Ghost as "the Lord and Giver of Life," His Church became a living organism, in which His people were united with Him, their Head, in Heaven. It was an organism in the truest sense of the word, because its whole life was centred in Christ in Heaven, and depended upon that one great Personality which lovingly overshadowed, without destroying the human personalities of His people.

It is an organism inspired by the one *mind* of Christ in Heaven, to Whose teachings His people rejoice to surrender their intellects, "casting down imaginations, and every high thing that exalteth itself against the knowledge of God, and bringing into captivity every thought to the obedience of Christ." It is an organism controlled by the one *will* of Christ in Heaven, through which His people become sanctified, and to whose rule they rejoice to surrender their human wills. It is an organism because, however the members of His Church may differ from one another in taste, disposition, and character, or in spiritual gifts, social spheres, or intellectual aims, the one united life purpose of all His people is to yield themselves up in body, soul, and spirit, as human organs, through which Christ in Heaven may continue His work on earth.

It was the intense realization and conviction of this organic life and organic unity of the Church of Christ on earth and of its inseparable union with Him in Heaven which inspired St. Paul to call it " the Body of Christ." And it is instructive to compare this description of St. Paul with our Lord's own words: "I am the Vine, ye are the branches." Clearly, Christ anticipated here His Apostle's illustration, for there is the closest resemblance between the two analogies. It is equally clear that our Lord could not, before His own Crucifixion, Resurrection, and Ascension, go so far as to adopt the language of St. Paul and call the Church " His Body " without being misunderstood and conveying a false impression to the minds of His Apostles.

But after Christ was in Heaven, and the Holy

Ghost had actually endued the Church with power from on high; after its organic life was objectively realized and recognized, St. Paul's description of that Church as "the Body of Christ" became the inspired interpretation of an existing reality. The objective life of the Church itself was a verification and corroboration of his words.

Let us now direct our attention more closely to this striking analogy of St. Paul's. It is all the more remarkable because the human body, as we know it now, is an earthly, not a heavenly thing; it is visible, not ethereal; it is physical, not spiritual; it is material, and subject to all the laws and limitations that govern matter. The human body, again, is a piece of mechanism in which all the functions are adapted to their environment, all the organs have their uses, and all the members, by a most wonderful adjustment, are correlated together. Indeed, when the Psalmist says that "we are fearfully and wonderfully made," he anticipates modern scientific discovery.

If St. Paul had employed this analogy only once or twice, we might dismiss it as a comparison that was not to be pressed. But he emphasizes it; he dwells upon it in detail; he recurs to it, again and again, as though it were something more than a mere illustration or metaphor, as it presented itself to his mind.

In the Epistle to the Romans he says: "We, being many, are one body in Christ, and every one members one of another." In the First Epistle to the Corinthians, he devotes a whole chapter to the subject, and says: "For as the body is one and hath many

---

[1] Rom xii. 5, *seq*.

members, and all members of that one body, being many, *are* one body, so also is Christ; for by one Spirit are we all baptized into one body."[1] In the Epistle to the Ephesians, he devotes again a whole chapter to the subject, and, after drawing out another series of lessons, he writes: "There is one body and one Spirit;" "Unto every one of us is given grace, according to the measure of the gift of Christ; . . . for the perfecting of the saints, for the work of the ministry, for the edifying of the body of Christ;" and holds up before us the ideal of growing "up into Him in all things, which is the Head, even Christ, from Whom the whole body, fitly joined together and compacted by that which every joint supplieth, according to the effectual working in the measure of every part, maketh increase of the body, unto the edifying of itself in love."[2]

Again, in the Epistle to the Colossians, He writes that Christ "is before all things, and by Him all things consist, and He is the Head of the Body, the Church."[3] He also warns the Colossians against the danger of false philosophies, and of not "holding the Head, from which all the body, by joints and bands, having nourishment, ministered; and, knit together, increaseth, with the increase of God."[4] We might also add here, that St. Paul's whole teaching in the third chapter of the Epistle to the Colossians flows from this analogy, nor can it be fully comprehended by those who do not realize that they "are called in one body."[5]

[1] 1 Cor. xii. 12, *seq.*
[2] Eph. iv. 4, *seq.*
[3] Col. i. 17, 18.
[4] Col. ii. 19.
[5] Col. iii. 15.

We have here the New Testament conception of the Church, as given by one of Christ's own chosen Apostles, and it stands out in vivid contrast to the ordinary Protestant idea with which we are familiar. In the popular religious thought of the day, at least in America, the Church of Christ is an inorganic society, whose sole bond of union is faith in the Lord Jesus Christ. As God is a Spirit, so the Kingdom of God on this earth is regarded as spiritual and invisible, and as an inward "Kingdom of Souls." It is looked upon as existing above and apart from all institutions, all ordinances, all human surroundings; as having, indeed, temporarily a visible form, but only by way of accommodation to human weakness.

Behind the visible church, men say, stands the invisible church; and behind the whole church stands the greater "Kingdom of Heaven." The visible is temporary, the invisible is eternal. The visible is the shadow, the invisible is the reality.

This modern idea is one of those side eddies that so often result from great historic movements. In the Middle Ages the swelling tide of power and influence in the old historic Church became so great that, in the visible reality of the Church's corporate life, Christians were not only in great danger of forgetting the right relation of the Church to Christ, her Prophet, Priest, and King in Heaven, but also of having their own individual free will and sense of personal responsibility destroyed.

The analogy of the faith was thus disturbed, and the great Protestant Reformation of the sixteenth century was the tremendous rebound from this abnormal development of the Church idea. Action and reaction are equal, not only in the physical, but in the moral world. The further the pendulum of human thought swings to one side of truth, the further it is apt to go, afterward, to the other; and in the reaction from the exaggerated conception of the power of the Church, and from the domination of her corporate life over the individual lives of her members, there grew up in Protestant lands a bitter antagonism to the very name of the Church, and a reverence for the sacredness of human personality which soon passed into the extreme of individualism. The peculiarly robust though one-sided type of Christian character developed under these Protestant influences, with its stalwart faith in God and its strong sense of personal responsibility to Christ, is a proof how necessary a reaction in this direction was. And the fact that Protestantism has held its own with such persistent power for three centuries, is an indication how deep-seated the disease in the Body of Christ must have been to require so prolonged a cure.

But the attention of the Christian world is now, at last, being turned from the past exaggerations of mediæval Christendom to the present exaggerations of Protestant systems. In the undue emphasis that has been laid upon the personal religion of the individual, a false feeling of independence has been engendered; the sphere of private judgement has been overestimated beyond all bounds; every man has become the maker of his own creed and the chooser as to what he ought to believe or not to believe.

A false perspective has been thus created, in consequence of which the sins of heresy and schism have been so completely ignored that sects have multiplied indefinitely, and the spirit of sect making has been fostered without restraint; the centrifugal or distributive forces of religion exceeding its centripetal or centralizing influences, have disturbed its equilibrium; the individualistic tendency to separation has smothered the catholic tendency to unity; individual religious life has taken the place of corporate religious life; while the Sacraments, the Creeds, the Ministry of the Church have been regarded as relics of a fast dying ecclesiasticism and "institutional" Christianity. It will be seen from all this that the whole office and function of the Church of Christ is as much undervalued, in these days, as it was disproportionately exaggerated in the Middle Ages. Indeed, this is as far removed from the New Testament conception of the Church, on the one side, as the ideal of Hildebrand or of Pope Innocent the III. was on the other.

Yet, the evil cannot be counteracted by holding up the true in contrast to this false idea of the Church, because the real difficulty lies far below the surface.

The reason for this wide divergence between modern views and New Testament teachings is to be found, not in different conceptions of the *Church*, but of Christ Himself.

When Christian believers comprehend that the Incarnation of Christ means the union of Heaven and earth, of the natural and spiritual, of the objective and the subjective, of the outward and the inward; and when they realize that the Ascension of Christ in His glorified Manhood, to Heaven, is the fulfilling of His Incarnation, all difficulties regarding the objective and visible Church, with her Creeds, her Sacraments, and her Ministry, will vanish.

We need not be afraid to press St. Paul's analogy that the Church is the body of Christ, for Church history and Christian experience have verified its accuracy and truth.

More than eighteen hundred years have come and gone since the Apostle lived; and in that time changes have taken place which he could not possibly have foreseen. The Church of Christ, which was then confined to the shores of the Mediterranean Sea, has spread itself over the whole world, and nations of every tongue and clime and age have flocked into it; yet to-day the wonderful fitness of his analogy is seen and appreciated as never before. Men as far apart as the saints in Nero's household are from American factory hands, have all been drawn together in the one Church by the one supreme desire to do Christ's will, to think as Christ thinks, to love sinners as Christ loved them, and to carry on Christ's work in this world. Thousands and hundreds of thousands of all sorts and conditions of men in all ages of the world have had no other ambition or life object than to serve Christ, and work as faithful members of His Body, as His hands, His feet, His voice, His eyes, in that state of life in which it has pleased Christ to place them.

If we were not so familiar with this fact, it would loom up as the most striking and wonderful phenomenon in all human history.

Side by side with this historic fact, there stands another that is equally marvellous. Christ said, " By this shall all men know that ye are My disciples, if ye love one another as I have loved you." For eighteen hundred years the idea of brotherhood has found in the Church of Christ such a realization as is seen nowhere else on this earth. All through the earlier part of the Christian era, as Milman so strikingly points out, the Church was the only really democratic institution known to man. Her cathedrals were the palaces of the poor, her parish churches were the homes of the people, and it has been chiefly through her benign influences that the social instincts of mankind have been developed. The New Testament teaches everywhere that we love God because He *first* loved us, and that Christ is the source and fountain of love in His Body, the Church. And when a disciple once surrenders himself to the influences of Christ's love, he *must* love others as Christ has loved him. For such love is one and the same power in the human breast, whether it takes a Godward or a manward direction. If it is increased in one way, it is increased in every way; if a Christian loves God, he must love his brother also. In the Church of Christ is witnessed the highest manifestation on this earth of those two Great Commandments of the Law, love toward God and love toward our neighbor.

And this truth is driven home to the soul with the intensity of a deep spiritual conviction, as the realization grows in the hearts of Christ's disciples that they are members of His Body; that every member has his own office and his own peculiar gift of the Spirit; that if one member of the body be exalted, all the other members are exalted with it; and that if one member suffers, all the other members suffer with it.

So closely are all bound together, that no one can reach his highest selfhood or attain the greatest possibilities of his own sphere of usefulness except through co-operation with others. He draws his inspirations not only from Christ, but from the society of believers, and both social and Divine influences contribute towards his growth in grace. If he attempts to live an independent existence, his development becomes one-sided; if he exaggerates his sphere in the Church, or refuses to take counsel of others, his higher life becomes dwarfed. As the laity must depend under God upon their ordained spiritual leaders, so the bishop in turn must depend upon his clergy, and the clergy upon their people. Each has his or her own place in God's Church, his or her own particular spiritual gift as a church worker, whether it be that of wisdom or understanding, ghostly counsel or strength, knowledge or godliness or the fear of God. St. Paul sets before us this high ideal of co-operation, in the unity of the Spirit and in the bond of peace; and it applies equally to all parish life, to all diocesan life, to the life of every national church, and to the Catholic Church of the ages. Only by following this ideal can we build up the Body of Christ and hasten the day when we shall all come, in the unity of the Faith, and of the knowledge of the Son of God, unto a perfect Man, unto the measure of the stature of the fulness of Christ.

That this body of Christ is objective as well as subjective, visible as well as invisible, social as well as personal, historical as well as spiritual, is shown by St. Paul's words, "By one Spirit are we all baptized into one body,"[1] as well as by all the other New Testament references to baptism. The risen Christ anchored this truth immutably, for all time, by proclaiming that to enter the Kingdom of Heaven we must be born of *water* and of the Spirit. By the use of the physical element of water our Lord has linked together Heaven and earth, the natural and the spiritual, so that it is impossible to mistake His meaning, and he who comprehends the profound significance of the doctrine of the Incarnation as it is revealed in the New Testament will have no difficulty in understanding why water is used in Baptism, or bread and wine in the Holy Eucharist; why there is a written as well as a living Word of God; why in the Christian Ministry there is not only the inward call of the Holy Ghost but the outward form of apostolic ordination; or why those who believe on the Lord Jesus Christ are associated together in an objective Church which is called in the New Testament "the Body of Christ."

[1] 1 Cor. xii. 13.

CHAPTER VII

THE VICAR OF CHRIST ON EARTH

IT is inconceivable that Christ should have gone back to Heaven without dealing with a subject of such supreme importance as this was, not only to the twelve Apostles, but to the whole Christian Church of future ages. Even if the sorrow-stricken Apostles did not, in their bewilderment, take in the full meaning of our Lord's repeated declaration that He was soon to be taken from them, Christ Himself knew that He was no longer to be their earthly Guide, and if He had kept silence as to Who would supply the distinct and irreparable loss of His own personal earthly Presence, when He went back to Heaven, the Christian religion would have remained to this day incomplete. Indeed, the New Testament Christians themselves would have been the first to feel the sense of loss. Its traces would and must have stereotyped themselves unmistakably in the Acts of the Apostles and their personal Epistles. But Christ anticipated the want before He left the earth. On the night before His Crucifixion He directed the attention of His twelve Apostles to this whole question, telling them plainly that He would send a Vicar to continue His work on earth. Furthermore, He gave an explicit and detailed description of the

Office and Ministration of this Person; all of which will appear later, when we come to the consideration of the details.

I

First of all, we should take notice that Christ describes this Vicar as taking the place of His own *Earthly* Presence. " These things have I spoken to you, *being yet present with you.* But the Comforter, which is the Holy Ghost, Whom the Father will send in My Name, He shall teach you all things." [1] " Nevertheless, I tell you the truth: it is expedient for you that I go away, for if I go not away, the Comforter will not come unto you; but if I depart, I will send Him unto you." [2]

That departure took place shortly afterwards, when Christ ascended to Heaven to commence His work there as our Reigning King. He ascended with His human body into the heavenly places, for only from a throne in Heaven itself could the Son of Man wield all power in Heaven and on earth.

Henceforth, though the distance between Heaven and earth made no difference to Him, Who was still to be to His disciples what He had always been, " Jesus Christ, the same yesterday, and to-day, and forever," present with His Church, " lo, alway, to the end of the world," it made an overwhelming difference to *them.* As Christ passed into the heavens, to stand henceforth with a glorified humanity, at the right hand of God, He passed into a spiritual realm where they could not follow.[3] He

---

[1] St. John xiv. 25, 26.   [2] St. John xvi. 7.
[3] St. John viii. 21; xiii. 33, 36.

was not separated from them, but they, by the very constitution of their nature and the limitation of their human minds, were separated from Him. Though, as King, He was closer to them than He had been when walking at their side, as Jesus of Nazareth, the carpenter's Son, they, on account of those human limitations, were shut out from realizing, or in any way recognizing, His heavenly Presence; and therefore, as time passed on, He would inevitably have become to them an absent, unapproachable Saviour, reigning in the far distant, invisible heavens, with an impassable gulf between Him and themselves, unless they were endued with some new "power from on high."

In a word, what the Apostles needed after Christ's Ascension was the personal presence, the personal influence, the personal teachings of a Vicar of Christ on earth, Who would show them how to reach their invisible King in Heaven, bring messages from their King to His Church on earth, accommodate His teachings to their earthly condition and limitations, show them, amid different earthly surroundings and the changing conditions of the times, how to conform to the example of Christ; and, above all, inspire them personally with the power of Christ's life.

Such must have been the want which the disciples felt after Christ's departure, and during those eager days of expectation which intervened between the Ascension and Pentecost. Yet nowhere do we gain the idea that this was a time of depression and gloom. On the contrary, St. Luke, who was probably the greatest and most accurate historian the

Christian Church has ever known, records that they spent those days in Jerusalem with great joy and continuous thanksgivings.[1]

There is only one way in which we may account for this strange joy. They were upheld by hope, and by that promise of the Father to which Christ referred just before His Ascension, when He reminded them of the words He had previously spoken[2] with such plainness on the night before the Crucifixion.

Then came the Day of Pentecost, when the Holy Ghost descended upon them in cloven tongues of fire. Now, for the first time, they realize what " the Promise of the Father" and the " Power from on high " mean. The Vicar of Christ, when He comes at Pentecost, is not a new Incarnation, because the Incarnation continues in Christ Himself, Who is now reigning in Heaven, as our Prophet, Priest, and King, our Saviour and our Judge. The Holy Ghost is sent by the Father "*in Christ's Name;*"[3] nay, He is sent by Christ Himself.[4] He is called by St. Paul the *Spirit of Christ.*[5] It is part of His Mission to translate the Revelation of God in Christ; or, to speak more accurately, to spiritualize the minds and hearts of believers so that they can comprehend it.

Furthermore, though the term "Vicar of Christ" is never used in the Gospels, Christ calls the Holy Ghost, the Paraclete; that is, the Advocate or Comforter; and the more we ponder the meaning of this comprehensive New Testament word, the more we shall realize its divine significance.

---

[1] St. Luke xxiv. 52, 53.
[2] Acts i. 4, 8.
[3] St. John xiv. 26.
[4] St. John xvi. 7.
[5] Rom. viii. 9.

It covers all the ground that the term "vicar" does, and at the same time signifies infinitely more. Read the Book of Acts and see how this was appreciated and felt by the Apostles and their contemporaries, and how they put themselves under the direction of the Holy Ghost. To a New Testament Christian, the bare idea of supplementing, by the human authority of any mortal man, this personal guidance of the Spirit of God Himself would have appeared nothing less than blasphemous.

Thus also was it in the post-apostolic Church. No one with any historical sense can read the Fathers of the first three centuries without distinguishing at a glance how impossible it would have been for them to tolerate the idea of a human vicar of Christ. The supposition involves an anachronism; for it presupposes conditions of thought utterly alien to the whole tone of church life at that early day. The contrast in this respect, indeed, between the periods A. D. 63–303 and A. D. 850–1225, is evident to every student of church history.

When, in Western Europe, Christian believers began to look no higher than to the authority of a human vicar of Christ, and substituted this for the divine influence of the Guide appointed by Christ Himself, the whole character of New Testament Churchmanship, as it had manifested itself in the former period, began insensibly to change.

II

The Vicar of Christ was to be an invisible Presence in His Church; an inward, not an outward Presence;

a Holy Spirit, revealing Himself only to spiritual men. All this is directly stated in Christ's own words: "If ye love Me, keep My commandments. And I will pray the Father, and He shall give you another Comforter: . . . even the Spirit of Truth, Whom the world cannot receive, because it seeth Him not, neither knoweth Him: but ye know Him, for He dwelleth with you, and shall be in you."[1]

It will be observed that our Lord lays especial emphasis upon the *invisibility* of the Spirit. The world cannot receive Him *because* He is unseen, and because He is beyond the world's power of perception. God, the Holy Ghost, hides Himself from the unconsecrated gaze of worldly eyes. His ways are not as the world's ways, neither are His thoughts like the world's thoughts. He manifests Himself only to those who love Christ and keep His commandments.

To these also He is just as invisible as to the outer world, but for a different reason. The sight revelation ended with Christ. There is but one Incarnation. There cannot be a second, for the Incarnation of Christ, as we have said, continues after He rose from the dead, and ascended to Heaven. Though in Gospel days His followers had known Christ after the flesh, they were henceforth to know Him so no more. The knowledge which began in sight was to pass beyond sight, and beyond the point where it was dependent on sight. It was to soar into higher, more spiritual regions of knowledge. It was to lift up their reasoning powers into the heavenly regions where Christ had gone before; it was to bring them a more satisfying certainty, and create in them

[1] St. John xiv. 15, 16, 17.

deeper spiritual convictions than could be created by the things that are seen and temporal. It was to enable them to realize the Presence of the unseen Christ, through the power of the Holy Ghost, in such a way that though now they saw Him not, yet, believing, they could rejoice with joy unspeakable and full of glory.

III

The Vicar of Christ was to bring no new revelation, but to interpret the one already given. " He shall not speak of Himself," was our Lord's plain, explicit declaration.

Christ alone was the Word of God; and St. John, in the prologue to his Gospel, reveals the fulness of meaning in that term. Without Him was not anything made that was made. He is the Alpha and Omega of all creation. When at last, after the evolution of untold ages, all created nature blossomed out in the Babe of Bethlehem, then He who had spoken heretofore through nature now spake as the Son of Man; and never man spake like this Man. Heaven and earth shall pass away, but His words shall not pass away. For they are the words of the Word of God. Eternal life and truth and power were in those words; and therefore He assured His disciples: " If ye abide in Me, and *My words* abide in you, ye shall ask what ye will, and it shall be done unto you."[1]

Furthermore, Christ's words were inseparably connected with His life. He was the Word of God, Who spoke both by utterance and by deed, for His example was His teaching translated into the object

[1] St. John xv. 7.

lessons of human actions, and both culminated in His Cross and Passion, His precious Death and Burial, His glorious Resurrection and Ascension.

The outward Revelation of God ended in Him, and was completed when He sent down, through the Holy Ghost, those messages recorded in the Epistles and the Book of Revelation.[1] The Mission of the Holy Ghost, the Spirit of Truth, was not to *add* anything to Christ's words: it was to reveal their truth; to deepen in the minds of believers the consciousness and conviction of their truth; to interpret and illumine their truth to successive generations of believers, by showing, as age followed age, how wonderfully true they continue to be to all conditions of human life and in all the progressive developments of human history. There was no need of any additional or supplemental revelation by the Holy Ghost, but there was need of educating the Christian world to a true comprehension of the revelation already given.

The history of the Church itself has brought out the reason for our Lord's prophecy that the Spirit of Truth " shall not speak of Himself, but whatsoever He shall hear that shall He speak."

There has been, indeed, a ceaseless advance on the part of the Church in Christian truth; an evolution of theology, a development of the Christian religion, a growth of the Church, a constant adaptation of Christianity to the changing conditions of the times, a progress in the apprehension of Christian truth correspondent with the progress of the world itself in art and science and literature, in inven-

[1] Rev. xxii. 16–20.

tion and discovery. But it is to be observed that, through all, Jesus Christ remains the same yesterday, and to-day, and forever; the Faith once for all delivered to the saints continues unchanged. In the evolution of theology, the faith which once was implicit becomes more and more explicit. In the development of the Christian religion, new and undiscovered meanings are found in the old facts of the Gospel; in the growth of the Church the wonderful description of St. Paul, in which he tells us that the Church is the Body of Christ, is discovered to have a profound depth of meaning that he himself could never have imagined, especially as regards the changing conditions of successive ages. And the lessons that the Church learns from the progress of science and literature in the outer world prompt it to cast off, not any part of the Christian Faith, but only the false ideas about science and history which have, from time to time, prevailed among Christians, in common with the rest of the world.

Through all, Christian progress has not been away from, but *in* the Faith once delivered to the saints; and how much higher is the plane of this progress, how much holier and more satisfying is this kind of inspiration, how much nobler is the education which Christians thus receive and the kind of character it develops in them, than if the outward revelation had not ended in Christ!

Therefore, New Testament Churchmanship requires that the One Holy Catholic and Apostolic Church must " be persuaded that the Holy Scriptures contain sufficiently all doctrine required of necessity for Eternal Salvation, and teach or maintain nothing, as required of necessity to eternal salvation, but that which she is persuaded may be concluded and proved from the same" (See Ordination Offices of Bishops and Priests in the Book of Common Prayer).

One has but to compare this teaching of Christ regarding the quiet influence of His Divine Vicar with the continuous utterances of a human vicar of Christ on earth to become conscious of a contrast that grows more irreconcilable the more it is realized.

IV

The Vicar whom Christ sent was to "reprove [or convince] the world of sin, and of righteousness, and of judgement."[1]

Here, let it be noted, appears a prophetic intimation of a kind of influence that the Holy Ghost will exert, beyond the bounds of the Church, upon the outer world itself. Though our Lord plainly stated that He is a Spirit that the world can neither receive nor know, *as a Divine Person*, here He tells us just as plainly that the world will be *unconsciously* influenced on the negative side against sin, if not on the positive side toward holiness, by His Presence in these three ways: (1) The Holy Ghost will bring to thousands of careless sinners who do not believe in Christ the conviction of sin; that is, the consciousness that they are yielding to a spirit of lawlessness and are living contrary to the will of God. (2) He will also, in the absence of Christ Himself, and of the direct influence of His words and example, " convince the world of righteousness;" that is, bring

[1] St. John xvi. 8.

home to the consciences of sinners the indirect influences of Christianity, filling them with a desire to do right. (3) He will "convince the world of judgement, because the prince of this world is judged."[1] While one hesitates about the exact interpretation of those last mysterious words of Christ, they seem to indicate that through the influence of the Holy Ghost worldly hearts will be inspired with a secret dread of coming judgements of God, and also with a certain capacity to see for themselves that wrong-doing always, sooner or later, brings its own punishment.

In the course of human history through eighteen Christian centuries, we seem to see a striking corroboration of this prophecy. While, on the one hand, we behold an unmistakable correlation between Christianity and civilization, at the same time we recognize, on the other, a plain differentiation between the Church of Christ and the civilized nations by which it is surrounded. The anomaly is one that has perplexed many thoughtful minds. In a certain sense a whole nation is christianized; in another sense, it is very far from being Christian. Perhaps, in this description of the work of the Comforter given by Christ we have the real explanation; namely, that civilization itself is actually but unconsciously inspired by the Holy Ghost with a hatred of the spirit of lawlessness or anarchy, with a love for moral law and order, and with a dread of immorality and its punishment.

And the remarkable effect of all this upon the Christian consciousness is, that while Christ's followers can on the one side affirm positively that cer-

[1] St. John xvi. 11.

tain essentials are generally necessary to salvation, such as repentance, faith and obedience, confession of Christ, Baptism, and the Lord's Supper, they dare not, on the other hand, deny salvation to those who do not fulfil these Gospel requirements; for Christ plainly assured us that the Holy Ghost would influence the world outside of His Church. There are numberless lives in this outside world which show the effects of the Spirit's working, and no human being can tell where the line of this unknown and mysterious influence ends.

V

The Vicar of Christ was to keep the remembrance of Christ's own life and teachings vivid and fresh in the hearts of His disciples. "He shall bring all things to your remembrance whatsoever I have said unto you;"[1] "He shall testify of me, and ye also shall bear witness;"[2] "Whatsoever He shall hear, that shall He speak."[3] The fulfilment of this prophecy is to be actually seen in the lives of the Apostles and first followers of Christ by their persistent preaching of Jesus. They lived upon His words and example, and then, before these first witnesses of Christ passed away, they were inspired by the Holy Ghost to write the Gospels and Epistles of the New Testament for those that came after. From that day to this, succeeding generations have treasured these writings; and as age follows age, the life, the words, the example of Christ are as fresh in the hearts of Chris-

[1] St. John xiv. 26. [2] St. John xvi. 26, 27.
[3] St. John xvi. 13.

tians as though He lived but yesterday on this earth. The New Testament has influenced the lives and characters of men, women, and children of all kindreds, nations, tribes, and tongues, as no other book has ever done. It has been the origin of the countless reformations which have taken place in Christian lands through all these centuries, inspiring Christ's followers with the intense desire to live as the New Testament Christians lived, and to follow Christ as they did, under the altered outward circumstances of life that have arisen in subsequent centuries. This remembrance of Christ's words is something more than a mere natural recollection. It is a *sanctified* remembrance. Under the influence of the Vicar of Christ, Christ's words have a living power. They become ever new and fresh. They are as applicable to the conditions of the fourth, or the fifteenth, or the nineteenth century, as to those of the first. They flash out new meanings, undreamed of before, as time goes on. They are interpreted by the passing events of each age. They become, under the power of the Holy Ghost, an inspiration to each successive Christian age, because they are the expression of universal truth.

Living in an atmosphere saturated with Christian teachings and associations, the very familiarity of facts like these is apt to blind one to their significance. But when we strive to stand aloof and view Christianity, as it were, from the outside, do we not find in these same facts of Christian history a remarkable fulfilment of that prophecy of Christ regarding this especial work of the Holy Ghost?

In this, we have an unmistakable criterion of the Presence and guidance of the Vicar Whom Christ appointed to take His place on earth; and in whatever period of Church History the Bible is neglected for other teachings, or is not the Book of all others placed by the Church in the hands of Christ's baptized followers, to mould their daily lives, this neglect is positive evidence that some outside influence has come between the Spirit of Truth and human souls, silencing His spiritual promptings and altering those normal conditions of Christian living, wherein He is constantly bringing to their remembrance whatsoever Christ has said unto them.

Yet here a distinction is to be carefully borne in mind. Our Lord told His Apostles that He would place them under the guidance of a Living Spirit of Truth, Who would thus bring His words inwardly to their remembrance. Christ said nothing regarding any *written* word. The Gospels are indeed the outward means adopted by the Holy Spirit for keeping the memory of Christ's spoken words in the hearts of His followers, but the New Testament itself needs to be constantly supplemented by the inward teachings of the Holy Ghost. Consequently, when, in the Middle Ages, western Christendom gradually learned to look for guidance to a human vicar of Christ, in place of that Divine Vicar Whom Christ Himself appointed, the Bible became more and more neglected, and the remembrance of Christ's words ceased to be felt, as a daily source of influence, in the lives of the people. Faith in Christ was, indeed, preserved, and the sacraments of the Gospel were administered. All over Europe faithful pastors were doing their duty in the towns and villages, and endeavoring to build up in other ways the religious life of the people. But somehow the void could not be filled, and the Christianity of the day fell far below the Gospel standard.

Then came the invention of printing, and the Word of God began to be quietly circulated in those towns and villages. The effect in England and Germany, and wherever the Bible was really read, was profound, and in less than three quarters of a century from the time when the first printed Bible appeared, the Protestant Reformation spread from land to land.

Then followed a strange but almost inevitable historical movement. The Bible, and the Bible only, became the religion of Protestants. They believed firmly it was true, in the guidance of the Holy Ghost; but they held that the only outward and visible channel of this guidance was the teaching of Holy Scripture. The Bible was the *only* organ through which the Holy Ghost authoritatively spoke, inspired the souls of men, and governed the Church. The written word was placed by them above the Sacraments, above the Ministry, above all the co-ordinated ways in which the Spirit of Truth had been guiding the Church of Christ into all truth through the Pentecostal Age of the Christian Era. A doctrine of verbal inspiration grew up, under these new limitations of Christian thought, which made Protestants the slaves of the letter while they forgot the spirit. As before the Reformation, their Roman Catholic forefathers had looked up to the Bishop of Rome as the infallible vicar of Christ on earth; so, since the Reformation, as a substitute for this visible authority, their Protestant descendants have looked up to an infallible Book on earth. As the Romanist has been obliged to invent artificial theories to support his ideas of an infallible human head of the Church, so the Protestant, in like manner, had to invent, to support his anti-Roman position, the theory of a mechanical verbal inspiration. And all the while both Romanist and Protestant have fallen so far below the primitive Church as to forget that the real Vicar of Christ on earth is God, the Holy Ghost.

VI

The Vicar of Christ is to *glorify* Christ. "He shall glorify Me: for He shall receive of Mine and shall show it unto you. All things that the Father hath are Mine: therefore said I, that He shall take of Mine and shall show it unto you."[1] Here our Lord prophesied that, under the guidance of the Holy Ghost, there was to be an advance in the knowledge and apprehension of that outward revelation which was complete in Him. It will be remembered that Christ's teachings were practically finished on the night before the the Crucifixion, when He said to His disciples, "Hereafter I will not talk much with you."[2] Henceforth, the *actions* of Christ's life were to take the place of His spoken words.

Yet this is the most important part of the whole Gospel history. The triumph of Christ's religion begins just where His teaching ends; namely, with the Crucifixion, the Death and Burial, the Resurrection and Ascension into Heaven.

Christ had, indeed, revealed to His Apostles the Divine Nature of that Incarnate Life which is the Life

[1] St. John xvi. 14, 15.   [2] St. John xiv. 30.

of the world and the Light of men. After His Resurrection, He had also revealed the fact that He was now the Almighty King, to Whom all power was given in Heaven and on earth, but He never opened His lips to *explain* to His Apostles all that the Crucifixion meant, all that the Resurrection meant, all that the Ascension meant. His explanations ended before the Crucifixion.

Christ had glorified *His Father* upon earth;[1] but how was Christ *Himself* hereafter to be glorified on earth?

The time of His glorification began at the very period when His own teachings ended. It began at His Crucifixion;[2] but the Apostles, before Pentecost, did not realize this. They did not comprehend that, when He rose from the dead, He was really glorified as the Resurrection and the Life of the world; or that, when He ascended His throne in Heaven, He was really glorified as the High Priest after the order of Melchizedek; and that henceforth He was to be the Reigning King under Whose power and authority, "in the dispensation of the fulness of times, all things shall be gathered together in one, both which are in Heaven and which are on earth."[3]

No truths or discoveries of science, philosophy, or history are comparable in importance with those stupendous realities which flow from the Crucifixion, Resurrection, and Ascension of Christ in His glorified humanity. Where, then, was the teacher to interpret these facts?

If Christ Himself did not explain these events, before their actual occurrence, in such a way that

---

[1] St. John xvii. 4. [2] St. John xii. 23; xvii. 4, 5.
[3] Eph. i. 10.

His disciples could comprehend them, it was impossible that any of the Apostles after His departure from this earth could fathom their divine depth of meaning. Christ needed something *more* than a human vicar on this earth to reveal the mystery of His glorified humanity.

Only that Person Who knows Christ *as He is now* in the unseen heavens, is capable of imparting this knowledge to mortal man on earth.

And if we glance back once more to our Lord's words, with these thoughts in mind, we shall perceive that this must have been what He meant when He said of the Holy Ghost: "He shall *glorify Me:* for He shall receive of Mine and shall show it unto you. All things that the Father hath are Mine: therefore said I, that He shall take of Mine and shall show it unto you."

When we turn from the Gospels to the Epistles of the New Testament, we behold the distinctive characteristics of the teaching of the Holy Ghost, the Vicar of Christ. There is in the latter a development of Christian truth that is far beyond what we read in the Gospel narrative. While the earthly life of Christ is constantly referred to and taken for granted, in these letters which the Apostles wrote to the churches under their care, the attention of the latter is ceaselessly directed to the risen and ascended Christ; to the power of His Resurrection;[1] to the connection between Baptism and the Resurrection;[2] to the correlation between the Resurrection and nature;[3] to the far-reaching effects of His Ascension

---

[1] Phil. iii. 1.   [2] Rom. vi. 4, 5; Col. ii. 12.
[3] 1 Cor. xv.; Rom. viii.

and our personal union with the Ascended Christ;[1] to the Church as the Body of Christ;[2] to Christ as the coming Judge;[3] to the nature of sin and the profound depth of meaning in the blood of Christ after His Resurrection and Ascension;[4] and to the continuous work of Christ as our Royal High Priest in Heaven.[5]

In our study of all these Epistles we shall observe, first, that through the teaching of the Holy Ghost the Apostles and New Testament Christians were continually discovering in the Resurrection and Ascension of Christ new powers; and, second, that there was in these Epistles a note of joy and of triumph that is absent in the typical religious life of our modern Christianity. Indeed, when we compare the Church of to-day with the joyous, triumphant Church of New Testament days, there is a contrast that is almost startling. Modern Christians are, in comparison, dispirited, lifeless and sad, showing that they have fallen below the level of the primitive Church, without being conscious of the cause.

The Roman Church, as we said in another chapter, stops at the Crucifixion, and Protestantism, at the Atonement on the cross. While both are technically orthodox in regard to the facts and doctrines of the Resurrection and Ascension of Christ, they do not appear to realize, as the writers of the Epistles did, what the Resurrection and Ascension mean; while both accept the letter, they seem to have lost the spirit. Practically, in their religious thinking they

---

[1] Eph. i., ii., iii.
[2] 1 Cor. xii; Eph. iv., *seq.*
[3] 1 and 2 Thess.
[4] 1 John.
[5] Epistle to the Hebrews.

do not go beyond the cross, and consequently have almost lost the conception of the glorified Christ. What is the cause? When we go back to the Reformation, the reason, I think, becomes evident.

Protestantism laid hold, with a mighty grasp, upon one forgotten truth, — justification by faith, — and holding to that one truth, it cast off the corruptions of Mediaevalism. But it was content with mere protests and denials. It never seemed to realize that there were other reforms even more necessary; that there were other forgotten truths besides " Justification by Faith," or that the whole standard of Christianity in the sixteenth century had fallen insensibly, in spirit, if not in the letter of formal orthodoxy, below the standard of Christianity in the first century; and that this was shown by the different way in which sixteenth century Christians and first century believers regarded the Resurrection and Ascension of Christ. And now, when we go a step further and ask the cause for this difference, we shall find that it antedates reformation times by several centuries, that it characterized the mediæval theology of the schoolmen, and that it began about the same time that the papacy put forth the claim of universal supremacy. Since that epoch the Roman Church, in her realization of Christian truth, has been apparently paralyzed in all her attempts to look beyond the Crucifixion. The reason for all those facts that we dwelt upon in the chapter on the Ascension is that the Church of Rome gradually began to lose the vision of the Glorified Christ from the day that she substituted a human vicar of Christ for that Divine Vicar Whom Christ Himself sent down into this world to take His place.

She confesses the letter, but has lost the spirit and the illumination of that Divine Guide Who reveals the Incarnation of Christ as a present fact, culminating in His Ascension to be our Reigning King, and in His future coming to judge both the quick and the dead.

If she had realized these great spiritual truths and all that flows from them, we should never have heard of the cultus of the Virgin Mary, of the mediæval doctrine of Transubstantiation, of the Invocation of the Saints, or of the distinctively Roman conceptions of the Christian Priesthood.

VII

The Vicar of Christ is the *Spirit of Truth*. On that same memorable night when Christ called Himself, "the Way, the Truth, and the Life,"[1] and when He prayed for His disciples to the Father, "This is life eternal, that they might know Thee, the only true God, and Jesus Christ Whom Thou hast sent,"[2] He also prophesied that the Holy Ghost should come to this earth as a "Spirit of Truth."[3] The juxtaposition of these terms must be something more than accidental; and the reiterated emphasis laid upon the fact that the Father is true, the Son is true, and the Holy Ghost is true, should not escape us.

The Holy Ghost is sent as the Revealer of Truth, to inspire, as a *Spirit* of Truth, all men who desire to be true, and thus enable them subjectively to realize the truth of the objective Revelation of

---

[1] St. John xiv. 6.   [2] St. John xvii. 3.
[3] St. John xiv. 17; xvi. 13.

Jesus Christ. As many as are led by the Spirit of God they are the sons of God. Unless one is true in spirit he cannot expect to be led by the Spirit of Truth. This explains to us the reason why so many of those who are baptized and confirmed receive apparently no gift of the Spirit, and why communicants of the Church continue to remain, in such large numbers, lukewarm and worldly, notwithstanding their frequent communions.

And when we pass from individual to corporate life, from the history of an individual soul to the history of the Church at large, have we not here the clue to many an ecclesiastical movement of the past? In mediæval times, the standard of truth which prevailed as a rule for centuries among the recognized leaders of the Church — although there have been always individual and conspicuous exceptions — was far below that spirit of truth which the Gospel enjoins and which animated New Testament Christians. For, side by side with the preservation of the form and the letter, there was manifested a spirit of casuistry, a tendency to substitute expediency for principle, and to make the end justify the means, which cannot but seem like disingenuousness.

It is also a fact that, to this day, the Papacy has not only made itself responsible for the code of morals taught by St. Alphonso di Liguori, but that it persistently countenances opinions, traditions of saints and relics, superstitions and historical inaccuracies, stories of past miracles and reports of present ones, which may help to glorify the Church in the popular mind, but which no accurate and unbiassed scholar and no strict lover of truth could ever accept.

These failings might be passed over in a spirit of Christian charity did not the whole Church of Rome profess to be governed by the earthly vicar of Him Who is the Way, the Truth, and the Life, and Who so expressly foretold that His Vicar should be the *Spirit of Truth.* Making that claim, it is but just and right that the whole Christian world should judge the ethical teachings of the Papacy by Christ's own standard.

Nothing in the Christian life is higher or more sacred than truth and truthfulness; and in an age of enlightenment like this, when all science, philosophy, and literature are pervaded by the supreme desire to be accurate and true, if the Roman Church under the leadership of an earthly vicar of Christ does not lead and inspire the world of science, philosophy, and literature by aiming for a still higher standard of accuracy and truthfulness, then Christians outside of her communion must apply to her Christ's own test of those prophets who profess to speak in His Name: "By their fruits ye shall know them."[1]

The Christian life from beginning to end is one of ceaseless effort in many directions, but the chief effort of all is the struggle to be true — inwardly true, under the eye of the Eternal Judge and through the guidance of the Holy Ghost. Such an effort necessitates a constant dependence upon an unseen, silent *Spirit* of Truth Who reveals His presence by no outward manifestations; and that dependence necessitates a natural feeling of uncertainty which, to a sinful heart, is always burdensome.

Sinners do not recognize that the uncertainty itself

[1] St. Matt. vii. 20.

THE VICAR OF CHRIST ON EARTH 157

arises from the conditions of human life, and that it is exaggerated by the spirit of unbelief.

There is no uncertainty about that positive outward Revelation of God which was completed in Jesus Christ; there is no uncertainty in Christ's Promises. Heaven and earth shall pass away, but His words shall not pass away. There is no uncertainty about the Presence, the inspiration, the influence of the Holy Ghost; but there *is* uncertainty regarding the interpretation of the principles of the Christian religion in meeting the problems that are ever arising in the advance of human thought, in the development of Church life, the progress of civilization, and the rule of right in personal human action.

It is not enough for doubting hearts that they have the certainties of the Gospel and the promised assistance of the Spirit of Truth, in working out those problems; they feel that all is insecure and vague, unless they have the additional certainty of an authoritative voice which will declare to them the will of God in things great and small as age follows age. It is an inexpressible relief to men, and often to the most intellectual of men, to escape the struggle of spiritual existence, the uncertainty of doubt, the divisions of Christendom, and the distracting theological systems of Protestantism, by submission to a recognized authority in matters of belief. The Roman Church offers an asylum where one may be spared all the pain and anxiety of thinking or deciding for himself and hence her fascination over multitudes of our race.

But count the cost. The type of Christian character developed under such influences stands out in vivid contrast to that which in New Testament times was moulded under the power of the Spirit of Truth. Those lesser uncertainties of life which the Romanist is saved from have, under God, their purpose and their use in stimulating Christ's disciples to reach out and grasp the deeper certainties of the Gospel. God Himself, to the Christian, is not unknowable. Positive truth, in all its essentials, has been revealed in Him Who is the Way, the Truth, and the Life. "This is life eternal, that they might know Thee, the only true God, and Jesus Christ Whom Thou has sent."[1] As, therefore, we press toward the mark for the prize of our high calling in God, we have in our Lord's own Promise that "the Spirit of Truth shall guide us into *all* truth," the assurance that we are on the pathway of highest truth and deepest certainty. And for those Christians who are treading this pathway the Holy Ghost is the only infallible Guide. It would be simply impossible for them to submit to any lower guide. This, of course, does not militate against the acceptance of the authority of the Catholic Church of the ages, because it was to the Church collectively as represented by her first Apostles to which Christ made that definite promise, "He shall guide you into all truth." It is through the guidance of the Spirit of Truth that the Church, by a slow gravitation of thought, gradually worked out the confession of her belief and formulated it in the Catholic Creeds. She was thus legitimately and rightly bearing her witness to the Faith once delivered to the saints; if various additions were made to the Creed by successive general councils, it was be-

---

[1] St. John xvii. 3

cause, in the intervening time, opposers had arisen to invent a new and strange interpretation to the old Faith, and it therefore became necessary to protect that Faith in its comprehensiveness and integrity by more definite phrase, against misconstruction.

The issue so often made between private judgement and church authority is a false issue. For the believer who most sacredly respects and reverences his own private judgement will be the one of all others to use his private judgement in accepting the united judgement of generations of other believers, as it has expressed itself in the catholic consent of the ages.[1]

That consent has been embodied and set forth in the Catholic Creeds. Only by yielding to an authority like this, which commends itself to every man's conscience in the sight of God as scriptural, rational, and moral, can that Unity of the Faith be preserved of which the New Testament so often speaks.

Those who yield to it are simply carrying on the continuity of the New Testament life. The authority to which they submit is that of the Divine Guide Who is the Vicar of Christ, and under it their Christian freedom remains and develops. Indeed, the more unreservedly they yield to it, the less can they obey any false authority. They can never rest satisfied with any doctrine of Papal Infallibility.

The Roman Church would deny, of course, that she substitutes a human for the Divine Vicar of Christ. She claims only that the pope is an authoritative human agent through whom the Spirit speaks. This, however, not only amounts to a real substitution for

[1] This subject has been more fully treated in "The Creedless Gospel and the Gospel Creed," chapter x., pp. 254-256.

the work of the Comforter, as described by Christ, but also results in the loss of that education of character which comes through the Spirit's guidance.

VIII

The Holy Ghost is the Comforter.[1] This Gospel word has well-nigh lost its original depth of meaning in the popular mind. "Comfort," in the ordinary sense, means rest and relaxation. As used by Christ it means to be *fortified*. This last signification is preserved and handed down to us in the Confirmation Office and in the prayer breathed over the candidates: "*Strengthen* them, we beseech thee, O Lord, with the Holy Ghost, the Comforter." The Comforter is the Spirit of Fortitude, Who is sent to strengthen Christians against that very tendency to unbelief and moral cowardice regarding the uncertainties of life of which we have just been speaking. They need courage to live up to their baptismal vows. Under His influence they receive power to fight manfully under Christ's banner, and to continue His faithful soldiers and servants unto their life's end. The comfort which the Comforter brings is therefore the reverse of that unspiritual ease which a worldly heart craves. It is the quietness and confidence that comes from inward strength and from the consciousness of being true. It is the exhilaration that comes from exertion and the joy of triumphing in the midst of hardship and warfare.

And the results are seen in the gradual development, in the followers of Christ, of a very marked

[1] St. John xiv.

and distinctive type of character, such as befits those who are become, in New Testament language, "a chosen generation, a royal priesthood, a holy nation, a peculiar people."[1] The very uncertainties of life are with Christians changed from stumbling-blocks into stepping-stones, and lead to a higher inward certainty of God that is hidden from the eyes of the world. By continual exercise, faith in Christ becomes heart-whole confidence; by continual, daily dependence on the Spirit of Truth, there grows up in a believer's breast a hatred for falsehood and unreality of every kind, an educated truthfulness in motive and speech, trained accuracy in thought and in judgement, simplicity and directness in action.

Continually facing uncertainty under the conscious guidance of an unseen Spirit of Truth, the Christian moves onward unto the unknown future as though it were well known. He is sure, whatever betide, that all things work together for good to them that love God. While inwardly depending upon the Spirit of God, outwardly he becomes among men more and more self-reliant, developing a character, through that Spirit's daily influence, that is singularly robust and strong. It is thus that the Comforter manifests His indwelling as the Spirit of Fortitude.

In vivid contrast to this, stands that type of Christian character which has been moulded under the influence of obedience to a human vicar of Christ. The pages of Church history and of Christian biography display before our eyes the different ethical effects of these two kinds of obedience. In just so

[1] 1 Peter ii. 9.

far as men or nations have yielded themselves up to subjection to a human vicar of Christ, their spiritual growth, as a rule, seems to have been arrested, retarded, dwarfed. A negative type of Christian character is developed among them which is lacking in robustness and mental vigor; and which, because it avoids the normal conditions of spiritual warfare, seems, in corresponding proportion, to be a stranger to the inspiring influences of the Spirit of Fortitude.

IX

The Vicar of Christ is the Spirit of Unity. Although this is not, it is true, directly stated in Christ's own description of the Comforter, it is more than implied in His high-priestly prayer recorded in the seventeenth chapter of St. John's Gospel, in which all His teachings on the night before the Crucifixion attain their climax. Surely, no words upon the subject of unity could be stronger than those with which this prayer ends: " That they all may be one; as Thou, Father, art in Me and I in Thee, that they also may be one in Us, that the world may believe that Thou hast sent Me. And the glory which Thou gavest Me, I have given them; that they may be one, even as We are One; I in them and Thou in Me, that they may be made perfect in One." [1]

Christ here sets forth first the everlasting truth that He Himself is the centre of unity between God and Man; and that all unity begins from above. It begins at God, not man. It begins with Christ's oneness with the Father; and it is a memorable his-

[1] St. John xvii. 21–23.

torical fact in the annals of the Church, that the first step toward unity has ever been the confession of the Doctrine of the Holy Trinity.

In the second place, Christ speaks of His oneness with His disciples; and this is the next step toward unity. Christians are never brought together until they acknowledge that Christ is "the Head of every man," and then recognize that superhuman Christ-like type of character which is created in human nature only by living contact with the living Christ.

In the third place, Christ speaks of the oneness of Christian believers with each other through their union with Him and His Father. It may seem strange that there should be no mention here of the Spirit of Truth, of Whose presence and work our Lord had been speaking so earnestly a short time before. But there was a reason for the omission. The basis of all Christian unity lies in the Incarnation of Christ. It is not spiritual alone; it is both spiritual and natural. It is objective as well as subjective, outward as well as inward.

In all ages we have witnessed an almost irresistible tendency on the part of believers toward the ideal of a spiritual, in contradistinction to an organic, unity; and down to the present day there are thousands of Christians who hold this false and unscriptural view. In Christ's high-priestly prayer this idea is conspicuous by its absence. The condition of all true Christian unity is union with the Incarnate Christ. It is only after the Church is formed as an organism, and after it has been recognized by the Apostles as the Body of Christ, that the agency of the Spirit, as a spirit of unity, is realized; and then the recognition appears to have come empirically through experience and observation of His presence in the organism itself. This is clearly brought out by St. Paul in his Epistles. For example, after writing to the Ephesians that they should endeavor to keep the unity of the Spirit in the bond of peace, he goes on to explain this unity by saying, " There is one body and one Spirit; . . . one Lord, one faith, one baptism, one God and Father of all, Who is above all, and through all, and in you all."[1] And then He reminds the members of the Church that they must keep looking up to the objective centre of unity, the Ascended Christ,[2] Who " gave some [to be] apostles; and some, prophets; and some, evangelists; and some, pastors and teachers; for the perfecting of the saints, for the work of the ministry, for the edifying of the Body of Christ."[3] Observe, that all the essentials of unity are here set forth, and that they all centre, through the power of the Spirit, in the Ascended Christ. Christ is the Head of the Body; unto Whom, the Body, or Church, is growing up "*in all things*,"[4] until it comes to the measure of the stature of the fulness of Christ.

Again, in the first Epistle to the Corinthians, St. Paul emphasizes, once more, the same intimate connection between the one Body and the one Spirit. " For as the body [*i. e.* the human body] is one and hath many members, and all members of that one body, being many, are one body, so also is Christ. For by one Spirit are we all baptized into one Body, whether we be Jews or Gentiles, whether we be bond

---

[1] Eph. iv. 4–6.
[2] Eph. iv. 7, 8.
[3] Eph. iv. 11, 12.
[4] Eph. iv. 15.

or free; and have all been made to drink into one Spirit."[1]

From this one Spirit, he tells us, every member of the Church, or of the one Body, receives personally and individually a special spiritual gift. In other words, the sacredness of human personality is recognized, and the power of each one's individuality is consecrated. Every member of the Church has a special work committed to him, a special gift of the Spirit to do that work, and a special responsibility to fulfil, as a child of God and an inheritor of the Kingdom of Heaven. But if he lawlessly separates from the rest of the body, exaggerates his special work, his special gift, his special responsibility, without regard to the work, the gifts, the responsibilities of others, then he is guilty of the awful sin of "*schism.*"[2] Only by working with others, under the direction of the Spirit, will his own personality be developed up to its highest point. To grow in the knowledge of Christ he must not only be one with Christ, but one with Christ's Body. To make the most of his own spiritual gift, and yet be one in spirit and in work, with the saints of all ages who compose the Body of Christ, the Christian must put himself under the daily influence and guidance of the Vicar of Christ, that "One Spirit" of Truth Who inspires all. For "there are diversities of gifts, but the same Spirit."[3] It is noteworthy how St. Paul, in verse after verse, keeps reiterating and emphasizing that phrase "*by the same Spirit,*" as though it were the one truth of all others that, in dwelling upon this subject, he would brand upon the hearts of the Cor-

[1] 1 Cor. xii. 12, 13.   [2] 1 Cor. xii. 25.   [3] 1 Cor. xii. 4.

inthian Church, until the ruling thought of each one, as he marks the contrast between his own and other's gifts, will be, "All these worketh that one and the self-same Spirit, dividing to every man severally as He will."[1] And the same truth that applies to individual Christians applies also to congregations of Christians. Such is the unity of the primitive Church as it is set forth in the New Testament. The unity of the One Holy, Catholic and Apostolic Church, as portrayed by the Apostles themselves, centres in Christ, begins and ends in the Ascended Christ, through the power of the unseen Spirit of Truth.

[1] 1 Cor. xii. 11.

CHAPTER VIII

APOSTOLIC SUCCESSION

THERE was certainly an Apostolic Ministry ordained by Christ Himself in New Testament times. To select a few of the many passages of the Gospels showing this, our Lord, in the earlier days of His ministry, told His disciples to pray that God would send forth laborers into His harvest; and then, after spending a whole night in prayer, He chose His twelve Apostles and sent them forth on their first Missionary Journey.[1] At the end of three years, after those Apostles had received at His own hands the most thorough and complete training any minister of Christ has ever received, He gathered them together the night before His Crucifixion, instituted the Holy Communion, and gave them that parting charge recorded in the fourteenth, fifteenth, and sixteenth chapters of St. John's Gospel, in the course of which He said, "Ye have not chosen Me, but I have chosen you, and ordained [or appointed] you, that ye should go and bring forth fruit, and that your fruit should remain."[2] Three days after, when He appeared to them for the first time after His Resurrection, He said, "Peace be unto you: *as My Father hath sent Me,*

[1] St. Matt. ix. 36, *seq.* [2] St. John xv. 16.

even so send I you. And when He had said this, He breathed on them, and saith unto them, Receive ye the Holy Ghost. Whose soever sins ye remit, they are remitted unto them; and whose soever sins ye retain, they are retained."[1]

Afterward, when the risen Christ revealed Himself unto them as the *King*, "to Whom all power had been given in Heaven and on earth," He said unto these same Apostles: "Go ye, therefore, and teach [or make disciples] of all nations, baptizing them in the name of the Father, and of the Son, and of the Holy Ghost, teaching them to observe all things whatsoever I have commanded you; and *lo, I am with you alway, even unto the end of the world, Amen.*"[2]

Again, in the Acts of the Apostles, we read that Jesus appeared, after His Resurrection, for forty days *"unto the Apostles whom He had chosen"*[3] taught them in the things pertaining to the Kingdom of Heaven; commanded them not to leave Jerusalem until the promise of the Father was sent; and at last, just before His Ascension to Heaven, commissioned them with these solemn words: "Ye shall receive power after that the Holy Ghost is come upon you: and ye shall be *witnesses unto Me*, both in Jerusalem, and in all Judæa, and in Samaria, and unto the uttermost part of the earth."[4] At first these Apostles became the recognized leaders of the Church and constituted its only ministry. But after Pentecost, the numbers of the baptized disciples of Christ grew so rapidly that the twelve

[1] St. John xx. 21-23.
[2] St. Matt. xxviii. 19, 20.
[3] Acts i. 2.
[4] Acts i. 8.

were obliged by pressure of work to resign the most unimportant of their duties to others.

I

The account of this first *extension* of the ministry is preserved to us in the Book of Acts. The Apostles told the people to select from themselves seven men of honest report, who were full of wisdom and the Holy Ghost. These were "set before the Apostles, and when they had prayed, they laid their hands on them."[1] Henceforth, therefore, there were two orders in the Church, — *Apostles* and *Deacons*.

After the death of St. Stephen a persecution ensued, which drove the disciples out of Jerusalem to proclaim the Gospel, and another extension of the ministry became necessary. Pastors, or parish priests, were needed for different congregations, and the Apostles assigned another and more important portion of their own work to a new order of ministers, called in the Book of Acts "*Elders*." It is not recorded when this second extension of the ministry took place; but as the first mention of "*Elders*" in the New Testament occurs in connection with the coming of a prophet to Antioch from Jerusalem to make known to them a future famine "in the days of Claudius Cæsar,"[2] it is to be noted that at this early date, when St. Paul was still called "Saul," and before the reign of Claudius Cæsar, there were already elders occupying a responsible position in the mother Church at Jerusalem. Furthermore, they are referred to in a

[1] Acts vi. 6.   [2] Acts xi. 28, 30.

way which indicates that they must have been for some time a recognized part of her organization. There were then, at this period, in Jerusalem, *Apostles*, *Elders*, and *Deacons*.

The very next chapter [1] gives still another glimpse of the organization of the mother Church. It records how, about that time, Herod, to vex the Church, killed James, the brother of John, and the first martyr in the Apostolic Band itself, with the sword; how, when he saw that this pleased the Jews, he proceeded to imprison the Apostle Peter also; and how St. Peter, released from the prison by an angel, in answer to the unceasing prayers of the Church, went to the memorable house of Mary, the mother of St. Mark, — the upper room of which one of the most important congregations in Jerusalem were most probably wont to use as a church, — and said to those who were present, "Go show these things *unto James*, and to the brethren," and then departed.

The way in which St. James is mentioned here by St. Peter is very noteworthy. Yet alone, and by itself, it might escape observation, were it not that St. Paul gives the same prominence to his name in writing to the church in Galatia [2] and even goes so far as to place it before those of Peter and John, in enumerating those who seemed to be pillars of the Church at Jerusalem [3] We also find that a few years after, when the Apostles and Elders came together in Jerusalem to consider the most important question that had ever as yet arisen in the New Testament Church, James was plainly,

[1] Acts xii. [2] Gal. i. 19. [3] Gal. ii. 9.

and beyond all manner of doubt, the presiding officer of this first recorded Apostolic Council.[1] The question now arises, Who was James of Jerusalem? For centuries it has been held, almost by common consent, that he was one of the original twelve Apostles.[2] Notwithstanding this popular and prevalent idea, there have been from time immemorial the following grave and really inexplicable difficulties connected with this supposition. First, our Lord gave to the original Twelve the plain, distinct commission and command to go and "make disciples of all nations;"[3] to go "into all the world and preach the Gospel to the whole creation;"[4] to go and be "witnesses unto Him, both in Jerusalem, and in all Judæa, and in Samaria, and to the uttermost parts of the earth."[5] It is very hard to understand how, in the face of these solemn charges, the Apostles should have detached and appointed one of their own number to reside exclusively at Jerusalem and spend his whole life in having a local superintendence over the churches at that place. Secondly, James of Jerusalem, as all the records show, was "James, the brother of our Lord." Even St. Paul calls him by this distinctive title.[6] But how could James *the son of Alpheus* be the same as James the Lord's brother? To meet

---

[1] Acts xv. 19.
[2] There were two apostles who bore the name of James (St. Matt. x. 2, 3; St. Luke vi. 14, 15), namely, James the brother of John, the son of Zebedee, who had been killed by Herod with the sword, and James "the Little" (St. Mark xv. 40, R. V.), the son of Alpheus and the brother of Jude and Joses.
[3] St. Matt. xxviii. 19, R. V.
[4] St. Mark xvi. 15, R. V.
[5] Acts i. 8.
[6] Gal. i. 19.

this difficulty, a plausible suggestion of St. Jerome has been adopted, that Alpheus or Cleophas married a sister of the Virgin Mary, who was also named Mary, and that their sons, who under such a supposition were really the cousins of our Lord, were called in the New Testament His brothers.

Bishop Lightfoot, in his masterly essay on "The Brethren of our Lord," has proved conclusively that this novel opinion of St. Jerome, first put forth three hundred years after the Crucifixion, is untenable, and that the older traditional view of the primitive Church — namely, that James and Joses, Simon and Jude, were the sons of Joseph by a former wife — is the simplest and only defensible interpretation of New Testament statements about "the brethren" of Christ. James, the Lord's brother, was not, therefore, one of the twelve Apostles. As late as the autumn before the Crucifixion, he stood among those who did not believe in Him.[1] But his conversion came with the events of the Passion or the Crucifixion; and after the Resurrection, St. Paul tells us that the Risen Christ appeared specially to St. James, who became a prominent figure in the New Testament Church. This solves for us the difficulty of supposing that one of the twelve Apostles had been appointed to a local supervision over the Church at Jerusalem.

We have noted how the different orders of the ministry were developed out of the Apostolate; how the twelve Apostles first resigned the least important part of their work to an Order of Deacons; how, at a later period, they committed other and more

[1] St. John vii. 3–5.

APOSTOLIC SUCCESSION 173

spiritual functions to an Order of Elders; but they did not stop there. The extension of the ministry was more rapid and went further, even in those early days, than is generally supposed. It is shown conclusively in the Book of Acts that the organization of the Church at Jerusalem included a chief pastor or presiding officer, who, while not one of the twelve Apostles, was yet somewhat different in position from the elders and deacons, and who therefore occupied an intermediate position between them and the twelve Apostles. Indeed, St. Paul even goes so far as to call him "an apostle"[1] not in the sense of classing him with the original "Twelve," but according to the more general use of the term that was then prevalent.[2] James was only an Apostle in the sense that Barnabas, Silas, Epaphroditus and others were Apostles.

We would call close attention to this fact, because, since the days of the Reformation, the statement has been unceasingly made, and reiterated and accepted by thousands, that Episcopacy was an after development of Church history, and that there is no clear and positive indication in the pages of the New Testament itself, either of its origin under the Apostles or of its existence in their day; and that consequently the Order of Bishops cannot be traced back in any way to their sanction and authority.

As a matter of fact, we find here, in the forefront of the New Testament, before the whole Church of Christ had been in existence a quarter of a century, a chief pastor, chosen either directly by the

[1] Gal. i. 19. [2] Acts xiv. 14; Phil. ii. 25, margin, etc.

twelve Apostles, or with their express sanction, to act under them as the presiding officer over the Church of Jerusalem. That person was James, the brother of our Lord, revered by all about him as one to whom Christ had specially appeared after His Resurrection.

It may therefore be truly said that James of Jerusalem occupies the unique position of the first bishop in the Church of Christ. For though He was not, of course, a "Diocesan Bishop" in our modern sense; though, from his intimate connection with all the events of the Gospel history and his peculiar personal relationship both to our Lord and the twelve Apostles, he held a different position from all other bishops of the Church; and though, at that very early period, it would be a gross anachronism to suppose that the growth of the Church, even in Jerusalem itself, had begun to reach that stage of development which was known in later days as Diocesan Organization, we cannot, on the other hand, ignore the fact that the same principle of development and extension of the ministry which led the twelve Apostles first to commit certain functions of their ministry to an Order of Deacons, and then other and greater functions to a second Order of Elders, led them also to commit a still more important function — the superintendence over these different Elders and Deacons and congregations in the local Church of Jerusalem to so wise and revered a follower of Christ as James, the brother of our Lord; leaving him to fulfil this responsibility, while the Twelve gave themselves "continually to prayer and to the ministry of the word," and obeyed their

Lord's parting command "to be witnesses unto Him in Jerusalem, and in all Judæa, and in Samaria, and unto the uttermost parts of the earth."

There are two classes of objections which might be raised against this statement that James of Jerusalem was, even in this inchoate sense, the first bishop in the Church of God. On the one hand, some will say that he was an Apostle similar to all the other Apostles. On the other hand, others, taking the opposite view, will affirm that he was only a presiding elder, who, though he occupied a position of authority similar to that of a bishop, yet never, as far as the records show, exercised the ordinary episcopal function of ordaining elders, and thus transmitting authority in Apostolic Succession. Let us take these objections in order.

(1) James of Jerusalem was not one of the original twelve; though the Risen Christ appeared to him especially, neither did he nor others put forth the claim so strenuously advanced by St. Paul regarding his own mission, of being specially chosen and sent by Christ to do an apostolic work similar to that of the twelve. It was the function of the twelve and of St. Paul himself to go into all the world and found churches everywhere, but St. James was anchored at Jerusalem, and his personal responsibility consisted in having the oversight and care of that one particular church. These are primary considerations, and they differentiate James the Just of Jerusalem from the original twelve and St. Paul. He clearly occupied a secondary position.

(2) In answer to the other objection, that he was only a presiding elder, who never exercised the

functions of the Apostolate in the transmission of orders, we would say that he was plainly reckoned as different from the elders. In the Epistle to the Galatians, St. Paul tells us that the first time he went up to Jerusalem to see St. Peter, and abode with him fifteen days, he adds, "But other of the Apostles saw I none save James, the Lord's brother."[1] When he went up to Jerusalem again, fourteen years after taking Barnabas and Titus with him, he tells us that "when *James*, Cephas, and John, who seemed to be *pillars*, perceived the grace that was given to me, they gave unto me and Barnabas the right hand of fellowship, that we should go to the heathen and they unto the circumcision."[2] In the history of the Council of the Apostles at Jerusalem, five times the phrase "Apostles and Elders" is used;[3] these and these only are the two Orders of the Ministry named. Is it possible, after we read what St. Paul had previously said of James, that he could have been reckoned among the elders or even as a presiding elder? Though there is no direct reference to his exercising the function of ordaining elders, we can hardly imagine that he who was called "an apostle" by St. Paul and reckoned by him as a "pillar" of the church with SS. Peter and John, should not have had this apostolic privilege committed to him; and the implication becomes certainty when we remember that Barnabas, who was also called "an apostle,"[4] ordained elders when he accompanied St. Paul on his first missionary tour.[5]

[1] Gal. i. 19.
[2] Gal. ii. 9.
[3] Acts xv. 2, 4, 6, 22, 23; xvi. 4.
[4] Acts xiv. 14.
[5] Acts xiv. 23.

APOSTOLIC SUCCESSION

But the case is set completely at rest when we turn to the pages of Church history, for Chrysostom, Hegesippus, Eusebius, and others, who lived in the days of fully matured diocesan Episcopacy, are unanimous in stating that James the Just was the first Bishop of Jerusalem.

While, therefore, we repeat, he was not a diocesan bishop, like those of post-apostolic days, James of Jerusalem was the prototypal bishop; for the organization of the mother Church at Jerusalem, with its Deacons, its Elders, and its chief Pastor; with its normal growth, and development under the influence and direction of the Apostles themselves before they separated to go to the uttermost parts of the earth, became, in process of time, the example and pattern that was followed elsewhere.

Forty years after Christ's Ascension, Jerusalem was destroyed by the Roman armies under Titus; the Jewish nation was scattered or carried into captivity to Rome; while Christians, heedful of our Lord's prophecy and warning,[1] fled to the mountains and escaped.

Shortly after this we find the Apostle St. John dwelling for a season, as St. Paul had done before him,[2] in Ephesus. Heretofore, as far as the records show, St. Peter and St. Paul had been the most prominent leaders in the Church of Christ; now, St. John stood forth as the aged patriarch, probably as the last survivor of the original twelve, to whom the rising generation of Christians should look for guidance and organization in that part of the Gentile world where St. Paul had labored a third of a cen-

[1] St. Matt. xxiv. 16.   [2] Acts xix. 8–10.

tury before. He carried with him to Ephesus the knowledge and matured experience that he had gained from the organization of the mother Church of Jerusalem, with whose history, before the fall of the city, he had become so familiar; and now he brought that experience to bear upon the organization of the churches in Asia Minor and its vicinity, adapting it to the different conditions of life that he found there.

For the next generation and even later St. John's disciples are the leading figures of the post-apostolic period; the churches of Asia Minor occupy in influence and example the place that the mother Church of Jerusalem once held, and everywhere the moulding impress of St. John's mind and hand are traceable in their life and organization.[1]

---

[1] The following extracts from Bishop Lightfoot's writings may be quoted here: —

"Unless we have recourse to a sweeping condemnation of received documents, it seems vain to deny that early in the second century the episcopal office was firmly and widely established. Thus, during the last three decades of the first century, and consequently during the lifetime of the latest surviving Apostle, this change must have been brought about."

"The evidence for the early and wide extension of episcopacy, throughout pro-consular Asia, the scene of St. John's latest labors, may be considered irrefragable."

"But these notices, besides establishing the general prevalence of episcopacy, also throw considerable light on its origin. . . . Above all, they establish this result clearly, that its maturer forms are seen first in those regions where the latest surviving Apostles (more especially St. John) fixed their abode, and at a time when its prevalence cannot be dissociated from their influence or their sanction."

"It has been seen that the institution of an episcopate must be placed as far back as the closing years of the first century, and that it cannot, without violence to historical testimony, be dissociated from the name of St. John."

"If the preceding investigation be substantially correct, the three-

There is another point regarding the condition of the ministry in the apostolic age that should be carefully noted. In answer to the objection that the episcopate was an after development from the presbyterate, it will be seen that the development was in an entirely different direction. It was not from the diaconate upward, but from the Apostolate *downward.* Each order arose only when the need for it became manifest. The need for the episcopate had not as yet arisen, in its fulness, in the day when the greater part of the Books of the New Testament were written. Only in Jerusalem, where the Church had reached its fullest development, was it felt. And there, as we have seen, it was at once provided for, by placing St. James, the Lord's brother, in a prominent position of responsibility in the mother Church. Elsewhere, the scattered churches in Judæa and among the Gentiles were still under the care of the Apostles themselves. St. Paul tells us this regarding the churches of his own planting, when he said that he had to bear, beside those trials and hardships that came to him from outer sources and missionary efforts, another special work in the matter of internal organization and discipline: "That which cometh upon me daily, the care of all the churches."[1] If it is true that he mentions only Deacons and Bishops (or Elders) in his Epistles,

---

fold ministry can be traced to Apostolic direction; and short of an express statement, we can possess no better assurance of a Divine appointment or at least a Divine sanction. If the facts do not allow us to unchurch other Christian communities differently organized, they may at least justify our jealous *adhesion to a polity derived from this source.*" — *Dissertations on the Apostolic Age,* pp. 241, 242.

[1] 2 Cor. xi. 28.

it is also true that he himself was, at this time, exercising over them both an apostolic and an episcopal supervision, and that here, as well as in other parts of the New Testament, an organization represented only by Elders and Deacons was regarded as incomplete. And this fact comes out even more strongly in the pastoral Epistles, when "Paul the aged," who through infirmities and imprisonments was no longer able to have the care of all the churches, gave to Timothy directions concerning Elders (or Bishops) and Deacons,[1] and said to Titus, "For this cause left I thee in Crete, that thou shouldst set in order the things that are wanting, and ordain Elders in every city, as I had appointed thee."[2]

It is unnecessary to pursue any further this branch of our subject, for, as the genuineness of the Epistles of St. Ignatius, through the efforts of Bishop Lightfoot, has been proved and accepted, the existence of the Episcopate in the post-apostolic age becomes one of the known facts of church history. After the days of Irenæus, its historicity has always been acknowledged.

II

But however strong the actual proof of an Apostolic Succession of bishops may be, there is another issue lying back of all ministerial succession, whether Episcopal or Presbyterial, that perplexes many minds. On what principle, it is often asked, does this ministerial succession itself rest? and

---

[1] 1 Tim. iii.   [2] Titus i. 5.

where is the authority for an institution in the Church which is not only self-perpetuating, but which creates a distinction between clergy and people that will continue to exist until the end of time? Not infrequently the secret dislike to such a distinction creates a prepossession in many minds which precludes them from recognizing, or giving due weight to, the fact that the distinction was created by Christ Himself when He selected the twelve Apostles from the rest of His disciples, before He left this earth. And there are three points in the commission which Christ gave to these Apostles which we should carefully note.

First, the commission was full and explicit. "Ye have not chosen Me, but I have chosen you, and ordained [appointed] you." "As My Father hath sent Me, even so send I you."

Secondly, it was not merely a charge to go into all the world and exercise a personal, moral, and spiritual influence among men; it was a commission to go and do certain specific acts; to teach, to baptize, to administer the Holy Communion ("Do this in remembrance of Me"), to be witnesses of His Resurrection, to remit and retain sins.

Thirdly, it was an authority that was to *continue* with these chosen ministers. Christ promised to be with them as they went forth to perform these acts of teaching, baptizing, etc., "*lo, alway, even unto the end of the world.*"

In the commencement of the Book of Acts, within ten days after Christ's Ascension, we read that the first act of the Apostles was to transmit the authority which Christ had given them to a new

Apostle. The election of St. Matthias shows the light in which the Apostles, at that time, regarded the commission they had received from Christ. They felt that they were authorized by Christ to select an Apostle to take the place of the apostate Judas, and thus to transmit to another the authority Christ had transmitted to them. Afterwards, in the same Book of Acts, it is recorded how they transmitted certain portions of this authority to others still; and in the Epistles we hear of yet later transmissions.

For example, when in St. Paul's directions to Timothy and Titus to ordain elders, and lay hands upon ministers whom the Apostles themselves did not select, we find most unmistakably that the persons to whom the Apostles transmitted authority were in turn not only empowered to transmit that authority to others, but were in fact directed to do so. Indeed, the only ministry of which we read in the New Testament is that which was developed out of the apostolate by the Apostles themselves. No one at that time is recorded as exercising spiritual authority or jurisdiction in the Church, save by their appointment.

It is, therefore, from the New Testament itself that we first learn the principle of the transmission of authority and of ministerial succession. It was first adopted by the Apostles themselves, through the guidance of the Holy Ghost, and was universally accepted by the Church, in the days of the Apostles, without a question. An Apostolic Ministry was the only ministry that was known, or even thought of, in New Testament times. More than this, it is implicitly taken for granted throughout the apostolic Epistles, that apostolic order, apostolic fellowship, apostolic doctrine were essential conditions of Church unity. And when we pass on to the next generation, we find that what was thus implicitly held, when St. John and St. Paul were still alive, was explicitly taught by the disciple of St. John, Ignatius of Antioch, and his contemporaries.

For fifteen hundred years thereafter, amid all the heresies and differences of opinion in the Church upon other matters, there was an undivided opinion and unanimous consensus in the Church regarding the principle of transmitted ministerial authority. Under such circumstances we may reasonably and in all charity ask, would this difficulty regarding transmitted authority ever have arisen to perplex Christian minds in the last three centuries, had there not been some anterior bias, prepossession, or prejudice to create it? If different Christian bodies since the Reformation had not organized a ministry of their own, which stands apart from a ministry that historically derives its succession from the Apostles, would this question ever have been raised?

Now that it has been raised, we should never forget that there are two classes of difficulties regarding the principle of ministerial succession. If, on the one hand, there are Christians who keep asking why the Church has not a right to constitute its own ministry, or why there should be such a division between clergy and laity as the doctrine of ministerial succession creates and perpetuates, there are, on the other hand, a far larger number of

Christians who ask, Has the Church the authority to organize any different kind of ministry, since Christ Himself has divided the ministry from the people by choosing the twelve Apostles, and since those Apostles have provided for the extension and continuance of that ministry? Has she the power to originate, at any period of her history, a new order of bishops, priests, or deacons? If so, what credentials has she to show, either from our Lord or His chosen Apostles? or what precedent in the history of the Church, for the first fifteen hundred years, authorizing such a departure from New Testament method?

Since the days of the Protestant Reformation, the heavy charge has been made again and again that the doctrine of Apostolical Succession is an unwarrantable and unscriptural assumption. In reply to this we ask again, in all charity, but for the sake of truth and real Christian unity, is it not, in reality, a *more* unwarrantable and unscriptural assumption to assert that the Church has the delegated authority from Christ to set up and originate a ministry of her own? Is not this claiming for the Church a power which has never been bestowed upon her? Is it not an effort to exaggerate the authority of the Church beyond its proper limits? Is it not, in fact, putting the Church in the place of Christ?

And when, in addition to this, we remember that such a plea was never set forth until the Church of Christ had been in existence for centuries; when we remember that in the whole of the intervening time between the Apostles and the Protestant Reformation of the sixteenth century — from Ignatius of Antioch, the disciple of St. John, and Clement of Rome, the disciple of St. Paul or of St. Peter, to Luther, Calvin, and Cranmer — the organization of the One Holy, Catholic and Apostolic Church throughout the world was founded upon the belief in a ministry deriving its authority and succession through the Apostles straight from Christ Himself, then we cannot but dismiss this other assumption as novel and unauthorized. "Whether bishops, priests, and deacons are or are not scriptural or exclusive orders of ministry is, on its own grounds, fair matter for argument; but antecedently to any such argument, I must submit that the principle in abstract form — that ministerial authority depends upon continuous transmission from the Apostles, through those to whom the Apostles transmitted the power to transmit — must be recognized as being from the time of St. Clement onwards a principle implanted in the consciousness of the Christian Church."[1]

The preface to the Ordinal in the Anglican Prayer Book is, therefore, strictly in the line of scriptural and historical precedent, when it says that "It is evident unto all men diligently reading Holy Scripture and ancient Authors, that from the Apostles' time there have been these orders of ministers in Christ's Church, — Bishops, Priests, and Deacons. Which Offices were evermore had in such reverend estimation, that no man might presume to execute any of them, except he were first called, tried, examined, and known to have such qualities as are requisite for the same; and also, by public Prayer, with Imposition of Hands, were approved

[1] "Ministerial Priesthood," by Canon Moberly, pp. 115, 116.

and admitted thereunto by lawful Authority." And the same Ordinal is a witness to the Catholic Faith, where it declares its *intention* that these orders should be "*continued*" by her.

III

Canon Moberly has well said, in the passage we have quoted, that ministerial succession is "a principle implanted in the consciousness of the Christian Church." This means that it is something more than an ecclesiastical tradition or a shibboleth of partizanship. Whatever is able to penetrate into the *consciousness* of the Christian Church, and preserve its continuity from age to age, must have a spiritual worth and a moral power to create religious conviction, — the kind of conviction that men are willing to die for.

The doctrine of Apostolic Succession has this moral and spiritual force. First, because it carries out the basal idea of the Incarnation and applies it to the ministry of the Christian Church. As in the Incarnation of Jesus Christ, Heaven and earth, divine and human, invisible and visible, subjective and objective, infinite and finite, inward and outward, are united together in one; as in the life of Christ Himself, in the preaching of the Gospel, in the two sacraments which Christ has ordained, and in the written Word of God, there are two elements, — the one of Heaven and the other of earth, the one spiritual and the other natural, the one divine and the other human, — so, in the doctrine of the Apostolic Succession there is both an inward call of

God's Spirit and the outward form of laying on of hands in Apostolic Ordination.

Secondly, this same doctrine creates in the breasts of those who are thus ordained that peculiar kind of moral conviction which was expressed by St. Paul when, in writing to the Galatians, who were choosing religious teachers of their own, he called himself an Apostle, "not of man, neither by man, but by Jesus Christ and God the Father, who raised Him from the dead,"[1] and said to the Corinthians, "With me it is a very small thing that I should be judged of you or of man's judgement. Yea, I judge not mine own self, . . . but he that judgeth me is the Lord."[2]

Those who feel that they are both inwardly called by God's Holy Spirit, and outwardly consecrated to the sacred Ministry by an authority which is derived by a chain of outward, visible, historic acts directly from the Apostles and from Christ Himself, have a much higher ideal of that Ministry than would be possible had they merely been admitted to it by an ordinance which the Church had originated for herself in post-apostolic times. For in the latter case, ordination means only authority conferred by the Church. And as the stream cannot rise higher than its fountain head, the ordained minister would, in his allegiance, look to no higher outward authority than that of the particular branch of the Church which, at some given historic period, instituted the ministry to which he has been appointed by her.

While in his personal loyalty to Christ he might be unfaltering in his efforts, individually, to live an

[1] Gal. i. 1. [2] 1 Cor. iv. 3, 4.

earnest Christian life, he would not, and could not, feel the same kind of allegiance to the Church regarding the official acts of his ministerial career. In his innermost thought he would differentiate between the authority of the Church and the authority of Christ Himself. And that distinction would lower the whole conception of the value of the sacraments and of his ministerial acts. The church, the people, the congregation whom he served, would have an abnormal place in his thoughts and motives; an abnormal power over his ministry.

But if one holds the deep conviction that through a ministerial succession in the Apostolic Church he traces his Orders as Bishop, Priest, or Deacon, straight back to Christ, that conviction creates a solemn, awful consciousness of the responsibility that he owes directly to the Head of the Church in Heaven. And the longer he lives, the deeper becomes his realization of the sacredness of his office. Woe be to him if he is neglectful of his charge, or unfaithful to his stewardship. It is Christ the Judge Who will call him to account for his sin at the Judgement Day. It is the indwelling Spirit of Truth Who will then bear witness against him.

He is appointed by Christ to be a Messenger of Heaven, a Watchman of Souls, a Steward of the Mysteries of God.

Belief in the Apostolic Succession gives him courage. He is spurred on, regardless of discouragement, unpopularity, or natural human timidity, to speak the Truth of God to human hearts. He dares not falter. He becomes instant in season and out of season, whether they will hear or whether they will forbear.

Thirdly, that same belief has the moral effect of deepening the sense of responsibility in *teaching*, — teaching nothing but Apostolic Doctrine and Bible Truth. When a man realizes that he is ordained to be a witness for Christ, that his office is not only a public trust but a Divine trust, that he has been trusted by Christ and His Church and placed in the official position of a recognized teacher in the Apostolic Church, that realization, in proportion to its intensity, restrains his individualism and checks each intemperate utterance. He dare not betray a trust, especially in so vital a matter as in teaching immortal souls for whom Christ died; nor does he dare to preach any other doctrine than that the Apostles themselves preached, or which may not be certainly proved out of the Holy Scriptures.

The fact that there may be few who follow this apostolic ideal out of the thousands of ordained ministers, is no more an argument against Apostolic Succession than that there are so few Christians whose lives correspond with the Sermon on the Mount is an argument against Christianity. There was a Judas Iscariot even among the twelve Apostles. It is enough for us if the ideal itself touches the deep moral convictions of our nature, if it corresponds with the spirit of Christ's religion and with what we read in the New Testament. With all the shortcomings of the clergy in these and other times, the history of the Church shows that this ideal has exerted a very marked influence over the ministry at large of the old historic Churches, and that it has evoked a deep moral sense of their responsibility regarding their ministerial duties which, without it, they would never have had.

Fourthly, if in New Testament days it was unceasingly taught that the unity of that Church of Christ which was built upon the foundation of the Apostles and Prophets depended upon union in doctrine and fellowship with the Apostles themselves, in the post-apostolic age it was equally emphasized that visible unity depended upon union with the successors of the Apostles. This truth is strongly brought out in the writings of Ignatius, the disciple of St. John. Indeed, he laid so much stress upon it, that it almost seems as though he felt it to be the only safeguard against certain dangers of disunion that were arising in the churches of Asia Minor.

Since that time, after eighteen centuries of Christian experience, it has been found that the Historic Episcopate is absolutely essential to organic Church unity. Instead of being, as so often represented, an impediment to the reunion of Christendom, it is proved by the facts of Church history that there can be no outward and visible unity of Christ's Church without it. This truth is becoming more and more explicitly recognized as time goes on. Yet it has been implicitly held, as through a Catholic instinct, for ages, and this is shown by the very names by which the Church has always designated or described her characteristic ministry.

"Historic Episcopate" is a modern term, and it is usually employed as a name for an institution or fact of Church history which does not commit us to any theory as to the meaning of that fact, like the phrase "Apostolic Succession." This older term, however, is much more profound; if anything, it is humbler and less assertive, for it does not emphasize the Episcopate at all. What it does emphasize is a *law of continuity* in the ministry of the Church of which the Historic Episcopate is only the outward and visible sign, — the effect of a cause. It is the same with the other term by which the ministry of the Church has been designated from time immemorial. Those holding these sacred offices have been called men in Holy Orders, because the apostolic ministry represents the principle of *order*, and because the Church has instinctively realized that without such order there can be no visible or organic unity.

IV

We come now to another fact which should be remembered as well by those who hold the doctrine of Apostolic Succession as by those who deny it. In the descriptions of the New Testament Church which are given in the writings of the Apostles, the threefold ministry of the Apostolic Succession will scarcely embrace all the ministerial functions that are there named. If, on the one hand, there are apostles, elders, and deacons, there are also, on the other, prophets, evangelists, workers of miracles, and those who speak with tongues. But when we look closer, we observe that there is a distinction drawn in the New Testament between the one and the other, clearly indicating that while the first are in an authoritative position of responsibility, the others are not.

For example, the Epistles of St. Paul are addressed (1) either to the whole Church collectively and to the "saints," who are its members, or (2) to the "Bishops and Deacons" with the saints, or (3) to individual men like Timothy, Titus, and Philemon. There is no mention of prophets or evangelists. Similarly, when St. Paul sends for the Elders of Ephesus to come to Miletus, it is to them, not to prophets or evangelists, that he delivers that solemn charge to feed the Church of God over which the Holy Ghost had made them overseers.[1] And again we are told that, in their first missionary journey, Paul and Barnabas "ordained" them Elders in every church;[2] we read the directions given regarding the life and duties of Elders (Bishops) and Deacons,[3] and the injunction given to Titus regarding the ordination of Elders.

And when we pass to the post-apostolic age, we find that the only Ministry that is emphasized as authoritative, and that is recognized as continuing from the apostolic times, is that of Bishops, Priests, and Deacons.

The Prophets and Evangelists are indeed spoken of in the Epistles of the New Testament as men who occupied a higher position in the Church than the workers of miracles or those who spake with tongues. But through all, their work was individual and their gifts personal. No prophet ordained other prophets; no evangelist transmitted authority to other evangelists.

[1] Acts xx. 17.   [2] Acts xiv. 23.   [3] 1 Tim. iii; Titus i.

As we look back upon the history of the Church through these eighteen centuries, we see plainly, unmistakably, that, unlike the power of working miracles or of speaking with tongues, these greater prophetic and evangelistic gifts have not ceased. We also note that they seem to be independent of the Apostolic Ministry itself, for sometimes they are possessed by the ordained clergy, sometimes not. Indeed, we find these functions possessed even by those who have no connection with any ministerial office. They are exercised by men raised up by God and filled with the Holy Ghost to do a certain kind of work in certain periods of Christian history. Oftentimes these men impress us deeply, not only by the greatness of their efforts, but by the saintliness of their lives and examples. They give themselves up to a life of prayer and of work in Christ's name; they hold to and preach the Faith once delivered to the saints as it is taught in Holy Scriptures, and also in the Catholic creeds; they bring thousands and ten thousands to Christ, and through their efforts the peculiar type of character that belongs distinctively to Christ's followers is undoubtedly developed. Such ministers may not have the outward call of Apostolic Ordination, but they have unmistakably an inward call of God's Holy Spirit for the individual work that God has raised them up to do, but without ministerial authority to transmit their functions. It is also a significant fact that, with a few exceptions, they themselves do not profess to exercise those functions of the Episcopate and of the Priesthood which from the first have been associated, in the Catholic Church, with the idea of ministerial succession; and perhaps, by and by, this fact may prove to be, not an obstacle, but a help toward ultimate Church unity.

While, on the one hand, Churchmen hold that Apostolic Ordination is essential to episcopal or priestly acts, and are prone to deny that outside of these there are any ministerial functions; non-episcopal bodies, on the other hand, hold that prophetic or evangelistic gifts are bestowed upon the Christian ministry irrespective of Apostolic Ordination, denying that there are any higher ministerial functions in the Church of Christ.

Both classes have positive convictions so deeply rooted and so persistently continuous on these points, as generation follows generation, that it is doubtful if either will ever change. After all, are not both right? Is it not, at the bottom, a question between two rights regarding the affirmations and of two wrongs regarding the denials? If both should continue to affirm their affirmations, and at the same time learn to deny their denials, what would the ultimate consequence be?

CHAPTER IX

CHRISTIAN SACERDOTALISM

AS among the ancient Romans the word "king" was ever associated with ideas of slavery and despotism, so in the minds of many modern Christians the word "sacerdotalism" is identified exclusively with a type of religion antagonistic to the spirit of the Gospel; with a kind of priestly power and domination incompatible with the glorious liberty of the sons of God; and with a priestly mediatorship between human souls and their Father in Heaven utterly at variance with the plain declaration of the New Testament that there is but one Mediator between God and man, even Jesus Christ our Lord.

Christian believers differing widely among themselves in their theological views, or ecclesiastical affiliations, all unite in an intense dislike and inveterate suspicion of the very name of "*priest.*" And as a proof that this honest dislike originates in no mere prejudice or narrow-mindedness, they point to the records of the past. Appealing to history, they affirm that wherever the spirit of sacerdotalism has prevailed, it has always blighted the pure religious life of the people and become the parent of superstition and degradation; that, among the ancient Jews, it was chiefly associated with outward forms, levitical rites and ceremonies, or perfunctory legal observances, which, they say, would have smothered the higher life of the people had it not been for the fearless prophets and reformers whom God raised up, from age to age; while many go so far as to attribute most of the corruptions that degraded the life of the Christian Church in the dark ages that preceded the Protestant Reformation, to the priestcraft and sacerdotal pretensions of the clergy.

Appealing next to the Gospels themselves, they show that at the head and forefront of those enemies who brought about the condemnation and crucifixion of Christ, were the high-priestly family of Annas and the priests of the temple; that in the New Testament there is an evident distinction drawn between the old Jewish priesthood and the Christian Ministry, and that, amid all the different terms used in describing the ministers of the Church, the word "*sacerdos*" is conspicuous by its absence. Though described as apostles and prophets, bishops, elders and deacons, evangelists, pastors and teachers, ministers are never called *priests*. Furthermore, it is affirmed that, as the word "priest" is distinctly derived from *presbuteros*, meaning *an elder*, it stands as a witness to the ages against any sacerdotal order in the Primitive Church; that only by a mediæval transposition of meaning does "presbyter" appear as the English equivalent for the Latin *sacerdos* or the Greek *hiereus;* and that the transposition was effected in the Middle Ages by those who — consciously or unconsciously — were blinded either by a desire for priestly power, or else by false and unscriptural ideas of the Christian ministry.

Lastly, it is affirmed that, though sacerdotal pretensions thus took shelter under an innocent name, the institution still preserved its old characteristics, and at last manifested so clearly its anti-scriptural tendencies that the word "priest" (presbyter or elder) aroused the same kind of prejudice and antagonism among the true children of God that the term *sacerdos* had done among their forefathers in days of yore.

We have striven to state these objections to the popular conception of sacerdotalism as fairly and honestly as possible, not only that the many earnest Christians who hold them may be satisfied that their views upon this subject have been impartially and adequately set forth, but that we may use them ourselves in differentiating between true and false ideas of Christian Priesthood. For we are persuaded that the time is fast approaching when this whole subject of Sacerdotalism will be investigated and studied by Christians in general in that impartial way in which men are learning more and more to approach all truth; and that this investigation will undoubtedly be one of the factors in the promotion of the future reunion of Christendom. The question now arises, Is there a true, Christian, Sacerdotalism?

I

The idea conveyed by the words "priest" and "sacrifice" undoubtedly corresponds to some inward want or religious instinct of human nature, whose universality tells its own story. A religion without a priest of some kind would be an imperfect, artificial religion, for it would violate a divine instinct of humanity. Modern science has taught us that the very presence of an instinct in animals or men is an indication of purpose or use. And it seems equally clear that the idea of sacrifice has always grown out of a human consciousness of guilt, or sin, separating man from God, and a desire for its removal; that such sin is intimately connected with the thought of life; and that blood is, as it were, nature's sacrament, which to all mankind represents *life*.[1]

It is true, that wherever in heathen religions we find the institution of priesthood and sacrifice, we find also priestcraft, and a kind of priestly domination that gives rise to superstition; but this arises, in every case, from *perversion*. All truth is liable to such perversion through the sinfulness of the human heart; all human experience shows that the greater a power, or the more sacred a truth, the greater is the tendency of man to pervert it.

It is so in physical life; it is so in social and intellectual life; and it is pre-eminently so in that spiritual life which comprehends and sanctifies all lower phases of existence. If the spiritual power of the priesthood

---

[1] Illustrations of this fact can be drawn from all human history. The shedding of blood has always a strange and mysterious power over human hearts. This is seen not only in religious sacrifices, but in the Roman gladiatorial shows and modern bull-fights. Again, in times of a riot or disturbance the populace can be kept quiet as long as they are simply restrained by superior force; but the moment the first drop of blood is shed they are instantly excited to a frenzy, for human nature feels intuitively that blood *always means life*.

has been perverted in the past, so has also the secular power of political rulers. But there is this distinction between the one and the other. In facing political power, the world has learned to distinguish between the thing itself and its perversion; that is, between the true and the false use of a power that God has given to man; whereas in sacerdotalism the perversions have been so unholy, conspicuous, and numerous, that the conception of a self-sacrificing priesthood has been well-nigh blotted out altogether from men's minds.

II

But we are not left to the study of comparative religions to discover that this institution of priest and sacrifice arose from a divine instinct in human nature, and had, therefore, a divine purpose and use. For, in the Old Testament, God Himself set His seal of approbation upon the institution; and whatever light the study of a Higher Criticism may throw upon the origin of the Jewish priesthood and various prescribed sacrifices of the ancient Jewish ritual, it is plain that they had not only a divine sanction as the expression of a true religious instinct, but an educational purpose and a prophetic significance in preparing the world for Christ.

The Jewish priesthood was a sacred order ordained by God. Korah, Dathan, and Abiram were destroyed for taking this honor to themselves without being appointed by God;[1] a similar sin had been committed by Nadab and Abihu; and now it was stated, with reiterated emphasis, that the blood of the prescribed

---

[1] Num. xvi. 1-35.

sacrifices really symbolized life, not death.[1] Henceforth, to every writer both of Old and New Testament days, as well as to the whole Jewish nation, from Moses to Christ, blood always meant life. The idea that blood means death only is entirely of modern origin, and from this cause, perhaps, more than any other, have arisen most modern difficulties regarding the Atonement; difficulties that disappear the moment the word is taken in the same sense in which the ancient Jews and every Christian believer who lived in New Testament days understood it.

But, notwithstanding all the increased light which the Jewish religion threw upon the institution of priesthood and sacrifice, it was felt, even by the people themselves, to be imperfect. We have only to read the words of the ancient prophets, stretching in a line back to Samuel, to discover that they felt deeply, increasingly, how impossible it was for the blood of bulls or of goats to take away sin. And when the writer of the Epistle to the Hebrews speaks of the imperfections of the Jewish Priesthood and sacrifices, he must have given expression to truths of which generations of his forefathers had been dimly conscious.

The Jewish law, which was a schoolmaster to bring men to Christ, developed moral aspirations it could not satisfy. Therefore, it is among the Jews themselves, more than anywhere else, that we find an intensity of desire, as well as an ever growing need, not only for an ideal Prophet and King, but for an ideal Priest.

No Christian believer will be found to dispute the

[1] Lev. xvii. 11, 14, etc.

fact that Christ in His Life and Death, His Resurrection and Ascension, fulfils to the uttermost the office of this ideal Priest. We must, therefore, look to Christ Himself, and to Christ alone, for the interpretation of the meaning of sacerdotal life and power. All true conceptions of priesthood centre in Him; and all kinds of Christian priesthood which are different from this great archetype must be unscriptural and false.

III

Christ was this ideal priest, first, because He was so by nature and inherent right. The author of the Epistle to the Hebrews dwells strongly upon this thought. Other priests were *appointed* to their office; Christ was made priest, not by the law of a carnal commandment, but because He possessed "the power of an endless life."[1] Other priests do not abide, — they are not only too imperfect in themselves to offer a perfect moral sacrifice, but they pass away, and others succeed them in office; Christ abideth forever, with an unchangeable Priesthood. Christ was not, therefore, and could not possibly be, a priest after the order of Aaron. His higher Order of Priesthood, indeed, comprehended that which already existed among the Jews, but it was infinitely higher, infinitely greater, infinitely more real. For this reason, we observe the strongest possible distinction drawn in the Epistle to the Hebrews between Christ and the Jewish priests. Never in the Gospel history do we find Him exercising the prescribed duties of

[1] Heb. vii. 16.

the Jewish priesthood. Though He calls the Temple "His Father's House" never does He participate as a priest in the services of the Jewish Temple, or offer any sacrifice upon the Temple altar.

Standing thus apart from that Jewish priesthood which so persistently claimed a priestly authority and power directly handed down from Aaron, Christ "glorified not Himself to be made an High Priest."[1] Indeed, there is not a single passage in all the Gospels where He, Who was really the Priest after the order of Melchizedek, directly calls himself a "*Priest.*" But He fulfils our human *ideal* of a priestly life in the three years of His ministry by His actions and example, and reveals the power of His heavenly Priesthood by His prayers, and His willingness, through suffering, to do the will of God on earth as it is done in Heaven.[2]

Christ was the ideal Priest because He offered up an ideal sacrifice for the sins of the whole world. "Every high priest is ordained to offer gifts and sacrifices: wherefore it is of necessity that this Man have somewhat also to offer."[3]

One reason why Christ is never spoken of as Priest in any of the four Gospels is because, before the Crucifixion, the time had not arrived for Him to exercise the functions of His high-priestly office. It was on the night of His betrayal that His glorification began.[4]

The only sacrifice for sin that Christ offered on this earth was that of His own Body and Blood on the Cross. Christ, therefore, was not only the One

---

[1] Heb. v. 5.
[2] Heb. v. 7-10.
[3] Heb. viii. 3.
[4] St. John xiii. 31; xvii. 1.

Priest of humanity, but the One Sacrifice, the One Lamb of God, that taketh away the sins of the world.[1]

In Christ's sacrifice all the separated and different parts of the Jewish symbolic sacrifices are gathered together in *one*. Christ was the Offerer, Who willingly offered His own human life for the sins of the world; Christ was the Priest Who made the offering; Christ was the Lamb Who was offered.

Christ's priesthood did not end with the one, full, perfect, and sufficient sacrifice, oblation, and satisfaction which He made on the cross for the sins of the whole world. That sacrifice of suffering for sin was, indeed, completed when He cried on the cross "*It is finished*," but He only *began* the exercise of His office as the High Priest on the day of the Crucifixion. He was Priest after "the power of an endless life."[2] Three days after He had poured out His life blood for the sins of the world He rose from the dead. The Lamb that was slain came to

---

[1] "This Oneness is dwelt upon by the writer of the Epistle to the Hebrews with great emphasis, and the more it is realized, the more it reveals by contrast the imperfection of the symbolic offerings of the Jewish law. In the Jewish sacrifices there was the following order: (1) the offerer slew the victim; (2) that victim being an animal of the brute creation slain for the sins of a human being; (3) its blood was poured out, as a symbol of life, and made available for others; (4) the priest sprinkled that blood, as a symbol of life, upon the altar to make an atonement for sin. The imperfection of such a sacrifice is shown by these facts: (1) the offerer, the priest, and the sacrifice, were separate and distinct from one another; (2) the victim was a dumb animal, slain not only for sins of which it was ignorant, but which were committed by another; (3) the blood was not life itself, but only a symbol of life; (4) it had no power of really imparting life after it had been poured out.

[2] Heb. vii. 16.

life again, the blood of sacrifice became life, and the living "power of the Resurrection." That blood was, henceforth, *in* the Priest and *in* the Lamb, as He ascended to Heaven, "the Holy Place not made with hands." There it is presented at the altar by the High Priest, Who ever liveth to make intercession for those who come to God by Him,[1] Whose Presence itself is a continuous intercession, and from Heaven that blood is imparted as life to men.

The sacrifice for sin is, therefore, only one part of that eternal sacrifice that Christ our High Priest offers. There is also the sacrifice of prayer and intercession for men, the sacrifice of praise and thanksgiving for men, the sacrifice of imparting His life to men.

If the sacrifice that Christ had to offer was only a sacrifice for *sin*, then Christ's Priesthood ends when sin ends. But this cannot be, for Christ remaineth *forever* a Priest after the order of Melchizedek. We would draw close attention to this truth, for it leads up to what follows.

If Christ the Priest is, at the same time, Christ the Lamb of God, then the power of His Priesthood is the power of Divine self-sacrifice. Christ has shown us that this is the secret and culmination of all priestly life. If priest and sacrifice are inseparable from one another, if the thoughts of sacrifice and sin, sacrifice and life, sacrifice and power, are, and have been from time immemorial, so intimately associated with one another by an ineradicable human instinct, then here, in Christ, the ideal Priest, we have the explanation and interpretation of this fact.

[1] Heb. vii. 25.

If self-sacrifice is thus the law of priestly life, it is because self-sacrifice is the Law of Love. "Love is not self-contained, but self-expending, and perfected in self-expenditure. The devotion of love in the sphere of Heaven is perfection of joy. But devotion of love to another in conditions of earth — even whilst it touches the highest possibilities of joy — means always more or less of pain. Devotion of self, in a world of sin and suffering, to the spiritual welfare of those who are enmeshed in suffering and sin, is forthwith, in external aspect, sacrifice, and in inner essence, love. There is no essential contrast between sacrifice and love. Love, under certain disabling conditions, becomes sacrifice; and sacrifice is not sacrifice, except it be love. Thoughts like these are, it seems to me, of primary importance if we would understand the sacrifice of Christ. It is the aspect which Divine love takes within the sphere of certain conditions, which conditions are *de facto* inseparable from our life on earth as it is. The heart of what it really is, is the holy offering up of life in love. Apart from sin it would have been all life and all love. But life that has sinned cannot offer itself perfectly to love without dying to sin. One aspect of love to God is hatred of sin. Man cannot love God without hating sin; nor love Him perfectly without hating sin even unto death. . . . Divine love, then, in the nature of man, takes the form of self-surrender to death. But so far from being, as death, the final object, this death is only real as a mode of love, and a passage from sin into holiness which is life. If verbally we confine the word 'sacrifice' to that which love becomes within the sphere of sin, we must recognize, at least, in doing so, that our word, so defined, expresses not the central essence, but what is really a secondary, if inseparable, aspect of that of which it speaks. The essential heart of sacrifice is love; pain and death are, so to say, its acquired conditions. . . . Sacrifice is love, within the sphere of sin, suffering and dying; and priesthood is the function of expressing and exhibiting that love, which, once for all, in the Person of Jesus Christ, has become within sin's sphere, self-devoting sacrifice. The Priesthood of Christ, then, is Divine Love under conditions of humanity."[1]

After sin is expiated, atoned for, blotted out forever, the other offices of self-giving love remain, expressing themselves in self-devotion to God and to man. And in such offerings Christ remains "a Priest forever after the order of Melchizedek," because for us men He is the Eternal High Priest of Love.

IV

Bearing in mind this thought of the intimate connection between priesthood and love, let us now pass to the Church of Christ. In the New Testament, Christ and His Church are spoken of as *one*. They are necessarily united in one because the Life of Christ is the life of the Church. Our Lord taught us that this union was like that of the branch and the vine, and that the moment the Church is separated from Him it becomes withered and dead,[2] for it has

---

[1] "Ministerial Priesthood," by Canon R. C. Moberly, D.D., p. 247, *seq.*
[2] St. John xv. 4–6.

no life apart from Him. "Without Me ye can do nothing." After Pentecost, when the Apostles had learned, both from the teaching of the Holy Ghost and from their own experience, what this union between Christ in Heaven and the Church really was, they were able to go farther. St. Paul teaches us not only that Christ is the Vine and they the branches, but that Christ is the Head, in Whom all fulness dwells, and that the Church on earth is His body.[1] By virtue of this union, and through the power of the Holy Ghost, the members of the Church are *in Christ*, in the heavenly places;[2] while Christ is *in them* on earth. His life is their life. They are dead with Him, risen with Him, ascended to the heavenly places in Him. If He is the Prophet, the Church is prophetic; if He is the King, the Church is royal and reigns with Him. If He is the Priest, the Church is also priestly. Indeed, this must be so, if, as we have said, Priest and Sacrifice are, in human language, the expression of self-devoting love.

Instead, therefore, of outgrowing sacerdotalism, the members of the Church should, in their personal life, grow up to it, and they will surely do so in proportion as they grow in grace and in the knowledge of Jesus Christ our Lord.

That true Christianity, of the New Testament type, is saturated with the spirit of sacerdotalism is shown by those words of St. Peter: "Ye are a chosen generation, a royal priesthood, a holy nation, a peculiar people; that ye should show forth the praises of Him who hath called you out of dark-

---

[1] Col. i. 18, 19; 1 Cor. xii., etc.
[2] Eph. i. 19-23. Compare ii. 4-6.

ness into His marvellous light;"[1] as also by these of St. John: "Unto Him that loved us, and washed us from our sins in His own blood, and hath made us kings and priests unto God and His Father; to Him be glory and dominion for ever and ever. Amen."[2]

This truth regarding the Priesthood of the Church has been obscured for a double reason. If there are some who have been afraid to recognize the priesthood of the clergy, there have been others equally fearful of emphasizing too much that of the laity, and the result has been not only that both causes have worked together in undervaluing one of the fundamental truths of the Christian religion, but that our modern religious life has fallen far below the New Testament standard. Why is it that so few of the laity feel that there is any responsibility resting upon them, as co-workers with Christ, for the spread of Christ's Kingdom on earth? Why are there so many who dissociate wholly their secular from their religious life and duties; so few who realize that their earthly profession is itself a high calling of God in which one is to do all in the name of the Lord Jesus? Why have our laity generally lost the idea of *worship*, — a worship of Common Prayer in which they are to offer up to God a real personal sacrifice of praise and thanksgiving? Why has the idea of "charity" and "almsgiving" so generally crowded out the higher idea of the stewardship of wealth, and of the consecration of all one's possessions to the service of Christ? Why do fathers of families so completely abdicate the position of priest in their own households? the difficulty is that the priesthood of

---

[1] Peter ii. 9.   [2] Rev. i. 5, 6.

the laity is not recognized. Our laymen do not realize their divine responsibility, their divine privileges as a chosen generation, a royal priesthood; a race of kings and of priests, consecrated in their baptism to be the religious leaders of their fellow men, and priests in their own households. The ruling idea of all priestly service is wanting in them. The priestly life is one of continuous joyous self-sacrifice, first, in the service of God, in the church and the home, in the daily life and calling; and secondly, in the service of man, in obeying Christ's new commandment to love one another as He has loved us. Such self-sacrifice leads to daily outward actions that correspond with the supreme inward motive; and never will the Church of Christ, therefore, regain its old-time New Testament power until the priesthood of the laity is realized.

V

We come now to the priesthood of the clergy. Notwithstanding the recognized evils of sacerdotalism in heathen nations and the manifest imperfections of the Jewish priesthood; notwithstanding the abuse of priestly power and the corruptions of priestcraft in the middle ages; notwithstanding the widespread antipathy to sacerdotalism that has prevailed in all Protestant lands since the Reformation, the One Holy Catholic and Apostolic Church has clung persistently to the doctrine that there is a *distinctive* priesthood in the Apostolic Ministry of the Church, and has declared it with unfaltering voice for eighteen hundred years.

A fact like this cannot be easily set aside, for it comes to us fortified by the authority of the ages. If we compare the history of this doctrine with that of other Christian doctrines that have similarly rooted themselves in the consciousness of the Church, we should judge that it plainly, by a Christian instinct, is connected with the Analogy of the Faith.

It is true that the whole Christian Church as the body of Christ, by virtue of its union with Him, the Prophet, Priest, and King in Heaven, becomes a race of kings and priests unto God; but it is also true that in that Church there are "diversities of gifts," "differences of administrations," "diversities of operations" created by that same Spirit Who divideth "to every man severally as he will"[1] and our Lord Himself divided ministers from people by the outward act of choosing an Apostolic Ministry before He ascended to Heaven.

This Apostolic Ministry must of necessity be priestly in character, because it is one with the Royal High Priest who commissions it, and one with the Church, which through union with Christ, is made a royal priesthood; but it cannot possibly be, in any sense, a *mediatorial* priesthood, coming between Christ and His Church, for this would imply that some kind of separation exists between the Head of the Church in Heaven, and His Body on earth. This negatives forever the idea that the priesthood of the clergy is different *in kind* from that of the laity; that it was ordained to offer up *any different sacrifices* from those that the Body of the Faithful offer; that it adds anything to, or is in any way a

[1] 1 Cor. xii. 4-12.

substitute for, the inherent priesthood of the Church itself. It is simply a representative priesthood.

The Apostolic Ministry is, in a word, the priestly organ of a priestly Body. Its members are commissioned by the Head of the Church to act for the Body in the discharge of certain priestly offices. They must be baptized and confirmed before they are ordained, and it is as members of a chosen generation, a peculiar people, a royal priesthood, that they are appointed by the Head of the Church, to represent that inherently priestly body, ordained to offer up spiritual sacrifices to God. The distinction between a false, or mediatorial priesthood, and the true representative priesthood of the Church, cannot be too strongly emphasized. If the priesthood were vicarious, the priest would be a personal mediator between Christ and the people; in the representative priesthood he is simply the minister of Christ's priesthood to the people, and the minister of the people's priesthood to God. If the priesthood were vicarious he would offer up a kind of sacrifice which the people cannot offer; in the representative priesthood he joins with them in offering the same sacrifice, and only differs from them in being appointed by Christ and His Church to act as their representative. A mediatorial priesthood would break the oneness of Christ with His Church; an organic representative priesthood, on the contrary, fulfils and gives perfect outward expression to that oneness.

If the Apostolic Ministry has been appointed to discharge certain priestly functions on behalf of the body, it is because the exercise of these functions is needful for the welfare of the body. Especially is this true with regard to the celebration of the holy Eucharist, in which the Church on earth unites with Christ in Heaven in pleading the merits of His one, full, perfect, and sufficient sacrifice, oblation, and satisfaction for the sins of the whole world. In this, her highest priestly act, the Church celebrates and offers to the Father, according to the institution of His most dearly beloved Son, the memorial which Christ commanded her to make, until His coming again, having in remembrance not only His blessed Passion and precious Death, but also His mighty Resurrection and glorious Ascension; and rendering unto God most hearty thanks for the innumerable benefits procured unto her by the same.

Bearing in mind what has been already said regarding the Holy Eucharist in its relation to the Ascension of Christ and His High Priestly Office (see Chapter V.), it will be recognized that the priestly character of the Church, the Body of Christ, is peculiarly sacred, by virtue of her close and intimate union with Him, her Head, in Heaven; therefore the Apostolic Ministry was ordained by Christ both to discharge and safeguard her priestly functions, especially in those things which pertain to the highest outward expression of her priestly life, but only in a representative capacity. Let it be distinctly observed that the whole Body of the Church has the inherent right to offer the same kind of sacrifice that the priest offers, and that the congregation *do* offer it through the ordained priest.

As Canon Moberly well says: "The Christian ministry is not a substituted intermediary — still less an atoning mediator — between God and lay people; but it is rather the representative and organ of the whole body, in the exercise of prerogatives and powers which belong to the body as a whole. It is ministerially empowered to wield, as the body's organic representative, the powers which belong *to the body*, but which the body cannot wield except through its own organs duly fitted for the purpose. What is duly done by Christian Ministers, it is not so much that *they* do it in the stead, or for the sake, of the whole; but rather that the whole does it by and through them. The Christian Priest does not offer an atoning sacrifice on behalf of the Church; it is rather the Church through his act that, not so much 'offers an atonement,' as 'is identified upon earth with the one heavenly offering of the atonement of Christ.' "[1]

There is, therefore, in the Church, ministerial *authority* derived directly from Christ, but there is no clerical *caste*. The difference between these two ideas should be carefully noted. Authority is one thing, caste is another.

St. Paul, when he calls the Church the Body of Christ, distinctly states that the Apostles — and the ministry that was developed out of the Apostolate — were themselves a part of the Body, comprehended in the Body, and exercised their particular ministry for the building of the Body. They are dependent upon the Body as much as the Body is dependent upon them. This truth is to be sharply emphasized. But side by side with it there is a counter truth that is to be recognized no less clearly.

[1] "Ministerial Priesthood," by Canon Moberly, p. 242.

"The fact that the organs represent, and live by, the life of the whole body does not mean that the rest of the body can dispense with the organs. If any organs are missing, it does not follow that all the rest of the body put together can discharge the special functions which the missing organs were made to discharge. A body, however otherwise complete, cannot see without eyes, hear without ears, or run a race without legs. Still less does it follow because the eye (say) is an organ of the whole body, living and seeing by, and not apart from, the body's life, that therefore, any and every other member of the body severally has the same functional power as the eye for seeing. Nor, again, does it follow because the life of the eye is the life of the body, specialized for a particular functional purpose, that therefore its sight-capacity is conferred upon the eye at the will or by the act of the body. Neither any other member in detail, nor the body as a whole, conferred upon the eye its capacity for seeing, or can transfer that capacity to any other organ, or can itself, in any other way, exercise the capacity for vision, if it should lose the eye. The eye is but an organ of the body by which the body sees: the hand is but an organ of the body by which the body strikes. But the body did not confer upon hand or eye their capacity of striking or of seeing for the body. It is therefore abundantly plain, that whatever may be true on other grounds, it most certainly is not contained as a logical inference within the principle that Church ministers are organs of the life of the Body of the Church, and not intermediaries between the Body and life; that, therefore, the rest of the Body, even all put together, — much less that any and every individual member of it, — is already *de jure* a minister, or that the authority of ministers to minister is derived from, or is conferred by, the mere act or will of the Body." [1]

[1] "Ministerial Priesthood," by Canon R. C. Moberly p. 68, *seq.*

To the fatal confusion between these two ideas of a scriptural ministerial or priestly authority and an anti-scriptural priestly caste, existing prejudice against sacerdotalism is largely attributable.

The Christian priest is a man among men; in every respect like the laymen by whom he is surrounded, save that of being among them in a position of authority and responsibility. In his private and personal religious life he and the laity among whom he ministers stand side by side. All are alike sinners in the sight of God; all pass through the same temptations and the same religious experiences; all must repent and believe, be baptized and confirmed in the same way, and enter Heaven by the self-same door. There is not one law for the clergy, another for the laity; one religious rule for the clergy, another for the laity; one social standard for the clergy, another for the laity. Anything that tends to confuse the mind regarding this truth becomes at once the gravest kind of impediment to the normal growth of the Church. And we hesitate not to say that the enforced celibacy of the clergy, in some branches of the Church, has had this disastrous effect. Originally adopted as a mere method of expediency, in times when there was danger of a hierarchy and of offices of the Church being handed down from father to son, it has become not only an anachronism, but a means of promoting that very kind of caste it was meant to prevent. Under any conditions in which it is wrong for the clergy to marry it should be equally wrong for the laity to marry also. This is but one illustration out of many that might be similarly adduced.

VI

We come now to a question that has been repeatedly asked: What scriptural authority is there for attributing sacerdotal functions to any office of the Christian ministry? Why is the very name of "priest" so plainly avoided in all descriptions of that ministry given in the Acts of the Apostles and the Epistles of the New Testament?

We answer: For the same reasons for which Christ Himself was never, in the Gospels, called the High Priest after the order of Melchizedek.

If the use of that name "Priest" as applied to Christ would have been premature and have caused confusion of thought until after His ascension to Heaven; it would have been still more premature, and have given rise to even greater misconceptions, if it had been applied to Christ's ministers in the times when the Epistles were written.

After Pentecost, though Christ Himself could now be recognized as the Priest after the order of Melchizedek, the difficulty remained, so far as the priestly character of the Church's ministry was concerned. So familiar were the Jews at that time with the associations and ideas connected with the Jewish priesthood, that if Christ's ministers had been called by this name there would have been the gravest danger of false, enslaving and antichristian conceptions of sacerdotalism. The Book of the Acts of the Apostles and the Epistles "were written at a time when sacrificial and priestly language were *de facto* identified with the symbolic, ceremonial, and unreal priesthood and sacrifices of the Mosaic Law. To have simply taken over the language while the Temple was standing and its worship in full force, *then* to have called Christian ministers as such ἱερεῖς, and the breaking of the bread simply θυσία, would have led to inextricable misunderstanding and confusion: what was possible without confusion, and what was necessary for apprehension of the truth, was to explain that that priesthood and those sacrifices were symbolic only and unreal; that Christ was the only true Priest, and His sacrifice the only real sacrifice, which, coupled with the basal Christian principle, that the bread and cup are the Church's ceremonial identification with Christ in His sacrifice, and that a real identification with Him in His sacrifice is the one *essentia* of the Church's life, constitutes the whole essence of sacrificial and priestly doctrine. All this the New Testament does emphatically teach."[1]

We have seen in later days how prone Christians have been to fall into error by drawing a parallel between the Jewish high priest, priest, and Levite, and the Christian bishop, priest, and deacon. How much greater that error would have been had Christian ministers been called "priests" in the New Testament itself.

Again, there was the still more important distinction between the eternal Priesthood of Christ in Heaven and the ministerial priesthood of his ordained servants on earth. This also needed to be plainly recognized and realized by the Church before its ministers could safely be called priests. But while the name itself

[1] "Ministerial Priesthood," by Canon Moberly, pp. 265, 266.

was thus, for a wise reason, passed over, the *functions* of a real priesthood, in the Christian sense, were undoubtedly exercised by the ministers whom Christ ordained; and this, as Canon Moberly truly says, is emphatically taught in the New Testament.

Not only are such functions directly implied when, as ministers of Christ's Priesthood, they celebrate and administer the Sacrament of His Body and Blood and obey His command, " Do this in remembrance of Me," but they are bidden to take heed to themselves, and to all the flock over which the Holy Ghost hath made them overseers, to feed the Church of God which He hath purchased with His own blood.[1] Again, not to multiply instances, the Corinthians are reminded by St. Paul that every man is to look upon the Apostles as Ambassadors of Christ, and, in Christ's own words, as " Stewards " of the Mysteries of God;[2] and then St. Paul goes on to say that the steward is required to be faithful to such a degree, that it is a small thing for him to be judged by those among whom he ministers or by " man's judgement," in comparison with the graver responsibility he directly owes to God, and with the way in which God will call him to give an account of his stewardship.

Though the word "priest" itself may not be used in the New Testament as applied to Christian ministers, it is evident that they are directly charged with the responsibilities of an office that can be nothing less than priestly, *in the New Testament sense*, that is, they are ministers of Christ's Priesthood as well as of Christ's Pastorhood. And this does not militate at all against the fact that as there is really but One

[1] Acts xx. 28.   [2] 1 Cor. iv. 1, *seq.*   Compare St. Luke xii 42.

Pastor of the Church of Christ, — the Good Shepherd *Who gave His life for the sheep*, — so there is but One Priest of the Church, even He Who once poured out His life-blood for the sins of the world and Who now ever liveth to make intercession for us. Indeed the words "pastor" and "priest" here melt into one another; and any idea of the ministry which stops short at the pastoral, and does not equally take in the priestly functions of the office, is an imperfect ideal, and falls just so far short of New Testament teaching regarding its responsibilities.

And it is to be noted that the Ordination Service of the Prayer Book, following exactly the same line as the Epistles of the New Testament, dwells so earnestly upon the *responsibility* of the office, — in contradistinction to the name itself, — that Roman Catholic theologians have emphasized the fact of that omission, as a proof that our ideas of the priesthood were unsound. There is no charge in the whole Prayer Book more solemn and weighty than that delivered to the ordinands before they are admitted to that which is called in the *beginning* of the service, "the Order of the Priesthood," and the "holy office of the Priesthood." Yet, in the charge itself — just as in the New Testament itself — the word "priest" is carefully kept in the background. It is upon the responsibilities of the office that the whole attention of the ordinands is concentrated: "Ye have heard, Brethren, as well in your private examination as in the exhortation which was now made to you, and in the holy Lessons taken out of the Gospel and the writings of the Apostles, of what dignity and of how great importance this office is, whereunto ye are called. And now, again, we exhort you in the Name of our Lord Jesus Christ, that ye have in remembrance, into how high a Dignity, and to how weighty an Office and Charge, ye are called; that is to say, to be Messengers, Watchmen, and Stewards of the Lord: to teach and to premonish, to feed and provide for the Lord's family; to seek for Christ's sheep that are dispersed abroad, and for His children who are in the midst of this naughty world that they may be saved through Christ forever.

"Have always, therefore, printed in your remembrance, how great a treasure is committed to your charge. For they are the sheep of Christ which He bought with His death, and for whom He shed His blood. The Church and congregation whom you must serve is His Spouse and His Body. And if it shall happen that the same Church or any member thereof do take any hurt or hindrance by reason of your negligence, ye know the greatness of the fault and also the horrible punishment that will ensue. Wherefore, consider with yourselves, the end of the ministry toward the children of God, toward the Spouse and Body of Christ, and see that ye never cease your labor, your care and diligence, until ye have done all that lieth in you, according to your bounden duty, to bring all such as are or shall be committed to your charge, unto that agreement with faith and knowledge of God, and to that ripeness and perfectness of age in Christ, that there be no place left among you, either for error in religion, or for viciousness of life."[1]

---

[1] See Service for the Ordering of Priests, in the Prayer Book.

VII

This brings us to our last point, the power of the Priesthood.

The real power of the Priesthood, as interpreted by Christ, is the greatest power that can be wielded by mortal man. It is the irresistible influence of self-sacrifice. And as self-sacrifice is the law of love, it is the power of a divine love and a great desire to bless, infused into human hearts *through Christ*. " By this shall all men know that ye are My disciples . . . if ye love one another as I have loved you." By virtue of this love, the whole Church becomes a race of kings, of leaders, of priests. By virtue of Christ's indwelling and their capacity of loving and sacrificing themselves for others, all devout believers become partakers of the priestly life with its priestly power.

And if so, the ordained ministry who are called by their office to be both ministers of the Priesthood of Christ, and ministers of the priesthood of the Church of Christ, are doubly called to a life of self-sacrifice. Never will they rise to the ideal of Christian priesthood until they take to themselves that message which Christ sent from Heaven when St. Paul was called, " For I will show him how great things he must suffer for My Name's sake "; [1] never can they hope to follow that ideal, until, in their personal lives, they bear patiently and uncomplainingly with the sinfulness and ignorance of human hearts, manifesting that quality of charity which suffereth long, envieth not,

[1] Acts ix. 16.

vaunteth not itself, thinketh no evil, rejoiceth not in iniquity, but rejoiceth in the truth; which beareth all things, believeth all things, hopeth all things, endureth all things; never can they exercise the real power of that priesthood, unless self-sacrifice becomes the ruling idea and spirit of their lives, spurring them onward in season and out of season, and at times when all others would fail, to do what their Office requires of them; to be faithful stewards of the mysteries of God, and unceasingly to deny self, in the service of that Master Who, for the joy that was set before Him, endured the cross, despising the shame, and is set down at the right hand of the throne of God.

How utterly at variance, this truth stands with popular, prevalent conceptions of priestly power, priestly ambition, priest-craft and self-seeking in every form, we leave the reader to ponder and see for himself.

CHAPTER X

THE BIBLE IN THE CHURCH

WHICH comes first, the Church or the New Testament? Which is the highest standard of authority, and which the ultimate court of appeal for the Christian world?

These are questions that are being mooted on all sides now. Some affirm and earnestly believe that the Bible alone, apart from the Church, is the divinely appointed fountain of authority; while others just as firmly assert that, as the Primitive Church existed many years before the first book of the New Testament was written, therefore the authority of the Church of Christ exceeds that of the Bible itself. Yet, strange to say, neither can prove their point; because, for the credentials of the Bible, we are forced to fall back upon the history of the Church; while for the credentials of the Church, we are equally forced to fall back upon the Bible. Each side, therefore, by undervaluing one of these sources of authority, is unconsciously weakening its own position.

The adversaries of Christianity are fond of asserting that, under these conditions, Christians are obliged to argue in a circle, proving the authority of the Bible by that of the Church, and, conversely, the authority of the Church by that of the Bible.

So far from denying the charge, we are eager to confess its truth; for as a matter of fact it is impossible to separate the Bible from the Church. They stand or fall together. They do not set before us, as so many suppose, two standards of appeal. They constitute together one united basis of authority; and the reason for this becomes evident at once, when we go back to the origin of the New Testament.

Before the days when there was either a Church or a Bible, the Risen Christ gave His Great Commission to His Apostles. The words of that charge, as rendered by St. Matthew, were: "All authority hath been given unto Me in Heaven and on earth. Go ye therefore, and make disciples of all the nations, baptizing them into the Name of the Father, and of the Son, and of the Holy Ghost: teaching them to observe all things whatsoever I have commanded you: and, lo, I am with you alway, even to the end of the world."

As given by St. Mark, the charge was: "Go ye into all the world, and preach the Gospel to the whole creation. He that believeth and is baptized shall be saved; but he that disbelieveth shall be condemned." Remembering that all nations are made disciples, or members of the Church, by baptism, we should take note that, in this commission, the ministry of the Word and Baptism — the Gospel message and the founding of the Church — stand side by side. However St. Mark's report may differ in other respects from St. Matthew's, this fundamental principle appears in both, and, after Pentecost, the same principle stands out as one of the marked characteristics of New Testament Christianity. The

THE BIBLE IN THE CHURCH 225

chief care of the Apostles, as they went forth establishing churches in various parts of the Roman Empire, was to be faithful witnesses of Jesus Christ to the world, by preaching, in season and out of season, the facts of His life, and receiving into the Church by baptism those who believed. And so unswerving was their fidelity to this Gospel message, that St. Paul even went so far as to say to the Galatians: "Though we, or an angel from Heaven, preach any other Gospel unto you, . . . let him be accursed."[1]

Within twenty-five years after St. Paul uttered these words, three of the four Gospels were written. And internal evidence clearly shows that this was the ultimate method which the founders of the Church adopted for perpetuating their witness for Christ and His Resurrection after they should be dead and gone, and for handing down to succeeding generations that primitive Gospel which they had heretofore imparted by word of mouth.

At the same time, they wrote other documents which are just as important. The Gospels set forth the life of Christ in this world before His ascension to Heaven, and then end abruptly. The very suddenness with which the story is broken off, and the sense of incompleteness which every reader feels, when he reaches the last verse, shows that this is not the end of the Gospel history itself. The abruptness was intentional; the Revelation was to be *continued;* and when we search for that continuation, we find it in the Epistles of the New Testament. The Gospels contain the message of the Son

[1] Gal. i. 8.

of Man to His followers while He was yet on earth. The Epistles proclaim the message of the Son of Man, sent down by Him to His Church after He had ascended to Heaven, and after all power had been given to Him in Heaven and on earth.

We behold, therefore, in the writers of the Epistles, — only in far greater degree, — the same unique, psychological phenomenon that is to be observed in the ancient prophets of Israel. For where the prophets cry, with a certainty that surpasses ordinary human knowledge, "Thus saith the Lord," the Apostles, in their writings after Pentecost, not only deliver the messages that Christ sends down through them, but proclaim, with united and unfaltering voice, a doctrine of the ascended and victorious Christ which must be true, if Christ is on the right hand of God, yet which is far in advance of the teachings of the Gospels themselves.

Bearing in mind the fact, that here was a revelation of Christ in Heaven sent through, and exclusively through, the Church on earth, we have before us the reason why the Church and the New Testament mutually depend upon one another for their credentials.

Again, just as the teachings of Christ in the Gospels are enforced and illustrated by His human example, so the doctrine taught by the Apostles, through the inspiration of the Holy Ghost, is enforced and illustrated by the example of the Primitive Church.

On the one hand, if we would trace the results of the Gospel history, we shall find them in the Church; on the other hand, if we would discover the practice of the early Church and the creed held by the Apostles, we must go to the records of the New Testament.

The New Testament is thus not only a witness for the doctrine of Christ, but a witness for the Faith of the early Apostolic Church; and this accounts for the position it has occupied through all subsequent days. We can see traces even in the writings of Ignatius, the disciple of St. John, of the kind of influence it afterwards exerted; and in the days of the General Councils it was enthroned, as a sign that the written Word of God was the supreme authority to which all bowed. Indeed this deep reverence for the Scriptures appears to have been universal at that time, for in the oldest church of Ravenna, built a century after the Council of Nice, the ancient mosaics represent four altars with the open books of the Gospels, and thrones with crosses.

Let us now pass to some other noteworthy facts.

In the Primitive Church the love for the Bible was so great that, although in that early day printing was not invented and Bible societies were unknown, Holy Scripture was translated for Parthians and Medes and Elamites; for the dwellers in Mesopotamia, in Pontus and Asia, in Phrygia and Pamphylia, and for every people that had been converted to Christianity. Eusebius tells us that it was studied by all nations throughout the world, as the Oracles of God. Chrysostom assures us that the Egyptians, the Indians, the Persians, and the Ethiopians translated the Bible into their own tongues, "whereby barbarians learned to be philosophers, and women and children, with the greatest ease, imbibed the doctrine of the Gospel." Theodoret says that every nation under Heaven had the Scriptures in their own tongue; and St. Jerome and St. Augustine affirm the same.

Again, Bingham assures us that it was a custom of the Primitive Church to place Bibles, translated into the vulgar tongue, in various parts of the churches for the people to read; and Constantine ordered fifty copies of the Scriptures to be thus distributed and used in the Church of Constantinople.

In addition to this, the people were not only encouraged, but earnestly exhorted, to read the Bible at their homes and with their families; and Chrysostom has a sermon upon the necessity of Bible reading, even by the lowly and uncultivated, which might have been preached from an American pulpit in the nineteenth, instead of from a Greek pulpit in the fourth century. Even children from their infancy were trained in the reading of the Holy Scriptures and in learning different passages by heart. The Bible was the first study of Origen and Eusebius in their childhood. Gregory of Nyssa tells the same story of his sister Macrina and his brother Peter; it was even taught to the children of charity schools in the early Church; and when Gregory, the Apostle of the Armenians, went forth to convert that nation, he set up, by the king's command, schools in every city to teach the Armenian children to read the Word of God.

Such was the use and influence of the Bible in the Primitive Church, down to the day when St. Jerome completed his translation of the Old Testament from the original Hebrew. This was between the years 400 and 404 A. D. In less than ten years from that time Alaric the Goth captured Rome; and thenceforward, in the Providence of God, new problems were before the Church, the solution of which would engross attention for many a coming century. In the words of Dr. Westcott, Bishop of Durham: "The normal processes of Christianity were in abeyance; organization prevailed over faith, and these new races were to be disciplined by act, before they could be taught the simple word. The Latin translation of the Vulgate sufficed for the teachers; and they ministered to their congregations such lessons from it as they could receive." These irruptions of the wild barbarians from the north, for the next three or four centuries, — of Goths and Vandals, Huns and Lombards and Norsemen, Danes and Angles and Saxons, — are an explanation, not only of this suspended activity, but of many others of the Church during the Middle Ages. But as soon as society became settled and Christianized the old instincts reappeared; and, strange to say, it was not in Greece or in Asia Minor, but in the far-off Islands of Great Britain, that those features of the Primitive Church which had been almost lost began most strongly to reassert themselves.

Among these was the intense desire to have the Holy Scriptures, in the vulgar tongue, distributed among the people. In the eighth century, the Book of Psalms was translated, probably by Aldhelm, Bishop of Sherbourne, into Anglo-Saxon; and about the same time the Venerable Bede, during his last illness, translated the Gospel of St. John. In the ninth century, King Alfred prefixed to the laws of the realm an Anglo-Saxon version of the Ten Commandments; and about a century later, the four Gospels were translated, probably for public use in the services of the Church and among the people. Then came the Norman invasion, which was another set-back. But all through the subsequent period, the ancient Church in the British Isles kept struggling for the mastery, with more or less success, against the novelties of Papal Mediævalism. And as generation after generation passed by, we can detect the old love for the Word of God continuously smouldering in human hearts. At last John Wickliffe, a learned priest of the English Church, and Master of Balliol College, Oxford, felt the God-given responsibility resting upon him, of rendering the New Testament into the English tongue; while his friend, Nicholas de Hereford, undertook the similar task of translating the Old Testament. Amid ceaseless opposition and misunderstanding, they completed their work. So that Wickliffe, who was now Vicar of Lutterworth, had the joy of seeing his life's task accomplished before he died, in 1384.

Within two generations, or scarcely more than sixty years after the death of Wickliffe, the printing press was invented. The first book of any size printed was Gutenberg's Latin Bible; and by the time that America was discovered, in 1492, Bibles were printed in Spanish, Italian, French, Dutch, German, and Bohemian. England had, as yet, only the manuscript copies of Wickliffe's translation; and we can, without doubt, trace the delay of the English people in securing a new translation to the power and influence of this older version. But soon another man arose, William Tyndale by name, filled with the spirit of the Vicar of Lutterworth in his desire to place an English Bible in the hands of the people. Like Wickliffe he was a graduate of Oxford, a priest of the English Church, and a man in many ways eminently fitted to continue Wickliffe's work; though by certain eccentricities and peculiar opinions, he awakened the antagonism of Tunstall, Bishop of London, and lost the confidence of other authorities in the Church.

Tyndale's translation was printed and circulated in 1525; and it produced a profound effect on the popular mind. Indeed, so great was the change of feeling in England within the next ten years that although Tyndale himself was martyred, a convocation of the Church of England, under the presidency of Thomas Cranmer, Archbishop of Canterbury, agreed to petition the king that he would "Vouchsafe to decree that a translation of the Scriptures into English should be made by certain honest and learned men whom the king should nominate, and that the translation so made should be delivered to the people for their learning." In the same year, or certainly within the next, Miles Coverdale's Bible appeared, with his own name, as the Bishop of Exeter, on the title-page, and with an open dedication to King Henry VIII. It is significant that although Coverdale's Bible was without the sanction of the civil authority, it was never suppressed; showing that there was no opposition in England, even in those early days, to a translation made by competent hands and set forth under the seal of authority.

Events now follow one another in rapid succession. In 1537, "Matthew's" or "Rogers' Bible" was issued; in 1539, "Taverner's Bible"; and in 1540, and in the following years, appeared in six successive editions, the "Great Bible," with a preface by Cranmer, Archbishop of Canterbury; and also with the name on the title-page of Tunstall, that same Bishop of London who had before condemned and burned the very Bible of Tyndale upon which this translation was founded. About twenty years after this appeared "The Bishops' Bible," set forth to be used in the cathedrals and churches of England by order of the Convocation. In 1604, or two generations after Tyndale, King James, yielding to the pressure of public religious opinion, responded, to the old request of Archbishop Cranmer and Convocation, "that a translation of the Scriptures into English should be made by certain honest and learned men whom the king (of England) should nominate;" and at last authorized a competent company of scholars in the Church of England to prepare a new version of the English Bible. They completed their work after seven years of labor, setting forth, in 1611, that commonly called "Authorized Version" which we all know so well. In 1870, two hundred and fifty years afterward, the Convocation of Canterbury organized another company of revisers for still another translation of the Bible, and this Revision was finished, the New Testament in 1880, and the Old Testament in 1884.

On the title-page of both these last versions, we

read that "*they were diligently revised and compared with former translations.*" The key to those familiar words is before us in the events we have been recounting. Looking back over the long period of English Church history, from the Venerable Bede to the present time, embracing an era of over eleven hundred years, we behold the gradual evolution of the English Bible, as age followed age, and its final culmination in the Revised Version. All these successive translations we have named were made by devout bishops, priests, and scholars of the Church of England, while the last two — the Authorized and Revised Versions — were made directly under the appointment of the Church itself. When we read, therefore, the history of that English Bible which is now exercising such an irresistible religious influence over the English-speaking nations of the world, and see how, from beginning to end, it was directly due to the English Church itself, can we marvel that belief in the Holy Scriptures "as containing all things necessary to salvation, and as the rule and ultimate standard of faith," has been set forth by the last two Lambeth Conferences as one of the four essential conditions for the reunion of Christendom? Many as are the points of similarity between the Anglican Communion of to-day and the early Church of Apostolic times, the Church in the post-apostolic age, the Church in the age of Augustine and Chrysostom, of Jerome and Athanasius, there is none more marked, or more characteristic of the continuity of Christian thought, than this English and American love and reverence for the Bible.

Let us now turn to the actual conditions as they exist at present. Thirty or forty years ago, and within the memory of many of us, the oft-repeated and ignorant charge was hurled against the Anglican Church that it placed the Prayer Book above the Bible itself; while, as a matter of fact, all through the past three centuries there has been no other church or Christian body on the face of the earth which enjoins by rule upon all the people so constant a perusal of Holy Scripture.

Three fourths of the Prayer Book itself are in the exact words of the Bible; and if its order for daily Morning and Evening Prayer is followed by parish churches in public services, or by individuals in private, the Old Testament will be read through once, the New Testament twice, and the Book of Psalms twelve times every year. For those who have not the time or the inclination to use the whole of the daily Morning and Evening Prayer, there is a Table of Lessons in the beginning of the Prayer Book indicating how they may read the four daily chapters of the Bible privately at home.

In addition to this, at the very commencement of the Christian year, there is a Sunday which, as Dr. Liddon well said, might appropriately be called Bible Sunday; and if any one is disposed to charge the Church of England with being adverse to the translation and circulation of the Bible in Reformation times, we have a direct witness to the contrary in that beautiful collect of the Second Sunday in Advent: —

"Blessed Lord, who hast caused all Holy Scriptures to be written for our learning, grant that we may . . . read, mark, learn, and inwardly digest them." The significance of this collect becomes all the greater when we remember that it was in the *First* Prayer Book of Edward VI., in 1549.

Anglican love of the Bible comes out even with greater prominence when we turn to the Ordination Services of the Prayer Book. In one respect these are the most significant of all, for it is at these times that the Church commits to chosen and tried men the awful responsibility of being her teachers in things pertaining to God. In the Ordination of Deacons the questions are asked of the ordinand: "Do you firmly believe all the Canonical Scriptures of the Old and New Testament, and will you diligently read the same to the people?" And immediately after his ordination, a copy of the New Testament is placed in his hand, with the charge to read the Gospel in the Church of God. In the Ordination of Priests a greater emphasis still is laid upon the belief in Holy Scriptures as containing all doctrines necessary to salvation; upon the necessity of instructing the people out of the same Scriptures; upon the duty of banishing and driving away all erroneous and strange doctrines contrary to God's Holy Word. In the Roman Church the sacred Communion vessels are placed in the ordinand's hand at the time of ordination; in the Anglican Church a copy of the Bible is substituted for the chalice and paten, immediately after the laying on of hands, with the accompanying charge: "Be thou a faithful dispenser of the Word of God and of His Holy Sacraments." So also, in the service for the Consecration of a Bishop, *one half* of all the questions addressed to the person to be consecrated relate to the doctrine, authority, sufficiency, discipline, rule of faith and of life set forth in the Holy Scriptures; and after the consecration of the newly ordained bishop, a copy of the Bible is handed him with a most solemn charge. Thus carefully has the Church provided that no deacon, priest, or bishop shall minister at her altars without being trained in the doctrine of the Bible and moulded by Holy Scripture. All her ministers are obliged to pledge themselves, in God's Presence, to be obedient and loyal to His Holy Word, before they are admitted to the privilege of teaching in the Church's name.

We find also in the Ordinal a marked emphasis laid upon the necessity of preaching the Word. The Word and the Ministry of the Word stand together in close connection. The Prayer Book gives no uncertain sound regarding the character of the sermons that the Church expects her ordained servants to deliver. Just as they are sent forth to "minister the sacraments" of Baptism and the Lord's Supper in such a way that the people will understand and be blessed and grow in grace through these divinely appointed channels wherein Christ imparts His life to the souls of men, so are they sent forth to "minister the Word" in such a way that the people will understand and be blessed and grow in grace through the Gospel, which is the good news which Christ brought down with Him from Heaven, and of which He said: "If ye abide in Me, and My words abide in you, ye shall ask what ye will and it shall be done unto you. Herein is My Father glorified, that ye bear much fruit; so shall ye be My disciples."[1]

[1] St. John xv. 7, 8.

The Prayer Book embodies the Christian experience of the ages, and it is part of that experience that the Ministry of the Word has a peculiar kind of spiritual power that is absolutely necessary for growth in grace. Listen how earnestly and solemnly the Church exhorts those who are to be ordained to her priesthood, with reference to this subject. "Forasmuch then as your Office is both of so great excellency, and of so great difficulty, . . . ye ought, and have need, to pray earnestly for God's Holy Spirit. And seeing that ye cannot, by any other means, compass the doing of so weighty a work pertaining to the salvation of man but with doctrine and exhortation taken out of the Holy Scripture, and with a life agreeable to the same, consider how studious ye ought to be in reading and learning the Scriptures, and in framing the manners both of yourselves and of them that specially pertain unto you, according to the rule of the same Scriptures; and for this self-same cause, how ye ought to forsake and set aside, as much as ye may, all worldly cares and studies, . . . that by daily reading and weighing the Scriptures ye may wax riper and stronger in your Ministry."

Similarly in the Office for the Consecration of Bishops, among the questions asked of the bishop elect is the following: "Will you then faithfully exercise yourself in the Holy Scriptures, and call upon God by prayer for the true understanding of the same, so that you may be able by them to teach and exhort with wholesome Doctrine, and to withstand and convince the gainsayers?" Then when the Bible is delivered into his hands by the consecrator, it is with the solemn charge: "Give heed unto reading, exhortation, and doctrine. Think upon the things contained in this Book. Be diligent in them, that the increase coming thereby may be manifest unto all men; for by so doing thou shalt both save thyself and them that hear thee."

What the Church means by the "Ministry of the Word" is here plainly set forth. Her clergy are not merely to preach from Bible texts or upon Bible themes, but they are to be "mighty in the Scriptures."

The mere delivery of a sermon upon some Scripture topic, the thoughts of which have been culled from historical, literary, or scientific sources on the one hand, or evolved from the active brain of the preacher on the other, is aside from the Church's purpose. However captivating in literary style, finished in oratorical delivery, or original in treatment such a sermon may be, it is poverty-stricken and thin, according to this high standard, if it does not draw from the unsearchable riches of Christ. Its polished elegance is but a makeshift to cover up the preacher's ignorance of the treasures stored away in the Word of God. Before her bishops and priests can be true ministers of the Word, they must know the Scriptures through and through. They must make the Bible their daily study. They must "be diligent in reading and learning the Scriptures." They must "draw all their studies this way." They must "think of the things contained in this Book, that the increase coming thereby may be made manifest to all men." Laying aside as far as possible all worldly cares and studies, they must get at the inner spiritual meaning of Christ's words, so that "by daily reading and weighing the Scriptures, they may wax riper and stronger in their ministry."

In other words, they must be so imbued by the Word of God, and saturated with its spirit, that they are full to overflowing with its glad tidings of salvation, feeling that they are impelled to deliver to others those messages which the Word of God puts into their mouths, and inspired by the irresistible desire to impart to others the knowledge of the love of Christ.

But there is a still deeper reason for this earnest emphasis upon the Ministry of the Word. It is not only that the Church of to-day may conform to the life and practice of the Primitive Church, but it is that her clergy may be imbued with the very spirit of New Testament Christianity and be ceaselessly renewed by the fresh springs of Apostolic Life. If these facts have not been rightly appreciated in the past three hundred years outside of the Anglican Church, it has been because Protestantism has been dominated overmuch by Chillingworth's maxim, "The Bible, and the Bible only, is the religion of Protestants." But now a reaction has taken place; popular thought is passing to the opposite extreme; and under the influence of the Higher Criticism, thousands have lost their faith in the Old Testament as the inspired Word of God.

Fifty years ago, in contrast with many Christian bodies around her, the Anglican Church seemed, to the popular eye, to undervalue the Bible, and to place it upon a lower level than the Prayer Book. To-day it is the exact reverse; in contrast to the present reaction in popular Christian thought, and, to the disintegrating process that is going on in many Christian bodies, the Anglican Church seems to stand out as the greatest bulwark and defender of the Bible which is to be found in all Western Christendom.

It is true that some of the greatest scholars in the Higher Criticism of the present day are in the ranks of the clergy of the Church of England; but there is a marked difference between these critics of the English Church and those of Germany, Holland, and elsewhere. The kind of Higher Criticism which emphasizes the value of the *Historic Method* of studying the Scriptures; which looks upon the ancient prophets of Israel as men, who, filled with the Holy Ghost, prophesied primarily of the burning issues of their own times, and applied to these issues those universal principles of Gospel truth which found a deeper fulfilment in Messianic days, is a kind of criticism which will ultimately increase our love for the Bible and make it seem more than ever the inspired Word of God. While the other and more destructive form of criticism which jumps at conclusions, dissolving historical facts into legends and ancient biblical characters into myths, will bring about exactly the opposite effect. And these two effects are even now manifesting themselves in contemporaneous Christian history.

While the faith of multitudes is so shaken that even Sunday-school children speak of the Scriptures with an irreverent freedom that would have amazed preceding generations, we behold in the English Church an ever-increasing hunger and thirst to know more about God's Holy Word. When the Speaker's Commentary was first published, about thirty years ago, Dean Plumptre told the writer that the publishers were in grave doubt whether the first edition would ever be taken off their hands. Since that time many commentaries have been issued — sometimes four in a single year; and to-day no kind of literature is more largely sought and read among English and American Churchmen than that which relates to the Holy Scriptures.

Such is the condition of religious thought in the Anglican Church at the present time. Nothing is more intensely interesting than to watch the effect of modern criticism and Bible study upon the devotional life of the Church; and, as it has been, so it will be in the future, only in greater degree. The more the Church knows about the Bible and drinks in the spirit of New Testament life, the more she will discover the law of her own life and the springs of her own health; for, to quote the words of Canon Mason of Canterbury: "It must never be forgotten that the Bible is a Church Book, written for Churchmen, under the inspiration of the same Spirit Who is leading the Church, so far as it is willing to be led, *into* all truth and *in* all truth."

CHAPTER XI

PUBLIC WORSHIP IN NEW TESTAMENT DAYS

IT is often said that as there is scarcely any reference in the New Testament to public worship, church edifices, or church services, these accessories of the Christian religion cannot claim the sanction of apostolic or scriptural authority; that they originated in a post-apostolic age, and are a development of the "institutional" in contradistinction to the Gospel type of religious life. But those who draw such a conclusion have not considered that the Acts of the Apostles, as well as most of the Epistles, were written within the first thirty years after Pentecost, when Christianity was still in its infancy and when congregations were composed entirely of fresh converts, chiefly taken from the lowest ranks of society. If there is little said in the New Testament regarding these institutions and external ordinances of Christianity, it is because in this period everything was inchoate, and in its first formative condition. Yet enough is revealed to give us a very vivid glimpse of the religious observances and habits of the early Church. After Pentecost, the Apostles and their followers attended the Temple services daily. When these were over, they went down to private houses, sometimes for "the Breaking of Bread," sometimes for united prayer.[1] At a later

[1] Acts ii. 42, 46; iii. 1; iv. 23-31; v. 42, etc.

date, Christians in Jerusalem and elsewhere met in those homes of believers where prayer was wont to be made; like the house of Mary, the mother of Mark,[1] of Lydia,[2] and of Philemon.[3] From this we learn that at that very early day, when there were neither Gospels nor Epistles, neither Prayer Book, church observances, nor church buildings, the first Christians (1) went up to the Temple daily to pray, and (2) there were regular meetings for "the Breaking of Bread."

Here we have two definite and important facts disclosed regarding public worship in New Testament times. Let us consider each by itself.

I

If we go back from the Book of Acts to the Gospels themselves, we shall discover the reason why Christ's disciples frequented the Temple services. We know how our Lord loved the Temple. When He was only twelve years old, and His sorrowing parents, after searching for three days, at last found Him in the Temple, His answer to them was: "How is it that ye sought Me? wist ye not that I must be in My Father's House?"[4] Eighteen years afterwards, when He began His public ministry, almost His first act was to go back to the Temple and drive out the money changers and others, saying: "Make not My Father's House an house of merchandise."[5] And finally, when that

---
[1] Acts xii. 12.   [3] Phil. 2.
[2] Acts xvi. 40.   [4] St. Luke ii. 49, R. V.
[5] St. John ii. 16.

ministry was over, in the last week of His earthly life, after He had made His triumphal entry as King of the Jews into Jerusalem, He once more cleansed the Temple. While the blind and the lame were waiting to be healed by Him, and while even the little children were singing in the Temple, "Hosanna to the Son of David," He cast forth the buyers and sellers, crying: "It is written, My House shall be called of all nations the House of Prayer, but ye have made it a den of thieves."[1] The significance of this final cleansing is enhanced by the fact that it occurred just before Christ left the Temple forever, saying first publicly to the Pharisees, "Behold your House is left unto you desolate. For I say unto you that ye shall not see Me henceforth till ye shall say, blessed is He that cometh in the name of the Lord;"[2] and then privately to His disciples, "Verily, I say unto you, There shall not be left here one stone upon another, that shall not be thrown down."[3] Clearly the second cleansing and the marked emphasis laid upon it, not only by the writers of the different Gospels but by our Lord Himself, had a prophetic, far-reaching meaning. It was a warning to the Pharisees of impending judgement for the past; it was also a lesson for the future, to be read and remembered by the whole Christian Church through coming ages. Christ not only loved His Father's house, but called it the House of Prayer; and He had also prophetically foretold that the time would come when worship like that of the Jewish Temple would be uni-

---

[1] St. Mark xi. 17. [2] St. Matt. xxiii. 38, 39.
[3] St. Matt. xxiv. 2.

versal.[1] At this time, when there were not, and would not be for many a long year to come, any Christian temples or houses of God, it is noteworthy that our Lord, gazing into the far future, should have spoken such words of the only House of God which His disciples in His own lifetime knew and recognized as such. The ideal of a House of God for all nations, of which the Jewish temple was the prototype, and which it failed so sadly to fulfil, was to be attained in after years in the churches of Christian believers; and the highest realization of that ideal is set forth by Christ Himself in those memorable words: "My House shall be called the House of Prayer for all people." He shows plainly here, both by word and action, how sacred every place of Christian worship must be. This simple conception of the ideal place of worship and its uses was so high, so pure, so comprehensive and lasting, that it soars above and embraces all those changes and additions in the forms of public worship, all those rites and ceremonies of the Catholic Church, all those hallowed associations and customs which have enriched the service of God through subsequent ages. It would be well if we could apply this ruling idea of New Testament Churchmanship to our modern Church life. There are in every congregation numbers of earnest-hearted men and women who are secretly hungering and thirsting that their parish church may become more and more of a spiritual home to themselves and to their families. Often both pastor and people are disappointed that there is so little of

[1] St. John iv. 21–23.

the homelike atmosphere in their church; yet they are unable to point out exactly why it is that the services seem so perfunctory and cold.

If all would only take more earnest heed to the prophetic charge of Christ at His second cleansing of the Temple, these unsatisfied longings would be met and all coldness would disappear.

From the time a congregation begin really to treat their Father in Heaven as a Living Person, and to make their Father's House a House of Prayer, the consciousness of their Father's Presence and of a home atmosphere in the sanctuary will naturally follow.

This intimate connection between prayer and the home feeling is, in fact, so simple and so much a matter of universal Christian experience, that it is self-evident to all devout minds. The moment a man *prays* in God's house, he begins to feel that somehow it belongs to him. It becomes a spiritual home to him at once, because he has *used* it as such. What, therefore, our modern congregations need most of all is to be taught to pray.

In God's own House of Prayer, secondary things are often put first. Either the ritual or the sermon, the architecture or the music, is the first consideration, while the prayers of the people and the inward lifting up of their hearts in acts of faith — in confession, and thanksgiving, in intercession and praise — are treated as of secondary importance. Earnest, eloquent sermons, a correct and reverent ritual, stately ecclesiastical edifices, and carefully trained choirs, are all important adjuncts to a perfectly appointed service; but their place, after all, is a subordinate one. The inward requires the outward for its expression, but the inward must never be sacrificed to the outward. The one thing needful to sanctify the whole is prayer. If Christ said, "My House shall be called the House of Prayer," it was because those things which prayer stands for — repentance, faith, obedience, charity, the determination to lead a new life — become, in prayer, the highest and most essential acts of Christian sacrifice. These are the realities of Christian service. If they are sincerely felt, the outward expression of this spirit of sacrifice becomes a necessity; but if there is the outward expression alone, in ritual or homily, while the spirit is absent, the whole congregation, by a true spiritual instinct, will detect that absence.

As the old Romans had their *Lares* and *Penates*, or household gods, who were present in the house so long as it was occupied by the family; as we know, almost intuitively, when we enter a house, or even one of its rooms, whether the family are wont to frequent and use it or not, so is it, only in greater degree, with our churches. We have said that a warm home feeling comes with prayer. It pervades mysteriously the atmosphere of every church which is habitually and daily used as a house of prayer; while, just as invariably, that home feeling is absent from those churches in which, however eloquent the Sunday's sermon or elaborate the musical service may be, other things take the place of prayer. A passer-by strays in at the door of a real house of prayer on a week day, and somehow the breath of prayer lingers on the walls; somehow the spiritual fragrance of prayer, which in the Bible is so often compared with incense, fills the quiet sanctuary. No other being may be present; but this stranger, who has never been there before, seems at once to feel at home, while the silent spell of the sanctuary falls full upon his soul, prompting him to sink on his knees and whisper, "This is My Father's House. This is none other but the House of God and the Gate of Heaven."

II

The Acts of the Apostles record that, after Pentecost, the first Christians were in the habit of coming often together in private houses for the Breaking of Bread. They had been Jews by birth and education before they became Christ's followers, and therefore very naturally they attended the services of the Jewish synagogues as well as that of the Temple itself. But the only distinctively *Christian* service held by them at that time was the one emphasized in the Book of Acts as the Breaking of Bread. And this accounts for that marked silence, throughout the New Testament, on the subject of public worship. We read, indeed, that the first Christians often came together informally for prayer, but they had only one service of public worship, — the Breaking of Bread; and that particular one is especially named and referred to not only in the Acts of the Apostles and the Epistles, but in the Gospels themselves.

We should never forget this historic fact, in contrasting nineteenth century days with New Testament days. If we would understand those times, we must not *read into* them, or take for granted, conditions and customs which have arisen in subsequent centuries, but simply take the record as it stands.

And the reason for this New Testament fact is evident. The Lord's Supper, instituted by Christ the night before His Crucifixion, was *the only service of public worship which the Lord Himself ordained.* And His dying charge to His followers concerning it was very explicit: "Do this in remembrance of Me."[1] In the earliest days, when Christianity itself was only known as "The Way," this service was called "The Breaking of Bread;" and the use of this term so exclusively in the first chapters of the Acts of the Apostles is an indication of the primitive character of that record. Soon after, St. Paul called it the "Lord's Supper"[2] and also, in the same Epistle by implication, "The Communion."[3] In the post-apostolic age, its distinctive name was "The Eucharist;" and this term also seems traceable, for its earliest use, back to St. Paul;[4] while the last name, used more especially by the early Christians of Rome, "The Sacrament," or oath, seems to have had especial reference to the "New Testament," or "New Covenant in His Blood," of which Christ so earnestly spoke.[5] These five names for the Holy Communion, all distinctly of New Testament origin, indicate how strongly it anchored itself in the life of the early

---

[1] St. Luke xxii. 19; 1 Cor. xi. 24.
[2] 1 Cor. xi. 20.   [3] 1 Cor. x. 16.
[4] 1 Cor. xiv. 16. Compare chapter xi. 24; also St. Matt. xxvi. 27; St. Mark xiv. 23; St. Luke xxii. 19.
[5] St. Matt. xxvi. 28; St. Mark xiv. 24; St. Luke xxii. 20; 1 Cor. xi. 25.

Christians, and how much it meant to them in its many-sided blessedness.[1] Instituted by Christ Himself, it naturally became their one supreme service of public worship. For it stood, in its comprehensive simplicity, (1) as an ever-present witness against the utter imperfection of all heathen sacrifices; (2) as the Christian substitute for all Jewish sacrificial services; (3) as the memorial of Christ's full, perfect, and sufficient sacrifice for the sins of the whole world upon the Cross; (4) as a service in which the risen Christ imparted to them His Divine life and the power of His Resurrection in such a way that they were made "one Body with Him;" (5) as a service in which the ascended Christ, the High Priest in Heaven, is united to His followers on earth and pledges to them the continuance of His self-sacrificing love; (6) as the "New Testament" or New Covenant in His blood that He makes with them; (7) as their sacrifice of prayer and thanksgiving to Him.

Standing for all this and more, the power of this particular service of public worship was such, in its direct and indirect influences, that as early as the beginning of the second century the younger Pliny wrote to the Emperor of Rome that, through the influence of the Christians, the Roman altars were being deserted and the Roman sacrifices in danger of being abolished.

[1] The word "*Mass*," though quite ancient, originated in a later period. It is derived not from the New Testament itself, but according to Cardinal Bona from a liturgical phrase, "*Missa est.*" It has no ancient or religious significance; and it has become identified with a doctrine of the Communion that was utterly unknown for the first seven centuries of the Christian era.

And when we pass on to a still later date, the Eucharist stands out as the foundation of all Christian liturgical worship; so much so, in fact, that for a long period it was the only service known distinctively as "the Liturgy." Though the beginnings of Christian, as distinguished from Jewish, liturgical worship are obscure, we find, in comparatively early days, four distinct groups or families of liturgies, which were traditionally and respectively known as (1) the Liturgy of St. James, used at Jerusalem; (2) the Liturgy of St. John, used at Ephesus and vicinity — and afterwards introduced by missionaries from Ephesus into France and England and Spain; (3) the Liturgy of St. Peter, used in Rome; and (4) the Liturgy of St. Mark, which was used in Egypt. In these Communion services there are a dozen or more distinct features that are common to all, though they are grouped together in different order of sequence. And, just as the likeness between different children of a family indicates that they are the offspring of the same parents, whose features they preserve, so the resemblances between these four liturgical groups point back to some common origin, or some apostolic nucleus of a Communion service used in the earliest days, but now lost. This essential nucleus of the liturgy consisted, at least, of the Benediction, the use of our Lord's words of Institution, the Breaking of the Bread, the giving of thanks, the taking of the cup into the hands, and the devout reception of the bread and wine, as is seen from the Gospel narrative.[1] In the first institution itself,

[1] St. Matt. xxvi. 26; St. Mark xiv. 22; St. Luke xxii. 19; and also 1 Cor. xi. 24.

our Lord also delivered a discourse[1] and a hymn was sung.[2]

While, therefore, it is true that as time went on the exact outward forms of ancient liturgies were gradually adapted to the varying and spiritual conditions of different nations, and that different centuries have contributed their liturgical features to the original use, nevertheless, we cannot fail to be impressed with the strict subordination of these to the primitive landmarks which have been handed down unchanged from New Testament times. Though many of these liturgical enrichments have been hallowed by the worship of fifty generations of believers inspired by the Holy Ghost, it is always to be borne in mind that, as these additions were utterly unknown to the first Christians, they are not necessary to the validity of the Sacrament itself.

Never were there holier Eucharists than those recorded in the Acts of the Apostles, in which the founders themselves of the Church, appointed by our Lord, took part; and we call earnest attention to these earlier and simpler celebrations of the Lord's Supper in New Testament days, as a reminder that the one thing needful above all others in the Eucharistic Service is the eucharistic offering of prayer and thanksgiving, whether the celebration be simple or rich in outward and liturgical expression. And therefore, when the whole body of Bishops of the Anglican Communion, assembled at Lambeth in 1888, set forth, as a basis for the reunion of Christendom, belief in the Scriptures and Catholic

---

[1] St. John xiii. 31; xiv., *seq.*
[2] St. Matt. xxvi. 30; St. Mark xiv. 26.

Creeds, in the Sacraments ordained by Christ and the Historic Episcopate, and, as with one voice, declared that for the validity of the sacrament of the Lord's Supper, as well as for that of Baptism, these two conditions were sufficient, (1) that they should be ministered with unfailing use of Christ's words of institution, and (2) of the elements ordained by Him, those Anglican Bishops were strictly in the line of New Testament Churchmanship, and their utterance falls on the ear with the force of the old apostolic ring.

III

On the first Easter Day the risen Christ appeared five times to His followers. At the time of one of these appearances, it is recorded by St. Luke that He walked with two disciples on the road to Emmaus, but was not recognized by them, until at eventide " He took bread and blessed it, and brake and gave to them, and their eyes were opened."[1] The similarity of this hallowed Easter interview, " where two or three were gathered together in His name," to that other service of the Lord's Supper, which He Himself had instituted three days before, is striking. And all doubt that it was regarded by the first Christians as a Eucharistic service is set at rest by their historian, St. Luke Himself,[2] when he records that these two

---

[1] St. Luke xxiv. 30.
[2] " Luke's style is compressed in the highest degree ; and he expects a great deal from the reader. He does not attempt to sketch the surroundings and set the whole scene like a picture before the reader; he states the bare facts that seem to him important, and leaves the reader to imagine the situation. . . . Hence, though his style is simple and clear, yet it often becomes obscure from its very

disciples hastened back to the Apostles at Jerusalem, and " told what things were done in the way and how *He was known of them in the breaking of the bread.*"[1] The earliest name for the Eucharist was " the Breaking of Bread," and the first time that distinctive name is used is in the description of how the risen Christ revealed Himself to the two disciples at Emmaus on the first Lord's Day of the Christian era.[2]

Once more this same first day of the week upon which the disciples were all assembled, *with one accord in one place*,[3] was consecrated by the descent of the Holy Ghost at Pentecost. When St. Peter, inspired by the Holy Ghost, had delivered his pentecostal message, we read that they who "*gladly received his word were baptized ;*" and, immediately after the verse in which we are told that "the same day there were added unto them about three thousand souls," comes the statement that these "*continued steadfastly in the Apostles' doctrine and fellowship and in breaking of bread and in prayers.*"[4]

For several years after this, in Jerusalem and its vicinity, the Jewish Sabbath, as a settled national institution, overshadowed the Christian Lord's Day. Very naturally, therefore, there is no mention of the

brevity; and the meaning is lost, because the reader has an incomplete or a positively false idea of the situation. It is always hard to recreate the remote past; knowledge, imagination, and, above all, sympathy and love are needed." (*St. Paul the Traveller and the Roman Citizen*, by W. C. Ramsay, D.C.L., p. 17.)

[1] St. Luke xxiv. 35, R. V.

[2] The second Lord's day was marked by the appearance of the risen Christ to Thomas and the other Apostles.

[3] Acts ii. 1.

[4] Acts ii. 41, 42.

latter in the Book of Acts, until later on, when Christianity had extended itself beyond Jerusalem. At first the two days were observed side by side,[1] but as time went on, the observance of the Jewish Sabbath decreased, while that of the Lord's Day increased; and the first time after Pentecost that the latter is directly mentioned in the Book of Acts, it is again associated with that service of public worship which the Lord Himself instituted. For St. Luke records that St. Paul tarried at Troas seven days to meet the assembled Church "*upon the first day of the week, when the disciples came together to break bread.*"[2] It is true that this phrase, "the breaking of bread," in the very beginning probably included also the Agapae or love feasts; but these were dropped at a very early day as not essential to the Sacrament. It is also quite possible that immediately after Pentecost it was the habit of the first Christians to receive the Communion daily as well as weekly; but we do not enter into these questions here. Enough for us is it to find in the New Testament record itself such ample ground for the belief which subsequently prevailed throughout the Church, that from the very first there was always a celebration of the Lord's Supper on the Lord's Day.

St. Chrysostom (A. D. 380) tells us that Sunday was anciently called, among other names, "*Dies Panis,*" the day of bread, because the Breaking of Bread was so general a custom in the Church on that day; and it can be shown from the Canons of many a Council of the Primitive Church that in the first

---

[1] Compare Rom. xiv. 5, 6; and Col. ii. 16, 17.
[2] Acts xx. 7.

ages it was a standing rule that communicants should be constant in receiving the Holy Communion once a week on the Lord's Day.[1]

[1] *Reception of the elements enjoined on all the Solemn Assembly on the Lord's Day*, Apost. Can., c. 10. "All communicants who come to church to hear the Scriptures read but do not stay to join in prayers and in *receiving* the Eucharist are to be suspended as authors of disorder in the Church."

Council of Antioch, Can. 2 (264). Let all those be cast out of the Church who come to hear the Scriptures read in the Church but do not communicate with the people in prayer or disorderly turn away from participation of the Eucharist.

Chrysos. (380) Hom. 3. [Ephesians]. All they that do not communicate are penitents, if thou art of the number of those who do penance thou mayest not partake, for whoever does not partake is one of that number.

Council of Eliber, Can. 28 (305). The Bishop must not receive the oblations of such as do not communicate.

First Council of Toledo (539), Can. 13. Those who come to church but neglect to communicate are to be admonished, and if they amend not upon admonition, they are to be reduced to a state of formal penance for their crime.

Justin Martyr, Apol. 1, cap. 67 (speaking of the Solemn Assembly of all the people on Sunday). "Then all the members participated of the Eucharist, and it was carried to the absent by the deacons."

Chrys. Hom. "I often observe a great multitude flock together to hear the sermon, but when the time of the Holy Mysteries comes I can see few or none of them, which makes me sigh from the bottom of my heart, that when I, your fellow servant, am discoursing to you you are ready to tread upon one another for earnestness to hear and continue very attentive to the end; but when Christ our common Lord and Master is ready to appear in the Holy Mysteries the Church is in a manner empty and deserted."

See also Calvin Inst., lib. 4, ch. 17, n. 46; condemning the popish custom of communicating once a year as an invention of the devil and pleading for a restoration of the primitive custom of communicating every Lord's Day, says: "Every week, at the least, the Lord's Table should be set before the assembly of the Christians. All should by heaps, as hungry men, come together to such dainties."

Time of celebration of the Solemn Assembly on Sunday. The third hour (9 o'clock) is mentioned by all the writers who say anything

IV

In vivid contrast to this ancient custom stands the modern way of keeping the Lord's Day holy that has prevailed among Protestants since the Reformation. The chief service of the Lord's Day — or, at least, that which is in popular opinion the most important service of the whole week — is not, as in the Primitive Church, for communicants only, but equally for non-communicants; and to meet the needs of the latter the one service of public worship which Christ Himself ordained is set aside for another kind of service of man's devising, in which the sermon is substituted for this Sacrament. The results of this change are as follows: —

First: Inasmuch as the spiritual welfare of communicants is disregarded and practically overlooked for the sake of non-communicants, Christ's most earnest followers, as a rule, find the chief service on the Sunday morning in their parish church far less spiritual in tone, far less helpful in effect, than some quiet, week-day service where two or three only are gathered together in Christ's name to praise and pray. For, in the Sunday's service, not only are they surrounded by the worldly and careless, who, by their evident want of sympathy with the spirit of prayer and praise, and by their cold indifference, are ceaselessly distracting the devout worshipper of

---

about it. In memory of the Holy Ghost coming upon the Apostles at this time, and of our Saviour's being condemned by Pilate at this time. Chrysostom says that the day is called Dies Panis, the Day of Bread. Sidonia Apoll., lib. 5, Epis. 17. "We meet at the third hour, when the priests perform the Divine Service."

God, but as the crowning effort of the pastor is to reach those who are not communicants already, this conditions the character of the sermons that are preached. The deeper spiritual truths of the Gospel, which to the devout believer are more real than all else in this world, are seldom or never dwelt upon, because they would sound as mere platitudes to those indifferent masses who are lacking in spiritual discernment. And, consequently, a communicant who is hungering and thirsting for the real ministry of the Word is obliged to listen Sunday after Sunday, while the Gospel message is toned down and presented in a way that will attract the attention of the careless or Gospel hardened, and while outsiders are urged to accept the truth that he has accepted years ago. Would such a method of education be tolerated for one moment in any human institution of learning?[1]

As an inevitable result, the whole spiritual tone of the communicant's life is lowered. He is neglected by the Church. No opportunities for spiritual education are afforded him over and above those held out to non-communicants, and he goes back to his home depressed by the morning service, disappointed that he cannot be in the Spirit on the Lord's Day, regretting the worldliness of the congregation, and the low spiritual tone of his rector's sermons,

---

[1] There are times in the Church when such appeals to the unconverted are not only necessary, but a true ministry of the Word, for Christ Himself taught the multitudes by parables; but when they were alone He expounded the mysteries of the Kingdom of Heaven to His disciples (St. Matt. xiii. 10–18, *seq.*), who thus received a special training at His hand. Can it be said that the communicants of to-day receive any similar training?

until at last he loses his desire to grow in grace and in spirituality.

Secondly, let us consider the effect upon the non-communicants themselves. In the Primitive Church these were, as we have said, separated from the communicants or "the faithful," because in that day there was not only a spiritual but a great *moral* distinction also between the lives of communicants and non-communicants. In the growth of that civilization which is a result of Christianity, times have, however, greatly changed. The kind of discipline that was needed in the early Church is no longer needed now, for the outward moral life of communicants and of the ordinary church-goer is practically the same. The discipline that the Church once exercised against gross immorality is now enforced by civilized society itself; if a man offends, he falls below the accepted standard of social respectability. But the *spiritual* distinction remains unchanged, nor can it be obliterated by any progress of Christian civilization. It is perfectly true that through the laws of Christian heredity, and also because of the social forces of their environment, non-communicants often attain a high standard of moral life. But does this afford a sufficient reason for the Church herself to go to the opposite extreme and adapt her services to them, rather than to those who openly confess Christ and obey His dying command, "Do this in remembrance of Me"? Such is, in effect, what is done when the Holy Communion is banished from the place it once occupied as the chief service of the Lord's Day. Even the monthly midday celebration for those communicants who have fallen below the primitive custom of weekly communion is placed in a subordinate position to the regular morning service. Those who refuse to repent of their sin and accept Christ as their Saviour are thus placed in an absolutely false position, in which they acquire a subtle sense of superiority over the communicants. When they behold the Church, on the one hand, preaching the supreme importance of repentance and conversion, of faith and obedience, of Baptism and the Lord's Supper, and then, to meet the needs of those who are not communicants, substituting for the one service ordained by Christ another kind of service, an impression of unreality is conveyed regarding all Church Doctrine, and particularly regarding Baptism and the Lord's Supper.

Is it any wonder that in view of such facts careless and indifferent people, whose judgements about religion are generally superficial, think that Confirmation is the end to which all the ministrations of the Church are directed? that when a person is once for all confirmed there is nothing more for him to do? and that the whole religious life thereafter is chiefly a matter of sentiment? Is it any marvel that under such circumstances popular impressions about the unreality of the religious life and the artificiality of the Sunday services become more and more prevalent?

Thirdly, even in her efforts to attract outsiders in whom the spirit of worship is lacking, the Church has sought to bring congregations together by appealing to a lower motive than that to which the New Testament Christians appealed.

The old message of the Apostles to the unconverted, echoed from the lips of St. John the Baptist and of Christ Himself, was, "Repent ye, for the Kingdom of Heaven is at hand," and they preached the "glad tidings" of the Kingdom to bleeding hearts and sinning souls with a power that surpassed all human eloquence. In painful, vivid contrast to that kind of apostolic preaching stands out the modern sermon, in which the Christian minister leaves the Gospel message he was ordained to deliver, to treat of those literary, social, and economical topics of the day which are supposed to interest a mixed congregation, but which fail to interest when they are the theme of a Sunday's sermon, for the simple reason that no clergyman can possibly speak upon secular subjects with the same force as professional lecturers who are experts in such special branches of knowledge. If, everywhere around us, the cry is going up to-day that the services of the Church are being more and more deserted by the people, the cause is obvious. In her efforts to reach the people by appealing to the secular motive the Church has lost her old-time power. Instead of spiritualizing them, she is not only in danger of becoming secularized herself, but the influences she has made use of have lost their spell, the lower motive to which she has appealed has come to the end of itself, the congregations she has drawn together have melted away. How far this neglect to preach the old Gospel message, in its power and simplicity, — how far, in a word, the Church's neglect to be herself "in the Spirit on the Lord's Day," — has contributed indirectly to the present secularization of Sunday, is a subject that deserves thoughtful consideration.

Sooner or later, the realization of this truth in its general bearings will be brought home to the Church of the future; and if she profits by the lesson, there will be a silver lining even to so dark a cloud as this.

V

What, then, is the remedy? The New Testament itself tells us. The Church can never convert the world by compromising with the world. Whenever she has tried to meet men by lowering her standard to attract the masses, she has failed; let her now return to the old Gospel way of elevating them to the plane of her own life.

If any spiritual result is to be accomplished, it must be through the *communicants themselves*. For they alone are responsive to higher motives; they alone are free and uncommitted to the bondage of sin; they alone have a sense of personal responsibility to Christ; they alone have faith in Christ's words and the discernment to recognize spiritual truths. It is chiefly through the direct and indirect influence of the lives of the communicants that the outer world is to be reached. They are the "light of the world," "the leaven that leaveneth the whole lump;" and when they begin to realize the profound truth so earnestly emphasized by St. Peter, that they are "a chosen generation, a royal priesthood, a holy nation, a peculiar people," when they begin to manifest the power of that priestly life of self-sacrifice which rejoices in enduring all things for Christ's sake, their influence will once more be felt by the outer world. What we need most of all in these days is not so much the extensive as the intensive influences of Christ's religion; not an increase of numbers from the many, but an increase of spiritual power among the few.

Many efforts in many directions have been put forth by those who recognize the gradual lowering of tone in the life of communicants, to quicken them to greater zeal, but these attempts have all been more or less disappointing. And is there not a plain reason for the failure? Is not Christ's own way, after all, the best way? No substitute of man's devising can take the place of that one Service which He ordained. Prayer meetings, communicants' union meetings, are all of them helpful in their way, but there is always a danger of self-consciousness and spiritual pride to be guarded against in such meetings; and this all experience proves.

What the communicants need most of all is to be brought to a higher, holier realization of the only Power that will lift them above self-consciousness into the region of God-consciousness, the Presence of Christ as our Everliving Prophet, Priest, and King. One reason why communicants do not stand out as witnesses and leaders for Christ, is because they are deficient in those elements of Christian character which depend upon the cultivation of the instinct of *worship*. Christian experience has shown conclusively that among all the public services of the Church, none exercises so powerful an influence upon the faithful in controlling their wandering thoughts, in fostering a spirit of prayer, or inspiring a consciousness of the Presence of Christ where two or three are gathered together in His name, as the

Holy Communion. If through the neglect of the Eucharist, therefore, the communicants lose this help to devotional life, not only is their own spiritual growth retarded, but the Church at large, which is ever depending upon their conscious or unconscious influence, is correspondingly impoverished.

No other service can take the place of the Holy Eucharist; and never shall we regain the earnestness, the joy, the abiding consciousness of the Presence of Christ possessed by the early Church, until we restore the Lord's Supper to its primitive position as the chief service on the Lord's Day.

It is true that hundreds of parish churches, for a generation or more, have had weekly celebrations of the Holy Communion upon each Lord's Day, without producing that kind of spiritual effect upon the lives of communicants which we have just described; but when we place these modern celebrations of the Eucharist side by side with those of the Primitive Church, do we not find a great difference between them?

If the Holy Communion is only celebrated either at a very early hour in the morning, when comparatively few can attend, or else after midday, when it has been preceded by a long service and sermon, it can hardly be called the *chief* service of the Lord's Day.

If, on the other hand, it is made "a High Celebration," with ornate ritual of a kind that was utterly unknown in the first three centuries, or at which the communicants are expected to be present without communicating, surely this is a kind of service entirely different from the Lord's Day Communions of the Primitive Church. If, again, those who advocate the modern practice do so on the ground of "fasting communions" (see Note A.), or of Catholic precedent, they should not only carefully compare what they call Catholic precedent with primitive precedent, but also seriously, conscientiously, and in the sight of God, face the fact that they are actually preventing the Lord's Supper from taking its place as the chief service of the Lord's Day according to *Anglican* precedent.

As it is set forth in the Book of Common Prayer, Anglican precedent is the nearest approximation to primitive precedent that exists in modern days; and this will be seen at once when we compare the celebration of the Eucharist, as it is set forth in the Prayer Book, with the celebrations of the post-apostolic Church in the middle of the second century, as they are described by a very trustworthy witness who wrote within fifty years after the death of St. John. That witness is Justin Martyr. Writing about A. D. 140, he says:—

"Upon the day called Sunday we have an assembly of all who live in the towns or in the country, who meet in an appointed place; and the records of the Apostles or the writings of the Apostles are read, according as time will permit. When the reader has ended, then the Bishop (ὁ προεστώς) admonishes and exhorts us in a discourse, that we should imitate such good examples. After that, we all stand up and pray, and, as we said before, when that prayer is ended, bread is offered and wine and water; then the Bishop also, according to the authority given him, sends up prayers and thanksgivings, and the people end the prayer with him. After which, distribution is made of the consecrated elements." (Justin Martyr, Apol. II.)

When we compare the Communion Office of the Prayer Book with the Eucharistic celebrations of the early Church, as here described, we discover a striking likeness between the two. In each, first things are put first; methods of administration and minute points of ritual are subordinated to those great spiritual and ethical principles of worship for which the Holy Communion stands. The service is in a language that the people can understand; the writings of the Apostles are read to inspire the hearts of the worshippers with the New Testament spirit; the Gospel message is delivered to the communicants by the lips of the bishop or priest as part of the preparation; then with prayers and thanksgivings, in which the congregation intelligently join, the bread and wine, or wine mixed with water, are consecrated and distributed to the congregation, who are expected on each Lord's Day, not only to be present, but to receive the consecrated elements according to Christ's command. It will be here distinctly noted that in both primitive and Anglican celebrations the service is in such a form as to help the communicants, not only spiritually, but morally and intellectually as well.

And this, after all, is the test of true worship. It must be in accordance with Christ's command, "Thou shalt love the Lord thy God with all thy heart, and with all thy soul, and with all thy mind;" it must be in accordance with the nature of Christ Himself, Who is the Eternal Logos, and with the principles of His Incarnation; it must be also in accordance with all that is highest and best in human nature, satisfying the demands of the reason and moral sense as well as the aspirations of the heart; it must, in short, bring men who are made in the image of God in living contact with the ascended Christ in such a way as to inspire them with the spirit of love and power and a sound mind. If the Eucharistic Service does not have this effect upon a communicant's life, or if, in any branch of the Church, it is interpreted and conducted in such a way that, while it may promote outward reverence and devotion, it does not strengthen the worshippers in a life of righteousness and intelligence, then this is a sure sign that such administration does not come up to the New Testament level or meet New Testament requirements. One cannot have true ideas of the Eucharistic Celebration who has low or false ideas of worship. For the Eucharist is the central act of worship of the Church of Christ, in which Christ's followers consecrate themselves, with all their physical, moral, intellectual, and spiritual powers, to His service; and confess that in all their earthly work, and their efforts to do that work, they are completely dependent upon Him. Nothing in all human existence reaches the height of this supreme act of faith, in which believers strive to surrender their lives to God as Christ gave His life for them, while they pray: "We earnestly desire Thy fatherly goodness mercifully to accept this our sacrifice of praise and thanksgiving, most humbly beseeching Thee to grant that, by the merits and death of Thy Son Jesus Christ, and through faith in His blood, we, and all Thy whole Church, may obtain remission of our sins, and all other benefits of His passion. And here we offer and present unto Thee, O Lord, ourselves, our souls and bodies, to be a reasonable, holy, and living sacrifice unto Thee."

VI

In the Book of Common Prayer we constantly meet with the phrase, "*The Ministry of the Word and of the Sacraments.*" Now in this connection, and then in that; now in the prayer for the Church Militant, and then in the different Ordination Offices, it appears with persistent repetition; and the profound reason why the Church so carefully preserves this balance between the Ministry of the Word on the one side and the Ministry of the Sacraments on the other, becomes evident when we look back upon the ecclesiastical history of the past and behold the one-sidedness, the forgetfulness of the Ascension of Christ and its meaning, the abnormal exaggeration of secondary above primary truths, and especially those low ideas of the blessed Eucharist, which reveal themselves so plainly in the religious life of east and west in bygone centuries. It was because the English reformers saw all this in their day that they embedded the sermon in the midst of the Communion Office. They had a wise and far-seeing object in so doing. Filled with the spirit of the Primitive Church, their aim was to provide for the Ministry of the Word, side by side with the Ministry of the Sacraments. The marked and significant position of the Sermon in the Anglican Prayer Book after the Creed — the confession of Faith on the part of the faithful — shows that the primary object of that sermon is to help the *communicants*. The present prevalent use of the Ante-Communion and Sermon, without the Communion itself, violates, therefore, the high ideal of the Prayer Book and defeats the very object it has in view; which is, that the whole Communion Office, as in the Primitive Church, should be used on every Lord's Day for those faithful and true believers who have responded to Christ's call, "Follow Me;" and that the best and most inspiring service of the whole day, with the most beautiful and devotional music, and the strongest, most spiritual sermon, should be the Sunday morning Eucharist, with a congregation composed of communicants. It is interesting to note here, in passing, that the "plain song" was also set forth at the same time by the reformers as a substitute for the less devotional music that preceded it.

Time enough is there on each Lord's Day, after this Eucharistic Service for communicants is over, for those ordinary Sunday services to which our church-goers have become accustomed (see Note B.) It is true that such services would thus take a secondary place; but so far from this being a loss, it would become spiritually an incalculable gain, for it would bring home to the unbaptized and the unconfirmed a realization of their true position in the sight of God. It would impress upon those who reject Christ the reality of their state of separation from God; it would reveal to them, by contrast, the danger of belonging to a Gospel-hardened class, and would show every non-communicant that there is a higher life, a holier companionship, an atmosphere of prayer and praise, beyond him and above him, from which he is excluded.

But the greatest gain of all would be to the communicants themselves. Restored to their true position in the Church, and that which believers occupied in the apostolic days; no longer held back by the lukewarm and indifferent, they would be free to worship God in spirit and in truth. Coming to the House of God as His children, to participate in the service which the Lord Himself appointed, the whole atmosphere of the sanctuary would be different from that of an ordinary Sunday morning's service. The congregation of communicants, bound together by a sense of Christian sympathy and companionship, would have the realization of the Communion of Saints, and be thrilled by the one supreme aim of doing the will of their reigning King in Heaven. They would recite the Creed as a real Confession of their Faith; they would join in the responses and the fervent devotional hymns as with one voice. They would listen to a sermon, the one object of which was to bring them closer to Christ, and which would inspire them with the consciousness that the one thing needful above all others in the Eucharistic Service is the Eucharistic offering of prayer and thanksgiving.

For the very first essential to a devout celebration is the realization what this one public service instituted by Christ Himself *means;* the realization that, for the time being, we are joining "with angels and archangels, and all the company of Heaven, in the worship of Heaven itself;" the realization that Christ unites *our* offering of bread and wine with *His* offering, in the Holy Place not made with hands, making the bread the Communion of His Body, and the cup the Communion of His Blood.

Those to whom the Eucharist means all this, and only those, will stand beside the New Testament Christians in their devotional life. Lifting up their hearts to the loftiest heights of prayer and thanksgiving, they will experience the consciousness of the Presence of Christ in the Communion Service as though, for the time being, they are not on earth, but in the heavenly places with Him.

They know, for they have Christ's own word for it, that Christ, their great High Priest in Heaven, Who ever liveth to make intercession for them, has, in this Service which He Himself ordained, come near to them, to bestow upon them every blessing which He promised in His own Eucharistic Discourse, after the Last Supper;[1] to give them His peace, to abide with them, and to fulfil His most gracious pledge, "Because I live, ye shall live also." And filled with the Spirit on the Lord's Day, those communicants will depart from the sanctuary in peace, inspired, satisfied, and willing now to comfort others with the comfort wherewith they themselves have been comforted of God.

[1] St. John xiii. 31–35; xiv., xv., xvii.

NOTE A

FASTING COMMUNIONS

THE objection will undoubtedly be made by some, that the effect of such a Eucharist as we have described would be to discourage and, perhaps, ultimately do away with the practice of fasting communions. For, it would be argued, few communicants would have the physical strength to come, while fasting, to a celebration at nine or ten o'clock in the forenoon, which, with its music, sermon, and other appointments, would become the chief service of each Lord's Day. All this may be true. But is not the emphasis so often laid upon the necessity of so-called fasting communions in itself an exaggeration? Fasting and abstinence are religious duties often referred to, often enjoined in the New Testament; but nowhere do we find exact and definite rules laid down regarding the *degree* of fasting that men shall observe; nowhere is it taught that fasting means total abstinence from food. It is always dangerous to be wise above that which is written, or to imitate the error of the Scribes and Pharisees in laying down specific rules of action where the Word of God has prescribed none, especially when the practice of the New Testament Church seems to have been, if anything, in the opposite direction.[1]

And when we turn to the Primitive Church and its practice in the first three centuries, we find that if any rule was clearly, definitely, and continuously laid down it was the injunction that Christians should never *fast on the Lord's*

[1] 1 Cor. xi. 34.

Day, because it was on this day that Christ rose from the dead, and that the Holy Ghost came down from Heaven. Surrounded by heathen nations everywhere, as the first Christians were, the observance of the Lord's Day was a witness, every week, to the truth of the Resurrection; and therefore the stress that was laid upon it. Saturday was also regarded as holy, because with the first Christians, especially in Judæa, it still retained somewhat of its hallowed associations as the Jewish sabbath. All this will be seen in the following quotations from the works of the Fathers and the records of the earlier Councils:—

Apost. Can. 64. Counc. of Gangra, Can. 18, A. D. 324. Council of Trullo, C. 55. 4 Coun. Carthage, C. 64. Anathematize all that under any pretence whatever presume to fast on the Lord's Day.

Augustine Ep. 82, to Jerome, speaking of the practice of Saturday fasting in preparation for the Eucharist at Rome, says: "If we say it is a sin to fast on the Sabbath, we shall condemn not only the Roman Church but many neighboring churches where the practice is kept and retained. But if we think it is a sin not to fast on the Sabbath, we condemn all the oriental and the greater part of the Christian world. We should therefore rather say it is a thing indifferent in itself, which a good man may perform either way, — without dissimulation, complying with the society and observance of the Church where he happens to be. No precept, however, concerning this practice is given to Christians in the Canonical Books."

Apost. Can. 65. If any clergyman is found to fast on the Lord's Day or on the Sabbath (excepting only the Sabbath before Easter, the day our Lord lay in the Tomb), let him be deposed; if he be a layman, let him be cast out of the Communion of the Church.

So also the 6th Council of Constantinople (692) confirms the above with this preface: "Forasmuch as we understand that in the city of Rome the Sabbath in Lent is kept as a fast contrary to the rule and custom of the Church, it has seemed good, etc."

Aug. Epis. 36, ad Casulanum, quoting St. Ambrose respecting this fast, says: "For when I go to Rome I fast on the Saturday as they do at Rome, but when I am here (in Milan) I do not fast. So likewise you, whatever church you come to, observe the custom of that place; follow the Bishop in this matter, and do as he does without doubt or scruple" (*i. e.* the Bishop as authority to appoint fasting or not in his own church).

The following words of a revered modern writer, in view of all this, are noteworthy. Christopher Wordsworth, Bishop of Lincoln, Church Hist., vol. 4, page 41. "Here we may remark that when a church, deeming actual communion to be necessary, and that the Eucharist is the crowning act of worship, and that early communion not being numerously attended, ought not to be the only Eucharistical provision for her people, has so ordered her services that the Communion is commonly administered at noon, it seems that Augustine, who declares it to be no small scandal to fast on the Lord's day (Epist. 36) and who commands every one to observe the practice of the church in which he lives, would not have advised any to enforce fasting as a pre-requisite for Communion."

It was not until the fourth century that the more modern idea of abstaining wholly from food before receiving the Eucharist began to prevail, and even then the injunction is ambiguous. We read, indeed, about this time, more and more of fasting communions, and occasionally this meant, literally, total abstinence from food; but we should not be guilty of the anachronism of *reading into* all those ancient records ideas that they were never meant to convey, or which were of much later origin. If "fasting" and "abstinence" are terms which even in this nineteenth century may mean either partial or total abstinence from food, the ambiguity was even greater then, as will be seen when the writings of different Fathers are consulted.

The whole object of fasting is to promote a devotional frame of mind, and there are physical reasons why communicants cannot be in a receptive spiritual state, or prepared for the concentrated religious effort which all true worship requires, after a hearty midday meal. The Primitive Church was, therefore, guided by simple practical experience of life in discountenancing afternoon or evening communions. When, in addition to this, it was sometimes enjoined upon believers to come to the Lord's Supper "fasting," we must remember the ordinary and conventional use of that term in those days. A man described himself as "fasting" or "impransus" if he had not partaken of the "prandium," even if he had taken the "jentaculum," or light morning repast. And correspondingly the communicants of the early church were regarded as "fasting" even if, like the French nation of to-day, they were accustomed at an early morning hour to partake sparingly of food.

All this appeals to one's reason; whereas the stress that is so frequently laid upon the necessity of fasting communions, in the sense of total abstinence, in order that the first food received may be that of the blessed Sacrament, seems to approach perilously near a kind of materialism, which is foreign to the spirit of the Gospels; which St. Paul touches with his profound thought in the second chapter of the Epistle to the Colossians, and which, in later days, developed into gnosticism.

Oftentimes in the very effort to make little of the body we make much of the body, and thus, inadvertently but really, divert attention from the spiritual to the physical. The highest Christian life is that which is so absorbed in the spiritual that it is unconscious of the physical; and this result cannot be reached if our bodily needs assert themselves abnormally, either through our self-indulgence or our self-denial.

When our Lord Himself said, "Take no thought what ye shall eat or what ye shall drink . . . but seek ye first the Kingdom of God and His Righteousness," He undoubtedly meant that His followers should be so filled with the high aim of seeking the Kingdom of God, that these physical needs would be subordinated and fall into the background of the Christian consciousness.

Again, Christ most earnestly warned His disciples against that universal human tendency to substitute a part for the whole, or the less for the greater, which was manifested so strikingly by the Pharisees when they substituted the gold of the temple for the temple itself; the gift on the altar for the altar itself; mint, anise, and cummin for the weightier matters of the law. Do we not behold modern illustrations of this self-same tendency in those who lay such an abnormal stress on the mere fact of fasting, that they will neglect the communion itself, for weeks and sometimes even months, if the circumstances of their lives are such that, because of illness or travel, or inconvenient hours, they are prevented from fasting before communion? Surely this idea is an exaggeration that will in the end defeat itself.

The more we reflect upon the rule for fasting laid down in the Book of Common Prayer, the wiser its provisions seem: "On Days of Fasting the Church requires such a measure of abstinence as is more especially suited to extraordinary acts and exercises of devotion."

There are many who hold as a simple matter of Christian experience, that it is for their own best spiritual welfare that they should always abstain from food before coming to the Holy Eucharist. And it is in accordance with the spirit of Christian liberty, that wherever it is possible, an early celebration should be provided on each Lord's Day for believers who feel this need. This, however, is a matter for the individual conscience. But if any are disposed to go a step farther, and make a principle of that which should only be a question of expediency, then they are refusing to others the very liberty that is accorded to them. To say that total abstinence from food before receiving the Holy Communion is a religious obligation imposed upon all true believers by Catholic usage and precedent, is to give a false idea of the teaching of the Catholic Church; for it does not include the Church in New Testament days or the Church in the post-apostolic age.

It prescribes, moreover, as a religious obligation, a rule about which neither Christ nor His Apostles have spoken, and which seems contrary to the whole spirit of St. Paul's teaching. Last, but not least, it is this idea more than any other which has in recent years prevented the Lord's Supper from being the chief service on the Lord's Day, with all the manifold blessings that would accompany such a devout following of the New Testament spirit.

NOTE B

SUNDAY SERVICES

THE question may very pertinently be asked, if the chief service on the morning of every Lord's Day should be a celebration of the Eucharist, what would become of that large class of church-goers who, while not communicants, are, through the influence of the more religious members of their families, or other causes, more or less regular in their attendance upon the Sunday services?

The answer is a very simple one. Let them have their familiar services of Morning Prayer and Litany, to which they have been so long accustomed, at the usual hour, with the usual music and sermon, conducted in such a way that they will feel no loss or difference. But, at the same time, it would be for the good of their own souls as well as for the benefit of the communicants of the parish, were they to understand distinctly that this service is strictly subordinate in every way to the Eucharistic Service or services for Christ's faithful followers, held in the earlier hours of the day. It is in accordance with the very spirit of the Prayer Book that these opening hours of each Lord's Day should be devoted to communicants, by having a quiet, early celebration for those who would find such a service most helpful, to be followed by "a Solemn Assembly of the Lord's Day," like that of the Primitive Church, held at the third hour or between nine and ten A. M.[1] As in the early Church, this celebration of the Eucharist should be the Chief

---

[1] The hour varied in the Primitive Church, as it was regulated by the rising of the sun at different times of the year.

Service of the Lord's Day, not only in outward form, but in inward spirit.

Then, at the noontide hour, or shortly before, would come the usual Service of Morning Prayer and Litany, with music and with a sermon for the ordinary class of church-goers; and for those communicants who might desire to remain over from the preceding service.

Sunday afternoon should of course be devoted to the children, with joyous Children's Services, Sunday-school lessons, and such public catechisings as the Prayer Book enjoins.

For psychological as well as religious reasons, the evening is as much the time for missionary meetings as the morning hours are for the communicants. On these Sunday evenings are needed short, bright services, with familiar hymns, hearty congregational singing, and rousing mission sermons to the unconverted. If deemed expedient, a few earnest, sympathetic lay-workers might meet each stranger at the door to introduce him to the clergy after service, or make him feel in other ways that the house of God has a homelike welcome for all, and a blessing for all.

In this way all classes in the community are cared for and helped, by services adapted to the needs of each.

www.ingramcontent.com/pod-product-compliance
Lightning Source LLC
Chambersburg PA
CBHW021954220426
43663CB00007B/817